Also by Herbert Kubly

AMERICAN IN ITALY

EASTER IN SICILY

by

HERBERT KUBLY

19   56

SIMON AND SCHUSTER

New York

LIBRARY OF CONGRESS CATALOG NUMBER: 56-9922

MANUFACTURED IN THE UNITED STATES OF AMERICA
BY AMERICAN BOOK—STRATFORD PRESS, INC., NEW YORK

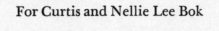

For Curtis and Nellie Lee Bok

CONTENTS

FOREWORD

BETWEEN *Europe and Africa in the Mediterranean lies the island on which Plato dreamed of establishing his republic.*

When I set out on the series of journeys which have resulted in this book, an American businessman who has lived in Palermo for many years said, "You will be talking with Sicilians. Do not believe them. Remember that Sicilians do not comprehend truth as we do. Sicilian truth is a relative mixture of legend and fantasy."

Living at the crossroads of both time and space, the Sicilian is the most enigmatic of Europeans. The twenty-seven hundred years of his recorded history is a roll call of invaders—Phoenicians, Greeks, Romans, Carthaginians, Byzantines, Vandals, Saracens, Normans, Spaniards, Garibaldi's red-shirted thousand and the Nazis and Allies of World War II. His blood is the blood of many races, his culture the repository of many cultures. His religion is a Christianity which incorporated rather than displaced the ancient paganism of his ancestors. His homeland is an Eden from which he has been cast by the sinful greed of landlords. He lives in a world of his own, escaping the brute reality of his material life into one of fantasy and legend.

Legends arise from nature; the Sicilian creates his from the landscape about him. It is possible even for a northerner to believe in the birth of Aphrodite as he looks down to the sea from the exalted perch of Erice; as he stands on the terrible cliffs of Enna, the abduction of Persephone is utterly comprehensible. From Aphrodite and Persephone to Mary the

Virgin Mother, from Charlemagne and the Norman heroes of the Crusades to the twentieth-century Salvatore Giuliano, the Sicilian peoples his life with gods and lives with them on intimate terms.

Sicily is the Easter island not in the limited Christian sense —though Sicilians will tell you that Jesus' first earthly appearance after the Resurrection was in Sicily—but in the sense of a reawakening of life. From January to June, Sicily is the land of spring, a campo dei fiori, *a field of flowers. These are the months Persephone lives on earth—in Sicily, of course. The months when she is underground with her abductor, Sicily is scorched with sorrow. Living close to the earth, a Sicilian is keenly aware of the Easter cycle of renewal: it makes him an optimistic and exuberant lover of life.*

When the businessman warned me about Sicilians, he meant that they are not always capable of comprehending the northerner's concept of black and white. Because much of this book comes from the mouths of Sicilians, I cannot verify that it is always factually true; about its spiritual truth I am confident. For the heart of the Sicilian, like the island on which he lives, is wondrous and awesome, closer to heaven and to hell than anything I know.

My friend Fra Giorgio Eldarov, O.F.M. Conv., of Rome, felt that in a previous book, American in Italy, *my attitude toward the Catholic Church was paradoxical, fluctuating between humanism and puritanism. He said:*

> *The Church is a social body. Her interest in the world is optimistic, her faith that God made all things good. Man is as much body as he is soul and through his body he is connected with a family, a society, a country, a world, and a universe. The Church, in working on souls, works for a better body and a better world. In some corners of our world people are still pagan; in others people remain fundamentally pagan with only a Christian varnish (and I am thinking of your story of the merry horses of Siena being blessed in church); in other places there*

are those who deliberately oppose the action of the Church. There are many of these people in your books. I must remind you they are human beings with both souls and bodies.

If my compassion for them is deeper in Easter in Sicily, *Fra Giorgio* must take the credit.

For valuable background material on Giuliano, I would also like to acknowledge my indebtedness to the Italian press and to the following books which deal sensitively with this subject: Eleanor Clark's Rome and a Villa *(Doubleday & Company, Inc., 1953) and Gavin Maxwell's* Bandit *(Harper & Brothers, 1956).*

Special gratitude goes to my former teacher, Helen White, who suggested both this book and its title.

HERBERT KUBLY

MacDowell Colony, New Hampshire, 1956

EASTER IN SICILY

PURSUIT

"When Christianity became the official religion of the Western world, these local aspects of heathen gods were not infrequently converted together with their worshipers. Particularly in the Mediterranean area, one often finds that the shrine of a local manifestation of an Olympian deity has been used as a foundation for the shrine of a Christian saint, whose characteristics are reminiscent of those of its heathen predecessors."
—RALPH LINTON, *The Tree of Culture*
(Alfred A. Knopf, Inc.)

CHAPTER 1

"A VIRGINIOUS QUALITY"

CHAPTER 1

"A VIRGINIOUS QUALITY"

ON FEBRUARY 22 I turned south from Rome for Sicily. Nearly one hundred and seventy years ago to the day, Goethe had departed from Rome on the same journey. His companion was a painter named Kniep, of whom he wrote, "My artist is a merry, truehearted fellow."

My companion was an Italian-speaking young South American named Franco Calorelli. "Frank," twenty-three, was the son of Italian immigrants to São Paulo. He had spent a year in an international school in north Europe studying languages and then traveled south for his first visit to the homeland of his parents. In Rome he had become fascinated by the film industry and was planning to organize a film company on his return to South America. One of our purposes in making a trip together was to speak Italian so that I might improve in the language. As it turned out we talked English almost exclusively. His newly learned English was so uniquely expressive that I didn't mind. He was occasionally sad, quite often serious, and very often merry. He was indeed a "truehearted fellow."

Since his arrival there, Frank had never left Rome. His parents had been Genoese and, like most north Italians, Frank thought of the south as a jungle of confusion and ugliness, of poverty and illiteracy, a place to avoid if possible. To persuade Frank to accompany me, I described ruins overgrown with bougainvillaea and clematis, donkeys decorated like pashas, Christian temples as lavish as mosques in *The Arabian Nights*. He was unimpressed. Frank's two passions were motion pictures and women. It was only when I told him of an earlier visit when I had seen Sicilian women with eyes as soft as the Ionian Sea that he became interested. He quickly decided to explore Sicily for a possible film story and came along.

The first lap of the trip from Rome to Naples took Goethe more than three days by carriage. In the Ford of an American embassy secretary it took us three hours. The morning we left, the Roman hills were covered with a thin film of snow. It was the beginning of the orange harvest; in the valleys between Rome and Naples farmers were building golden mounds of fruit. Our diplomat seemed a mild man; his wife a strong woman. Their five-month-old baby slept in a pink-beribboned basket. Much of their conversation en route to Naples was an argument as to where the Washington's Birthday holiday should be spent. Our host favored Capri; his wife preferred Sorrento. The diplomat, a religious man, crossed himself whenever we passed a church or a funeral on the road. This became hazardous as we entered Naples. On the Via Foria, past the cemetery on the hill, we met one hearse after another. Neapolitan funerals are social occasions of pomp and pageantry. A first-class corpse rides in a hearse carved with cherubs and skulls, or on an open caisson pulled by four or six horses; the second-class corpse rides behind two horses, and the third-class body usually rides a lowly motor hearse. Hearses for children are completely white. "What a wonderful experience it must be," said Frank, "to die in Naples!"

The diplomat finally won over his wife; we last saw him mounting the gangplank of the Capri boat with the pink baby basket under his arm.

Since the night boat which Frank and I were taking to Palermo did not leave until nine we went in search of some food. We found a little *trattoria* where the owner waited on us. His half-dozen children followed him to and from the table like a litter of puppies; in a back room his pregnant wife cooked. We ate a fine veal stew with vegetables and drank a quart of Chianti. When we were finished we set out to explore the town.

The weather was *capriccioso*, with alternating fits of sun and rain. At the moment it was sunny. "Naples at first sight leaves a free, cheerful, and lively impression," Goethe wrote. "Numberless beings are passing and repassing each other." In that respect, at least, we found things unchanged. People were still passing and repassing. Each narrow little street was as noisy and bustling as a fair. At the Piazza del Plebiscito, there was great excitement. A daredevil cyclist was stringing a rope across the piazza to the dome of the great church of San Francesco. On this he was going to ride a bicycle.

Hundreds of barefoot, ragged children waited eagerly. They cadged cigarettes or smoked the butts they picked from the streets. Among them were the usual Italian war souvenirs, Negroid *bambini*, now ten to twelve years old. Hucksters drove their silver-yoked donkeys through the throngs as if they were sheep, and flocks of pigeons swooped over the piazza like wind gusts. Just as the cyclist was ready to begin his feat, a black cloud appeared, and it began to hail. Ice crystals clattered on the pavements like machine-gun fire. An old man claimed he couldn't remember when it had hailed such large stones. The children picked them up and gazed at them as if they were jewels. The daredevil announced the postponement of his performance until evening.

We waited out the storm under the porticoes of San Francesco. When it stopped, we set out for the port to buy our boat tickets. Before we made it to the harbor, the storm broke more fiercely than ever. So we ran into a water-front bar for shelter. It was a dark cavern in which several young men, apparently habitués, were gathered around the *padrona*, a fat *signora* who lorded it over them like a queen. She was dressed in silks; her feet, tiny as a Japanese's, were enclosed in dainty pumps. I marveled that they could support such a hulk of flesh. On each finger she wore three or four glistening rings.

The light in the bar flickered. Outside the streets were dark; rain lashed against the door. Since we ordered our wine in English it did not occur to the *signora* and her circle that Frank and I might be eavesdropping. All Italians love to travel, Neapolitans most of all; they have been rovers ever since they went up to Milan centuries ago to sell oranges and other fruits of the south. These idle young men gathered around the *signora* and spent hours watching the arrival and departure of great ships. Emigration was their favorite subject of conversation. America was their paradise. They were dream wanderers for whom the harbor was the end of the journey, as close to paradise as they would ever get. The *signora*'s dingy bar was their haven; there they could lament their frustrations and spin their fantasies. One of them was asking the current price of something.

"Five hundred thousand lire," the *signora* said.

"Who has five hundred thousand lire?" another jeered. "Only in America it is possible to earn so much."

It was black-market passports they were discussing. The *signora*, apparently, was an agent.

"Go to South America," she said. "São Paulo is an Italian city where Italians are welcomed. For fifty thousand lire I will have you on a boat for South America in two weeks."

"Who wants to go to São Paulo!" the first young man said scornfully. "Just like Italy. Nothing but Italians. I prefer to go to the United States and become an American."

"You will rot here." The *signora* grunted. She spat on the floor beside her dainty feet and scratched her head with a long darning needle. She crossed her feet prettily and said,

"In New York the Italians are as poor as they are in Naples. It is impossible for an Italian to get a job without belonging to a labor union, and labor unions do not take into membership Italians. In São Paulo there are jobs for all. For Italians there is great riches and position in society. I tell you the story of Seppe Petrucci who went to São Paulo after the war without a clean pair of drawers to change into. Now he is *padrone* of a hotel more grand than the Excelsior. When he came home, he brought his poor old mother a diamond ring. Pina Petrucci who never in her life had an honest wedding ring now has a diamond! I tell you, go to São Paulo."

"São Paulo is a *villaggio*," the youth said. "The greatest city in the world is Brooklyn."

"Brooklyn!" The *signora* snorted. "Nothing but Sicilians! In Brooklyn there is so much snow people must tunnel from their doors to the streets." The *signora* laughed loudly. "Imagine a Neapolitan tunneling his way through the snow! In São Paulo there is no snow. The weather is as warm as in Italy."

The young men looked sullenly into their glasses of vino and listened to the storm at the windows. The *signora* raised her jeweled hand and with her needle probed deeply into her ear. Then she started to knit.

"I do not believe it about the snow," one of the young men mumbled.

It was after eight o'clock. We emptied our glasses and ran through the rain to our boat, which was loading in the harbor. The agent at the ticket window was determined that we should buy first-class tickets. The difference in price between first and second class was two thousand lire.

"*Lei è un Americano, vada in prima classe,*" the man argued. By persisting, Frank finally succeeded in buying a pair of second-class tickets. Most of the passengers were laborers and peasants traveling third class. As we had guessed, first and second class were the same; there were a few people in second class and almost none in first. In buying second-class tickets we had simply saved ourselves some money.

Our *cabina* was spacious enough for four people. It was clean and quiet. We began our voyage with dinner. The dining room was small; there were no more than a half-dozen diners. The waiter served us spaghetti, veal fried in olive oil, spinach cooked in olive oil, and some cheese. It was hardly a meal to put into one's stomach before a stormy night on a wild sea. But we ate it and then went outside for a walk. The deck was wet and dark; the cold wind pierced our clothing. Behind us Naples was only a glimmer. Goethe's passage to Sicily on an American-built sailing ship took him more than four seasick days and nights. Our voyage was to take a single night. Frank made an exploratory tour of the boat and returned with the disappointing news that there were no unattached women aboard.

Women were necessary to Frank's mental serenity. "When I have a girl to think at I think better," he explained to me. "When I have no girl to think at I think like I have nothing to do. If I have a girl to think at and I know I see her at six o'clock, I begin to work at two o'clock and work until six o'clock, but if I have no girl to see at six o'clock, then I pass the day drinking coffee and smoking cigarettes and being very nervous. But having a girl I do lots of things." At the time of our journey his thoughts were with an American Fulbright student—a girl named Genevieve who was studying art in Rome. Frank took a dim view of most of the Fulbrights he had met. "Many are spiritually displaced persons," he said. "I think your committees select them by sticking pins in a telephone book at night." Nevertheless, Genevieve had made a sufficient impression for him to carry her photograph in his suitcase. It showed her to be extremely pretty, with pert, elfish eyes. About the depth of his affections for her, Frank had doubts. "She is American and I like that very much," he said. "She is a girl deep in soul and very confusing. She has very great ambitions to be an artist and will, I think, place her career before her emotional life, which a woman should never do. So I am undecided about her."

Our oily supper lay heavily on our stomachs. My own held a tenuous peace, but Frank's was threatening disaster. The small boat rocked violently and we lay in our beds trying to calm our insides. Frank passed a fitful night and was up with his stomach several times. In the morning we went out on deck early to watch the landing. The dawn was clear and cold; a tart salt wind brought the color back to Frank's pale cheeks. In the rising sun, gray Pellegrino, taking shape in the mists over Palermo, had a lavender sheen. On the deck were crates of cabbages. Frank tried to explain to me the difference between *cavolo*, which means "cabbage," and *cavallo*, which means "horse"; we spent some time practicing the pronunciation of one and two *l*s.

On billboards at the edge of the harbor we saw posters advertising two performances that day by an American Negro dance troupe. Frank was carried away by the prospect of "seeing the niggers." To break him of using this American vulgarism I called him "Dago" every time he repeated it. It didn't work. "Nigger" is commonly used by Latin peoples. Frank, who had a strong sense of social justice, was not speaking in contempt or derision. He simply couldn't remember the American connotation of the word any more than I could keep in mind the difference between horses and cabbages.

After checking in at our hotel Frank urged me to call the Negro troupe's manager, whom I had known in New York, and reserve a pair of seats for the evening. The seats set aside for us were in the center of the first row, uncomfortably close to the orchestra but ideal for Frank to feast his eyes on the girls. There were six of them, light in color and extremely pretty. Frank picked his favorite and from his program identified her as Doris. He fidgeted nervously in his seat. "When I go to theater, I am an artist," he said. "I experience what I see. Now I like to jump out of my seat and do something." At the intermission he said, "Now I am awakened in my pants. I want to live." He begged me to take him backstage, suggesting that since Doris would certainly be impressed with nobility, I introduce him as Principe Francesco. He said, "I will look sad and Doris will ask me, 'Why do you seem so sad?' and I will look away and say, 'I am thinking of the poor nigger peasants in Alabama.' That will touch her heart. Then she will want to discuss with me race relations and I will say, 'No. I would rather not discuss race relations. I would rather have some race relations.' "

Things didn't work out. Doris had been in Europe long enough to prefer commoners with pockets full of lire and francs to impoverished nobility. She was cool to Principe Francesco.

After the performance Frank was frustrated and restless. Later on at a restaurant he made a visit to a washroom. When he returned to the table he said, "It is a very small toilet I visit, and on the window there is a cat saying 'meow.' It was beautiful. I felt very strange standing there while this cat is saying 'meow' in the window. I began to cry. When the artist in me is aroused, little things mean so very much." He drank a glass of wine and looked reflectively into the bottle. "I am terribly sad," he said. "I think maybe five of the nigger girls have lovers. But there is one who has no lover and she will be in bed by herself, crying because she has no lover. Life is very, very sad."

Back in our room, Frank took from his suitcase the framed photograph of the American Fulbright painter and set it before him on the table. Then he took pen and paper and began to write, "My angel, Genevieve . . ." Having written these words, he turned to me and said, "I try myself to keep a virginious quality, but life is hard running from one trouble to another. I always have need of new raw material. I would like to get married, but where is there a girl who has remained pure? She is very difficult to find. It is very sad."

He returned to his letter. "My darling," he wrote, "I am like a bird flying through the dark night of life and I think it is the time to think of the dawn and of you and me. You are with the angels and I am with the Devil. . . ."

He wrote the rest of the night.

CHAPTER 2

THE GOLDEN SHELL

IN SICILY I hoped to find the Madonna with a female Jesus.

I had read of such a statue in the journals of a nineteenth-century English traveler who reported having seen it in a church in the vicinity of Enna. That such a statue might exist is not surprising; it could have come down from ancient times when Enna was the seat of the cult of Demeter and her daughter Persephone.*

To Anglo-Saxon Christians the idea of pagan ancestors for Mary and Jesus may be startling. To Sicilians it is not. Demeter was the goddess who made the earth fruitful; she came to them from the flat Eleusinian cornlands of Greece. She was also a mother; her daughter Persephone rose from the underworld to become goddess of the soul's immortality. Each springtime when the earth flowered, pilgrims journeyed to Sicily from all over the ancient world to celebrate Persephone's resurrection in Enna's temple of Demeter.

When Christianity spread to Sicily, the legend-loving Sicilians didn't abandon one set of deities for another. Instead they were quick to see the kinship of the two mothers and

* Named by the Romans, Ceres and Proserpina.

their sacred children; they added one to the other, with the result that the Virgin cult of the Catholic Church flourished in Sicily. As the springtime fertility rites had been the principal festival of the pagan year, so Easter became the climax of the ecclesiastical year.

Sicily is the home of the female deity. Rosalie is the patroness of Palermo, Agatha of Catania, Lucia of Syracuse, and Mary of Messina and Trapani. No male god can inspire the veneration Sicilians feel for their Virgin goddesses. The reason is, in a word, *Mother*. The Sicilian male venerates his mother above all things and believes himself an unworthy son as he believes Jesus was unworthy of Mary. It is motherhood which is worshiped. Whether the child be male or female does not seem to matter.

To prepare ourselves for the journey around the island Frank and I passed a fortnight in Palermo absorbing the sights, sounds, and bright colors of the city. Sight-seeing would, we hoped, give us a sense of history and put us more closely in touch with the people. Toward this end the uniformed staff of our hotel offered no help. Their function seemed to be to protect foreign guests from Sicilians. One morning a large country family of men, women, and children tumbled through the revolving door and gazed wide-eyed at the marble halls. Their spokesman explained they had never seen a hotel; they had come down from the mountains to see this one in which an American cousin had recently spent a honeymoon with a Sicilian bride.

They did not stay long. "This is no museum," the doorman scolded, and whirled them back into the street, laughing at their awkwardness in coping with the revolving door. When I asked the clerk for the address of a Sicilian puppet theater he was astounded that we would want to go to one. "Do you have your pistols with you?" he asked. "One can't go into those streets without pistols for protection. People are always being attacked." We went twice to the theater without pistols or mishaps.

The elevator operator, a good-looking, slender youth, wore a tight black glove over an artificial left hand which he held stiffly before him as if he were always about to bow. More striking than the hand was his curiously dual personality which seemed to change with Jekyll-and-Hyde punctuality at sunset. His daytime personality was quiet and modest. When I questioned him about his missing hand he replied, "An accident of the war," and spoke no more of it. But at night he would turn sullen and bitter and speak so arrogantly of a *"bombardamento Americano"* that English-speaking passengers felt guilty about the missing hand. I credited the almost uncanny transformation of his personality to physical fatigue, for he seemed to be working around the clock.

Despite the hotel's protection, Sicily got through to us. Though we were only two blocks from the opera house, which is the heart of the city, the bloodcurdling braying of donkeys combined with crowing cocks and bleating goats being driven to housewives' doors for milking was our morning alarm. "We are sleeping in a zoo," Frank said.

When we opened our windows beggars and peddlers called up to us from the street. An old lady came daily to tell us our fortunes. "Young people need to know their fortunes, M'Lord," she said, speaking in Italian but adding "M'Lord" in English.

"We already have good fortunes," I said.

"I am a poor feeble old woman without any money to buy bread. You are young, *signore*, you do not know the curse of the aged. Once I was a midwife, delivering four babies a week, and had much money. Now that I am old no one trusts me, though I can draw forth the *bambini* as well as ever. Young people are hard," she accused. "Young people are cruel."

I threw her a ten-lire note, which she stashed away in her cloth bag. I could see from above that it was filled with small currency. "May God bless you," she sang as she departed. "May the saints grant you a long life. . . ."

It rained often, but whenever the sun flashed through for an hour we went out to explore the town. The streets were even more of a turmoil than those in Naples. There was a great deal of building going on. Badly bombed during the war, Palermo was rising defiantly, if tardily, from the rubble. The great baroque church of San Giuseppe, destroyed by bombs, was restored to a new and shining richness. More than any other city in Europe, Palermo is a city of contrasts. It has pavilions and palaces that are Oriental in splendor, surrounded by Oriental squalor. The economic barriers between rich and poor are as strong as racial barriers in the American South. On Sundays, a day of *passeggiata* for all, the rich close the shutters of their palaces. Their withdrawal is like their selfishness, a self-protection. They are frightened of the miserable poor.

Visitors meet the rich only by having letters of introduction. Society operates according to a medieval ritual going back almost a thousand years, when the Normans made Palermo into a dazzling capital. The glory continued into the eighteenth century when Queen Maria Carolina, sister of Marie Antoinette, entertained those dilatory residents Admiral Nelson and Lady Hamilton with parties and balls.

Since Frank and I had no such letters, we met only the poor. Our walks were invariably convoyed by beggars, peddlers, pimps, and thieves. The people of the streets were a human potpourri, for Palermo has conquered all ravishers with her passivity. One sees faces so Greek and Roman they might have been struck from ancient coins. Moors and Spaniards, Oriental Semites of Africa, fair-haired Normans—all these are here. Despite the variety of faces, genes have blended with expedience to produce a distinctive personality. Palermons are a heady combination of Asiatic subtlety, African mystery, Latin braggadocio, and Celtic fantasy. They are beachcombers: the flotsam and jetsam they comb are the visitors the seas bring to their shores. No other people, not even the Neapolitans, are so skillful in the art of living parasitically from their guests. They hover over the harbor like flies on offal. Ships, especially those from America, are greeted with a celebration, for Americans are their favorite visitors.

One day I set out to find the work of Sicily's two great artists, Antonello da Messina and Giacomo Serpotta. With Antonello this was easy. His paintings have traveled far. But "Annunciation" is in Palermo, and it is probably his masterpiece. It is a small painting standing on its own pedestal in the center of a room in the beautifully appointed National Gallery. It portrays a calm and peaceful Madonna, a brown, dark-eyed Mediterranean peasant girl, simple and trusting, yet strong and lovely as the mother of Jesus must have been. Her head is covered with a cool, bright-blue shawl. One sees women all over Sicily as darkly beautiful, and with the same trusting, peaceful acceptance.

The work of Giacomo Serpotta, however, can be seen only in Palermo. His statues, modeled in plaster, are mounted on the walls of churches and oratories. In the great flowering of Sicilian baroque, Serpotta is famous for his busy and agile *putti*, or cherubs. Travel books devote long chapters to the three oratories dedicated to Saints Lorenzo, Zita, and Domenico which Serpotta decorated. They are not easy to see because almost no one in Palermo knows where they are, and, once found, they are usually locked up. On two previous visits to Palermo I had missed them.

These chapels are hidden away in the Quartiere Arabo, a crowded casbah of markets and slums. One fruitless afternoon, directed by natives, I trudged through the rain from one church to another searching for Saint Lorenzo. I finally gave up. Next day, returning with a local artist, I realized that I had passed it several times. Its entrance was through a private court which was used as a poultry yard. Inside was a gallery alive with animated sculptures. There were scenes from the lives of Saints Francesco and Lorenzo; around the ceiling there were statues posturing like the painted youths of the Sistine Chapel. The joy of the room was a precocious kindergarten of sophisticated, naughty infants tumbling over one another, riding pickaback, posing in costumes, yanking at one another's hair. One could almost hear their shrieking bedlam.

It was the same in the oratory of Saint Zita, where the walls were covered with a bewildering pattern of historical and religious subjects, flippantly supported by the mischievous infants, who held them as if stone were so much silk. The elusive Saint Domenico oratory turned out to be the most diverting. From the Saint Domenico Church we were led by a curate through a maze of dark alleys into an evil-smelling, dirty corridor, where by holding my thumb on a bell I was able to arouse an old grandmother with whom we negotiated an entrance as if it were an evil transaction. Here Serpotta's irreverent infants were busy as an ant colony. In the foyer four groups were play-acting the passion and crucifixion of Jesus. Impish infants made ribald charades of the crown of thorns, the carrying of the cross, the episode of Veronica's veil and the entombment. Each panel was a naughty game played as children do in a spirit of mockery, catching the essence of things and converting it to impious hilarity.

Frank was no lover of baroque. He said, "Here we have it, the hypocrisy of Sicilians. They are not religious at all; they just like the game of it, the carrying of statues through the street, the play-acting, the excuse for a *festa*."

He was, I think, not quite right. The most charming quality of Serpotta's infants is a rollicking, childish innocence which redeems them from blasphemy.

In his religion as in everything else, a Sicilian is an activist. His church is his theater, his recreation, his social center, and when he participates, it is to the fullest possible degree. Participation, worldly and spiritual, unites the individual with man and God. By keeping the spirit in the body, where it rightly belongs, the Sicilian finds, through human experience, his place in the cosmos.

"I am of course a Catholic," Frank said. "Though not a very good one, for I see too clearly all the social and economic ills of the church."

"They are the ills of human nature."

"You are a better Catholic than I am."

"I am not a Catholic at all."

"All the same, you are a better Catholic," Frank said. "There are things for both of us to learn in Sicily."

Another day we went by bus into the hills to Monreale and the Norman cathedral of King William the Good. We passed dwellings with cloth hangings for doors. Drawn apart, they revealed squalid rooms shared with goats and chickens; outside, five or six children played in barren plots of three or four square yards. Frank was checking the death notices against the birth notices in a morning paper. There were fifty-six births and eighteen deaths. "It is here even worse than in Italy," said Frank, whose innate Genoese pride never permitted him to accept Sicily as Italy. "Each set of parents has from six to ten children, of which about seventy-five per cent survive. Those babies that die are the lucky ones. They have nothing to do but play tennis with the angels. Those that live have a whole lifetime of troubles."

We passed through a belt of ripening orange groves, blossoming almond orchards, and silver forests of olives, but the idyl ended quickly when we entered Monreale, where the poverty was even drearier than in Palermo. Monreale is a town built on a ledge, with the mountain descending to Palermo in the front and rising in the back to jagged gray bluffs where bandits hide. At the time of the building of the cathedral in the twelfth century it was a rich and bustling capital. Today its fifteen thousand people, many idle, live in chimneyless hovels with only a hole in the wall for the smoke to escape. There is no sanitation in Monreale, and the only telephone serves the municipal offices. A row of tourist busses in the cathedral square was surrounded by the citizenry come to look and beg. Dirty children with sores on lips and legs blocked the paths of strangers with pathetic little dances. Crippled old men displayed their infirmities, hoping to open purses with the horror of them, and ancient women, more mummy than human, droned their sorrows from inside black shawls. It was as if all the misery of the world had gathered on the cathedral steps. Near a placard which read, "Women with sleeveless dresses or low cut not admitted to cathedral," two men were nonchalantly urinating against the wall. No one paid any attention. We passed inside, where the sun streaming through high windows illuminated the nave like flames.

Monreale, like Chartres Cathedral in France, is a human miracle, an almost perfect thing. Its mosaics are a composition of millions of carefully cut bits and pieces, most of them gold. Where fragments have crumbled away there has been, in modern times, little restoration. The overpopulation and cheap labor which could build golden temples still exist, but the great, simple faith which drove men to sacrifice themselves to minute, painstaking work because they believed their rewards would be heavenly ones does not.

The guidebook says the Monreale mosaics cover more than seventy thousand square feet. Such figures are meaningful only to statistics lovers; better to say that the imagination is staggered. "A thousand and one nights," said Frank, and so it seemed, though actually it is the story of the Bible from the Creation to the Crucifixion depicted in gold.

It is an animated toy world with perspective all akilter. The most lively section is the Noah cycle, with its solemn processional and recessional of animals and its teeming ark resting precariously on the peaks of three toy mountains. The destruction of the cities of the plains is a Halloween bonfire with Lot's wife a salt statuette. Frank's favorite showed Adam viewing for the first time his newly created Eve. "Jesus Christ," Frank somewhat figuratively quoted Adam in English. "Look what God gave me. She have none of the things like me and lots of things I don't have."

The cathedral is dominated by the great Christ-head gazing down from the concave shell of the apse. It is the last of three such Christs in Sicily, the first and most celestial being in the cathedral of Cefalù, the second in the Cappella Palatina in Palermo. All three Christs, dressed in the rich trappings of Byzantine patriarchs, grasp the Gospel in their left hands and raise the fingers of their right in solemn benediction.

They are worthy monuments to the most intriguing of Sicily's historic epochs, the reign of the Normans from Hauteville. The one at Cefalù, built in the twelfth century by Roger I, last of the Tancred brothers to come from France, is the most impressive. The Christ in the Palatine, built for Roger II, and the one in Palermo for his son, William, do not have the fearsome omnipotence of the first; they are less awesome copies set in more lavish surroundings. All three have the same searching eyes; they follow you no matter where you stand. The Normans were wise and forceful tyrants. They knew the spell that such a godhead would cast on their subjects and that the penetrating eyes would seek out every dark corner of the soul as intensely as they search out the dark corners of the church. They placed Christ Male above that of Mother Female, creating Him in their own fair and vigorous image. Their concept has influenced the world's portraiture of Christ as the Hellenist Demeter has influenced the world's concept of the Virgin.

My neck ached from looking up. English-speaking guides were herding groups of tourists; an old lady tottered across the shafts of sunlight attacking each marble pillar with her cane, shouting furiously, "*Tutto marmo* [pure marble]!" exalting in beauty in her own way.

I collected Frank, who had gone into the village, and we returned to Palermo, where I had been invited to share the opera box of the United States Consul. The great red and gold theater—Palermons claim it to be the largest in the world —is florid rather than beautiful. *La Traviata* was as colorful and sweet as Sicilian pastry. The applause was restrained. Because of the rigid social barriers in Palermo, opera is a social rite rather than the popular art it is in continental Italy. Prices, higher than in Milan's La Scala, exclude all but the rich. The house was "sold out," yet almost half of the stalls were unoccupied.

After the opera I was invited to a party at the apartment of the representative of an American oil company. Sulking unhappily in a corner was a young engineer from Virginia named Charles Dobbins. After some drinks of American whisky he finally told me what was troubling him. It was a girl, or rather it had been a girl—a shy, sloe-eyed thing named Cecilia with whom he had struck up a somewhat inarticulate friendship—since he spoke hardly any Italian and she spoke no English—one afternoon in the public garden. The friendship had blossomed into love within twenty-four hours. On the second evening, when Dobbins returned lightheartedly to the gardens to keep an engagement with his new-found love, she arrived with two men whom she introduced as her father and her brother. Dobbins referred to them as the Berlitz family. Speaking English, the two men said they were happy to meet the good *Americano* and were most lamentably sorry it had to be for such sad and serious business. "We hope not to have to speak to the police. It would be very embarrassing," the brother said gravely, and the father added, "Cecilia is only a *bambina*, having no more than eighteen years. The police are very severe in such cases." Cecilia stood quietly in the shadows looking at her shoes while her new American suitor trembled with fear under a street lamp. The father dolefully continued that unfortunately nothing could be done to restore the deflowered Cecilia, a condition for which Dobbins doubted his responsibility. *"Naturalmente* I understand the hot blood," the father said with what appeared to be compassion. "I was myself once young and impulsive. But facts are facts, a father's daughter has been robbed of her most prized possession. If the *gentile Americano* will give her three hundred thousand lire to comfort her in her sorrow and pay for a novena to ask forgiveness of the Blessed Virgin, all will be forgotten." The brother hastened to add, "And two hundred thousand lire to buy myself a shoemaker's shop. For no one will marry Cecilia now, and if she doesn't become a nun she will remain a brother's liability forever. Who can say how many liabilities? Perhaps there will be a *bambino.*"

It was a situation to make any young American sweat ice, and Charles Dobbins did just that when he told me about it. He had only recently arrived in Palermo. Being a stranger in the city and speaking no Italian, he had no idea how to raise a half million lire. There was no one in America who could send the money. His mother was a widow of modest means.

When he failed to keep a second appointment in the park, the Berlitz family had come to his hotel. The next day he had changed hotels, but the brother, seeing him on the street one night, had followed him to the new address. To keep them from returning to the hotel, he had made an appointment to meet them in the park the following night. In the meantime he had managed to raise almost a hundred thousand lire, mostly by borrowing at a high rate of interest against his salary. He hoped the Berlitz family would settle for that.

I told Dobbins that he was the victim of a rather naïve blackmail trick. Most visitors in foreign countries are terrified at the prospect of becoming involved with the police. Realizing this, a family with an attractive daughter might well prosper by blackmail. Knowing how afraid Italians are of their own police and the great respect they have for American officialdom, I advised Dobbins against giving the Berlitzes any money and to report the incident to the American Consulate. But the next day was Sunday and the consulate was closed, and he had promised to meet the Berlitzes that night. So I volunteered to go with him and pose as an American lawyer. The money I told him to leave at home.

Sunday it rained and turned cold. The appointment was for nine o'clock in a street behind the opera house. When we went to keep it the lamps glowed dimly in the mists and the rain beat in our faces. I sent Dobbins ahead and waited in the shadows until the Berlitz family appeared. Almost at once three figures stepped from the shadows where they had been hiding. The girl hung back so that I could hardly see her. She never spoke. I walked out and Dobbins presented me as a lawyer. "*Lei, chi è?*" the father asked. "I am legal adviser to an American oil company," I said, and took from my pocket an official-looking document. It was a pass from the Italian government in Rome giving me free entry to theaters and museums. It was too dark to read the type, but the government seal was conspicuous. When they saw it, the father and son became as polite as Japanese servants. "I suggest that you go to the American Consulate on Monday," I said. "You can report the matter then."

"Sir, it will not be necessary," the father said. "It is all a misunderstanding. We are good friends of the young American."

"You are quite right in wanting the police to know about this," I said. "I shall arrange for them to be there so you can tell your story."

"There is no need, sir. No need at all. We do not wish to embarrass the young man, nor bother you. . . ."

"It's no bother," I said. "Justice must be done."

"You know how girls are—ashamed of their own foolishness.

It is possible she does not tell the truth, and I beg the pardon of the young man." In the shadows I caught the flash of Cecilia's eyes.

"Then the case is closed," I said.

"*Finito,*" said the father, bowing to me. "*Grazie, signore, grazie.*"

"*Grazie,*" I said. "*Buona sera.*"

"*Buona sera,*" they said.

The two men insisted on shaking hands with both of us. Then they disappeared into the gloom, forgetting about Cecilia, who trailed silently behind.

Dobbins and I started back toward the lighted heart of the town, each of us deep in our own thoughts. Suddenly Dobbins shook his head and said ruefully, "And to think that I never have any news for my mother when I write to her. She thinks nothing ever happens to me."

It had started to rain again. As I sloshed back to the hotel, my spirits were as damp as my coat. I was pleasantly surprised to find that the elevator operator had forgotten to change into his night personality. He was smiling as if the sun had never set.

"You are happy," I said.

"I am always happy," he replied.

"In the daytime," I said, "but not at night. You were not happy last night or the night before or the night before that."

"I was not here last night or the night before," he said. He then proceeded to unfold a comedy of errors. I discovered that there were two operators, unrelated, but in appearance as alike as twins. Each had lost a hand during the civilian bombings of World War II. The sullen night boy was a child of eight when he was caught in a Palermo street explosion; the happy day youth was only six when a bomb had hit his house in Trapani. Now Palermo was having his night off and Trapani was working his shift. Because of their differences in temperament they were not even close friends.

"He is sad that he has lost his hand," said Trapani. "I am glad I am alive."

He reached over his black left hand to open the door.

"Good night," he said. "Sleep well."

CHAPTER 3

THE DAY THE FLEET ARRIVED

WORD SWEPT THROUGH the city like a holocaust. The U.S. Navy was coming to Palermo!

For three days the town prepared for the big event as if for a saint's *festa*. Shopwindows were filled with miniature donkey carts and dolls in peasant dress. The prices of post cards rose from twenty to forty lire; cab drivers removed their meters and hotels their rate cards. Funerals were hastened or postponed, so that all men could be down at the harbor on the great day. Café and bar men studied American cocktail recipe books, virgin daughters were confined to their rooms, and the opera house, as a tribute to the American Navy, scheduled a performance of *Madama Butterfly*.

A few of the politically minded grumbled about "the iron club," but they were a small minority. In the excitement no one remembered that it was merely one aircraft carrier and two destroyers that were coming, or that they represented, not the U.S., but NATO.

Palermo's feverish hospitality toward visitors dates back to the war, when the bombed city lived from spurts of prosperity brought on by free-spending American soldiers and sailors. For several weeks the town had been in a state of high tension as citizens watched the newspapers for the progress of the NATO Mediterranean Fleet good-will tour. They noted stops at Cannes, Malta, Genoa, and Naples; in Greece there had been an American aircraft demonstration for the King and Queen. Now, Palermo at last! *La Marina Miricana* was to be the biggest invasion since the war.

The Sicilians had the weather in their favor. After a week of constant rains, the day dawned gloriously. The three vessels had crept up in the night and anchored in the harbor. With the first light of morning the men of the town, plus a few elderly women no longer concerned for their good names, arrived on the docks to greet them. Bands of young men played music and sang Sicilian folk songs. Vendors set up booths loaded with guitars, mandolins, dolls, pastry, toys, cognac, brass jewelry, fruit, and nuts. "Oriental" carpets with camel and sphinx designs lay on the pavements. Everything was scandalously priced. Money-changers' pockets bulged with lire, real and counterfeit, and wads of currency padded with newspaper cores. Horse cabs black as hearses were lined up as far as the eye could see. Enterprising cabbies raced their beasts into a lather across the harbor plaza to attract the visitors' attentions. There was some delay in granting liberties, but the seamen—five thousand of them—were lined up on the railings of the ships. Said Frank, "The sailors on the ships and the Sicilians on the shore are like two opposite sides of monkeys staring at one another, wondering if they are going to fight or be friends."

To keep the lid on the town, no more than a third of the seamen were to be on liberty at one time. The ships were staying three days and each sailor was to have one day's leave. Officers were allowed longer liberties, with the privilege of taking hotel rooms, all of which had been reserved for weeks. Motor launches were finally lowered from the ships and the first wave of seamen chugged toward shore, about a hundred and fifty to a load. The sailors were young; for many it was their first cruise. They were happy and high-spirited. They received a warm welcome and the "Joe" chorus started at once. "Hey, Joe, change *moneta*; Joe, you see catacombs; you wish a guide, Joe; show town, Joe; wanna taxi, Joe; dirty pitchers, Joe, show everything; bottle cognac, Joe; wanna buy lire, Joe, I make good change; wanna woman, Joe, niza pissa ass, Joe . . ." The words "genuinely first class" were used to describe everything from brass rings and bottles of Marsala to chenille bedspreads, prostitutes, and phony "Parker" pens. Since it was still early in the morning, the sailors displayed a healthy skepticism and business was bad. The people of Palermo were not dismayed. They willingly bided their time, waiting for the collaboration of their good ally, alcohol.

Guides and cabbies, however, did not have to wait. Sailors paid as much as ten dollars apiece, or forty dollars for a load of four, for a two-hour carriage tour of the town. If they had Italian currency, they paid two thousand lire for a trip into the heart of the town, a distance of five or six blocks. Almost every group of sailors was accompanied by a young Sicilian. If they started off without one, a *giovane* usually leaped onto their carriage as they drove away. The shrewd lads promised "protection from the crooks" and they promised girls which very few of them could deliver. Little children lined the streets to stare, as if the Americans had green skins.

The heart of Palermo is small. Within an hour the city was filled with sailors. On the Via Maqueda and other crowded thoroughfares phonographs blared "Give Me Five Minutes More" and "I Love You for Sentimental Reasons." Conscientious sailors made sight-seeing trips to the cathedral and the Cappucini tombs. A few pious ones even set out for the shrine of St. Rosalie on top of Mt. Pellegrino. But most of them milled aimlessly about the streets. Determined to make the most of the day, they began drinking at once. The cinemas did brisk business even though the houses were empty, for sailors, having bought tickets to Abbott and Costello and

Lana Turner films, discovered that they couldn't understand the dubbed-in Italian and left at once. The whores of the town were ready and did a land-office business, but they were too few, and only a small number of sailors were able to buy the illusion of love. Despite the festive displays in the shops and the forced gaiety on the streets, it looked as though the great and glorious leave might turn out to be a sad and empty visitation.

By midafternoon the town had turned into a sort of bedlam. Being themselves neither heavy nor good drinkers of hard liquors, the Sicilians watched with awe and happy anticipation as the drunken sailors reeling through the streets began to turn out their pockets for scarves, pillows, dolls, and musical instruments at prices which were ten times their value. Bars and cafés were filled with sailors in the custody of Sicilian chums who, with shrewd sobriety, drank soft drinks or poured their liquor into shavings on the floor. Many sailors became sentimental; putting their arms around their new friends, they showed their wallet photographs of girls in Buffalo, Denver, or Chicago. The Sicilians admired the photographs exuberantly. "Oo-la-la!" they said. "Very nice!"

Liquor prices were shocking and the behavior of waiters scandalous. Hardly any of the sailors understood Italian currency. The waiters, shrewdly gauging their state of drunkenness, took vast sums and shortchanged mercilessly. When I saw a waiter return two thousand lire from a ten-thousand-lire note for a fourth-rate bottle of champagne, I could stand it no longer. I went to the table of three sailors and three young Sicilians and explained I should like to help them if they made any more purchases. The Sicilians were as hostile to me as I expected them to be. The youngest American, a seaman third class from Georgia, began telling me sadly how he had to send pay money home to help support his sister's illegitimate child by another sailor. As he talked he began to weep from homesickness. Another, a Nebraskan, was giggling foolishly with a Sicilian over some pornographic pictures. The eldest of the three was a pharmacist's mate from Texas. His eyes narrowed suspiciously. He was remembering security warnings about strangers and was taking no chances. "Who the hell are you and how come you talk English so good?" he asked me.

I said I was an American.

"Where you from?" he asked. I replied I was from Wisconsin. He asked me a series of questions about American geography, obviously testing me. He looked at my tweed jacket. "Where did you get that?"

"In Chicago," I replied.

"You're lying," he said. "That ain't no American jacket. That's a British tweed."

I couldn't convince him. "You might as well get along, Buddy," he told me. "I ain't gonna tell you a god-damned thing. But I'll say this for you, you're the smoothest god-damned dago I ever met."

At our hotel, Madame Reymond, a handsome retired French schoolteacher wintering in Palermo, was distressed at the Sicilian assault on *"ces doux garçons innocents* [those sweet innocent boys]." She put on some rouge and lipstick and her best hat and went into town to "protect them like their mothers would," as she put it. She could speak no English, and the sailors, unable to understand either French or Italian, mistook her for a procuress and mobbed her with their eagerness. She returned to the hotel with both her hat and her illusions battered.

On the streets sailors were racing rented motorcycles through the town in terrifying fashion, and those in carriages were racing the horses. In the driver's place one sailor would hold the reins and another would lash a whip on the panting beast like a parody of a Ben Hur chariot race. In back seats shouting sailors waved wine bottles and cabbies huddled in fright, wondering what was going to happen next. Whips cracked, wheels locked, and drunken sailors spilled into the streets.

In a bookstall, displaying for the occasion a shelf of American twenty-five-cent paperbacks, a quiet, sober sailor with red hair was earnestly trying to explain something to the owner. The boy's softness of speech suggested that his home was somewhere in the southern Appalachians. He seemed greatly distressed, so I asked if I could be of some service. "I would like to know if he has an English Bible," the boy said. I translated the request into Italian. The shopkeeper looked as if he thought both of us bereft of reason.

"You make a joke," he said.

"Quite the contrary," I said. "The young man wants a Bible." The man burst into ribald laughter. "Five thousand Americans want a woman," he said, using a vulgar idiom. "And he wants a Bible!"

Madama Butterfly was a roaring success. The soprano, though musically undistinguished, was young and pretty. Lieutenant Pinkerton, a squat bushy-haired, mustachioed tenor, was hardly well cast, but he sang passably well and the sympathies of both Sicilians and Americans in the audience were with him rather than with the geisha bride whom he drove to suicide by his betrayal. The house, for once, was exuberant and the demonstration which followed was as much for the United States Navy as for the artists. A few seamen were scattered in the house, but most of the Americans were officers, called by Italians "*borsalini*," after Borsalino hats, the Stetsons of Italy, which they wore. Officers wore civilian clothes on shore presumably to impress Europeans with the democracy of the United States Navy. "Their elegance must make the poor underpaid Italian officers very sad," Frank said. Not all officers, however, were at the opera. Some were at the fashionable Della Palma Hotel having a party with American women, many of whom were wives who had flown down from Rome.

The enlisted men whose entertainment was left to the people of Palermo tired early. At eight o'clock they began straggling back, bearing the trophies of the day: bottles, boxes of pastry and candy, embroidery. A fog had fallen over the sea, obscuring the ships in the harbor. The only lights were vendors' torches flickering in the wind. From a booth a recording of "Night and Day" blared over the port. The whole town had come down to the water front for the leave-taking. Bedraggled seamen, drunk and weary, their money and illusions spent, lined up for five hundred feet waiting for their turn on the landing boat. The boat plied silently in and out of the fog. It was a chilly night, and the boys, dressed for a sunny morning, shivered as they waited. Faster than the boat could haul them away, they poured into the harbor. Propping up each other, they came by motor taxi and they came by foot. Some were escorted by shore police, who guided the delinquents with good-humored sympathy. The noisiest came by carriage. In the distance one heard frenzied shouting, the cracking of whips and clatter of hoofs on the cobblestones. Horses, foaming at the mouth, emerged from the night pulling carriages with white-clad sailors bent over the buckboards like ghosts.

Vendors and hucksters were making their final pitch. The rugs, "genuine first-class quality," were spread out on the pavements with salmon-colored chenille bedspreads "guaranteed from Arabia." Drunken sailors bought up the feminine symbols of home and security as fast as the merchants could unpack them; each time they were sold out another pile appeared mysteriously from the dark. Two seamen reversed the tables and talked a wily old mandolin seller into accepting for payment an American watch that didn't run. Another plagued a villainous fruit merchant into counting out a hundred tangerines four times because he suspected him of cheating. When the sailor was certain he had all his fruit, the paper bag split and the tangerines scattered all the way to the landing boat.

The queue waiting for the boat swayed back and forth like a long white serpent. Men were sentimental, silly, or surly, depending on their dispositions. Some shot popguns; others played with toy snakes. Many were sad, and one or two very young drunks were crying. Most were bareheaded. (Next day half the *ragazzi* in town wore white caps.) Some shivered inside tasseled shawls and blankets bought for mothers and sweethearts. Their morning gaiety, like their money and the starch in their uniforms, was gone. Gregarious, friendly, and trusting, they had arrived ill-armed to conquer the shrewd old city. Battered they now were, but defeated they were not. They left a wake of good will behind them and this was their victory.

The sea lapped blackly against the cement wall and the fog thickened. Shortly before the last boat left, the clatter of a carriage stopped with a thud. A foam-flecked old horse fell dead, spilling sailors and driver in a heap over the beast. The shore police rescued the sailors and put them on the boat. The launch chugged away, its cargo of weary men huddling together under bedspreads and shawls. Those that still wore caps wore them like halos as they slid into the Stygian night. The people of Palermo snuffed their lamps, folded their wares, and crept away to rest up for two more days of American sailors.

It was two o'clock and quiet and dark. The only sound on the dock was the cabby sobbing over the corpse of his horse as if it were his mother.

CHAPTER 4

BENNY

SICILIANS are facile linguists and English is their favorite language. Frank, who was often mistaken for an American, enjoyed sparring with them. Even though he occasionally got into some tight situations, I never lost my confidence in Frank's ability to talk his way out. He met his match, however, in a youth from Bagheria called Benny.

Outside the eccentric villa of the Prince Palagonia, I found Frank trying to shake off the usual circle of persistent natives.

"We don't need a guide," he was saying in Italian. "We guide ourselves."

"I am not a guide. I am a friend." The speaker was a young fellow dressed in an American Army field jacket, American dungarees rolled to the knees, and American sport shirt. "I do not want money."

"What Sicilian does not want money?" Frank asked.

"You are a guest in my town, and it is my duty to be hospitable."

The young man turned and spoke to me in English. "My name is Benvenuto," he said, "but you will call me Benny. Benny is my American name."

For a moment I thought he might even be American. But

his Oriental olive skin, his large black eyes and black curly hair were quite Sicilian. I judged him to be about eighteen. He was small but strongly built; on his upper lip was a scraggly mustache, on his chin a few wisps of beard. His clothes were fresh and clean. He had a warm, flashing smile and a nervous personality that contrasted sharply with the pitiful congregation of woe and misery about him. Having failed with Frank, he now went to work on me. "I like very much Americans," he said. "America is the nicest country in world and Americans are nicest people. If there is any way I can help you on your visit I should be very happy."

"There is no way," Frank said firmly. "We have already seen the villa."

"You have not seen our town," the boy said.

"As much as we wish," Frank said, and added for my ears, "Sicilian friendship has the dollar mark on it. Be careful."

I asked Benny where he'd learned English. "For one year, I have studied at the Palermo British Institute," he said.

Why then, I asked, did he speak American English rather than British English?

"I have many American friends," he said. "I have even an American girl." From his pocket came a letter postmarked Cleveland and signed "Janey." "She came with her mother to see the villa and I met her here," he said. "For a year we are writing letters."

And the American clothes?

"I have an aunt in America sends them. From Cleveland. Is big Sicilian colony in Cleveland," Benny said. "You live in New York?" he asked.

I replied that I had.

"That's what I like, Madison Square Garden and Broadway," he said. "I have only American friends and wear only American clothes. In Bagheria everyone is Communist. I talk always how wonderful a country is America. All the people say how well they like Russia. You are crazy, I say, you should like America. So I am not popular. I have no friends. They call me 'L'Americano' and laugh at me."

I asked about his family.

"They live outside the town—my grandmother, my father and mother, and two brothers and two sisters. I am the first. My father works in the country and is paid twenty-five thousand lire a month. Is not much."

It was hardly forty dollars. Benny drew from his pocket the usual fat wallet of photographs and showed us pictures of his parents and brothers and sisters, the youngest of which was a baby. Most of the photographs were of himself, including one in the uniform of an American sailor. "I borrow the suit from a sailor who is my friend," he said, admiring the picture. "It is my greatest wish one day to wear one for Uncle Sam."

It was time to eat. I asked Benny if one could buy lunch in Bagheria. He knew a place, "not for tourists, so it will be cheap." I invited him to lunch and he accepted eagerly. He led us into some narrow back streets, chattering breathlessly and with touching eloquence. "In Sicily life is empty of everything but sorrows. People have no money and no work; they are rich only in empty hours. I do not go to school since I am twelve years old because there is not enough money. I look for job, but there are no jobs and my father is very angry with me because I do not work. You understand? When I am on the streets with nothing to do I am a bad boy. I cheat. I steal. I do not like myself when I am bad. I want to be a good man. Understand?" Benny punctuated his conversation with "understand," each time looking me hard in the eye, defying me to meet his glistening gaze. Then his face would melt into an animated smile, a split-second transition from aggressive persuasion to bubbling friendliness. "When people are poor they hate each other," he said. "I do not like hatred. I like for people to be kind to each other. In America I think everyone is kind and is friends with everyone. It is my dream to study engineering in America. Every night I pray to the God in heaven to make it possible for me to become an American. But to go to America one must have American friends to sign the papers. Understand? God cannot sign papers and I have no friends in America. So is no good, the praying."

"Perhaps your aunt in Cleveland could help," I said.

"To sign papers is necessary money in the bank," Benny said. "My aunt is poor lady."

We passed a small building with a sign which said, *Partito Comunista Bagheria*. "Bloody reds," Benny muttered.

"You know song, 'America I Love You'?" he asked.

I didn't, so he sang it for me at the top of his voice. "I am very happy today," he said. "I am always happy when I have an American friend. Is last year in Palermo an American journalist. You know him, Mr. Burke? I work for him. I make interviews and translate. When he goes away he said, 'Benny, you are my friend. I will write you. Maybe I can arrange for you to come to America.' He never writes. He forgets me *subito*. But Benny does not forget a friend. Mr. Burke is always my friend. I read only American books and journals —the *Time* and the *Esquire* and the *Silver Screen*. I like American movies and American phonograph disks. When I like something like I like America, then I want to get it all. Understand?"

His ardor included American girls. "I have heard in America girls go out alone with boys before they are engaged," he said. "Is it true?"

I said it was.

"In Sicily if you go with girl you are engaged, and all her family go with you. You take her to the movies, you take also her mother and sisters and maybe even the aunts. Who can afford?" He drew a letter from his pocket and with the air of a bored Don Juan invited me to read it. It was from Syracuse, and signed by a girl named Lucinda. "You are the dream of my heart and I will love you *eternamente*," I read.

Benny shrugged. "She was in Bagheria with her mother to

make pilgrimage. For five minutes I speak to her through a bus window. I tell her my address and she writes me."

I said that in America such a letter would indicate considerable intimacy.

"Italian girls are foolish," he said. "They are all right for *amore*, but I cannot like a girl who is not American."

In the street of the butchers we weaved through the bloody carcasses and brushed against festoons of sausages. Freshly killed kids hung with their white skins turned inside out and their kidneys exposed like plums; blood dripped from their tiny snouts; the smell of blood was everywhere and live goats played in the sun. People peered at us through holes in their walls with unfriendly eyes.

"Bloody reds," Benny said. He led us into a dank cellar below the street. The place stank of fish and oil, sour wine and unwashed bodies. There were two rooms. In the first, piled ceiling high with wine barrels, a conclave of men was silently eating fish—old, hungry men slobbering juice from a brown bowl on the table. Each had a mess of fish skeletons before him. Behind the barrels a baby yowled and other *bambini* rolled on the floor with mangy dogs. We entered a second empty room and sat among more barrels at a table covered with a filthy cloth. Immediately the *padrone* brought us a liter of dark wine. It was good. We drank liberally. Though it was understood I was paying for the meal, Benny took over and acted as host. An astounding repast began with chunks of salami rich with garlic and fat. Next came bowls of spaghetti. Benny, bending low over his plate, took it in like a vacuum cleaner and made almost as much noise. The red sauce which remained on his mouth he wiped on the dirty tablecloth. Three dogs of varying breeds begged scraps under the table. Flies gathered on the wineglasses and food. I recalled doctors' warnings about dysentery and I ate less and drank more wine as a precaution.

Benny's hospitality was offended. "Do you not like it?" he asked. "Is it not good?"

He ordered a salad, a curious assortment of lettuce, fish, olives, and orange sections swimming in oil. The fish, with heads, tails, and viscera intact and eyes that looked at me, I dropped to the dogs, but the rest I ate. Benny sopped up the rich oils in the bowl with pieces of bread and polished it shining clean. He ate as lustily as an animal at a kill storing up for a leaner day. The wine he took in great gulps, letting purple rivulets course over his lips and drop from his chin whiskers onto the table. Between courses he lit a cigarette, and when more food came he carefully extinguished it and tucked it behind his ear for later use. The next dish was a special delicacy, a small fish called *nunnatella*. My stomach winced. What was set before us was a loathsome mass of silvery-gray slime. The fish, tiny and transparent, had been stirred into a gelatinous, uncooked mass which Benny and Frank scooped up with relish. Next came eggs fried in oil. When a bit of yolk dripped on Benny's trousers he wiped it off with bread, which he then popped into his mouth. The meal came to an end with more wine and a bowl of oranges.

Benny was in expansive good spirits. He began to sing—first the United States Marine Hymn, then a half-dozen verses of "Roll Me Over"; finally he broke into "My San Antonio Rose" with a Gene Autry twang. He started "She'll Be Coming Round the Mountain," and Frank and I fell in. We sang an assortment of cowboy songs and finally "Oh! Susannah." Then Benny, falling into a deep drawl, asked, "You all from Alabam?" and Frank, in a broad midwestern accent, replied, "I'm from *Ioway*."

"Ahm from the Deep South," said Benny. "Sugah cane country."

I hardly believed what I heard.

Benny asked about my family in America. When I said I lived alone he said, "When I come to America I will live like a brother with you." I laughed. A hurt look crossed his face. "You must forgive me," he said. "I want so much to be an American I can think of nothing else. Understand?" He told me he had tried to get a job with the American Consulate and several American firms, including the American Express. "Is my dearest wish to work for Americans," he said. "Now I have nothing to do. I am a bum hanging around the piazza doing bad things which I do not want to do because I have no lire for cigarettes. Is impossible for a Sicilian to get a job with Americans unless he knows a big shot. Will you help me?"

I said I was hardly a big shot but that I would do what I could. He was flowery in his gratitude. "To have you for a friend will make me a good man," he said.

He walked with Frank and me to the bus. I suggested that he meet us several days later in a Palermo café. I wanted to avoid giving him the name of our hotel. He looked very sad, and I asked what was troubling him. "I am so happy that you are my friend," he said. "When I am happy I must think how happy I am and when I think my face is always *serioso*. Understand?"

A few days later I went to the American Consulate to see what could be done about a job for Benny. The officer I talked with was not encouraging. "There are half a million like him in Sicily," he said. From the consulate I went to the offices of an American company where the American-born representative was as pessimistic as the man at the consulate. He was amused that an American should have been taken in by the eloquence of a Sicilian.

"When a Sicilian tells the truth, it's an accident. Of course, when a Sicilian lies to you, you know he's lying, but you listen without ever hinting that you know he's lying. Even if he knows that you know he is lying, he is deeply hurt; he is insulted and even angry when you do not trust him. It's all a sort of elaborate game you play with him."

Nevertheless, the man promised to speak with Benny and to help if he found him worthy. I was brooding about his cynicism on my way back to the hotel when I saw walking ahead of me a pair of backs that gave me an uneasy turn. I moved faster to make certain of their identity. They were, as I feared, Benny and the brother of the Berlitz family, from which I had helped rescue the American engineer, Charles Dobbins. When I told Frank about it he was not surprised.

The next morning Frank started out for the harbor. In a moment he was back in the room to report that he had met Benny with two men in the lobby of our hotel. One, well dressed and prosperous, Benny had introduced as his American uncle; the other, a sad, pinched little man, as his father.

Within a few minutes there was a knock on our door. Benny bolted into the room, very excited. He was flashily dressed in an American zoot suit. "My American Uncle Sam is arrived unexpectedly," he said. "I have come to tell you I cannot meet you tomorrow because I must be with my uncle. Last night I stayed with him in the Villa Igea. Beginning today my uncle has taken a room in this hotel. This moment I go to meet my uncle at the Villa Igea."

I asked where in America the uncle lived.

"In Cleveland," he said.

I remembered that the aunt had been poor. I supposed there could be other, more prosperous, relatives. Still I was skeptical, and Benny sensed it.

"You do not believe me," he said, deeply pained. From his pocket came a new set of photographs. Uncle Sam had brought them, he said. There were several of the "uncle," a beefy, round-faced man; some of "my aunt," a housewife in a gingham dress; and some of two young people in their late adolescence, a girl and a boy. "My cousins," Benny said proudly. "This is Janey, and this is Billy. Billy is eighteen. He has the same years as I have."

"Is Janey the one you correspond with?" I asked.

He hesitated a moment, then replied, "No doubt there are many Janeys in America."

I repeated my question: Wasn't the Janey on the photograph the same Janey who had written him the letter, the Janey whom he had met in the piazza at Bagheria?

Without backtracking on his original story, he admitted she was. "You do not believe me, my *buon' amico Americano*, to whom I can tell no lies?" he exclaimed with a look of anguish which put me at once on the defensive. "Is it an American trait to doubt one's friends?" He launched into an elaboration of his original story, adding evidence like a fibbing child, and the fantasy grew.

"Janey came to Sicily on a tour with students and naturally she wished to make a visit to her relatives in Bagheria," he explained. "She likes me and writes me foolish letters." He passed this off like a man of the world and offered as proof Janey's latest letter, which he said the "uncle" had brought.

"I was glad to get your picture so now I see what you look like and you are even handsomer than I thought," I read. Why, I asked, did Janey need a photograph to see how handsome Benny was if she had been in Bagheria?

"She forgets," Benny said. "Is a long time. Three years."

How old was Janey?

"She has seventeen years," Benny said.

I was thinking that fourteen had been a young age for a girl to be on a student tour.

"Are many nuns along," he added, figuring that this would convince me.

None of the people on the photographs appeared particularly Sicilian. I asked if there were any pictures of the other aunt, the poor one.

"Is none," he said. "She is old lady and don't like her picture taken."

Photographs of the uncle's new fieldstone home in Shaker Heights and of a large new Buick had the air of ostentatious bourgeois wealth. Benny said, "Tomorrow my uncle wishes to go to Agrigento and the next day we will go to Enna. On Sunday my uncle will leave, and I will come to see you. You are my true and dear friends. Is unfortunate my uncle has come this week."

Then he tried to borrow five hundred lire so he might take a carriage to the Villa Igea. I pointed out that the Villa Igea was on a tram line.

"Is true," he said, "but it is the highest class hotel in Palermo. One does not arrive at the Villa Igea in a tram. Is necessary a carriage. Understand?"

Frank and I tried to make some sense out of the strange fabric which Benny had woven for us. We found no logical design, only false clues, dead ends, and unnerving effrontery. "It is a baroque tale," Frank said uneasily. "I do not like the baroque. What I do not understand frightens me."

That evening in the dining room, Frank, looking over my shoulder, said, "Here they come—Benny and his uncle. Now we must be very dignified." They came straight to our table. The American uncle was certainly the man in the photographs, a beaming, red-haired man who appeared more Irish than Italian. He wore a double-breasted, pin-striped navy-blue suit.

"Hello, boys!" The uncle greeted us heartily. Without being invited, he and Benny sat down at our table. "So you're with the U.S. Government, perfesser," he said to me.

I said I wasn't.

"Well, you're diplomatic, aincher, perfesser?" he said. He was nervously ill at ease, his geniality was pure bravado. "I'm from Cleveland, perfesser. Where you from?" He produced another picture of the fieldstone house and still another of a brick house. "Used to own this down in Cleveland," he said. "Didn't have any zoning when we bought it fifteen years ago. Nice enough neighborhood then but you know how it is, perfesser. All the scum started moving in and niggers. So I got out from under before it was too late and built this in Shaker Heights."

Benny said nothing; it was obvious that the uncle had decided to carry the conversational ball alone. I said Benny's family must have been very surprised, having an American uncle drop in without warning.

"Never bother to let anyone know, perfesser. Just like to pop in. That way you can always do as you like. Anyone says traveling is cheap these days ought to have his head examined," he noted. "They say Rome's a dead city, and believe me, perfesser, it is. So dead it stinks. Spent my first night here in the Villa Igea. Most expensive in town and there wasn't no soap in the bathroom."

Was he traveling for business or pleasure? I asked.

"Strictly for pleasure, perfesser. Couldn't make a tour last year on account of business being too good, but otherwise I make it every year for my nerves. If I didn't make the tour I'd crack up. I figure it's cheaper buying airplane tickets for my nerve tours than payin' doctors' bills."

"In two years Benny must have changed quite a bit," I said.

"Yeah, the kid's growing up. He's a bright boy." Benny beamed happily. "Bright as a whip. Sure would like to get him over to the States. I figure yer bein' a perfesser, perfesser, and in wid dem diplomats, maybe you can help me get Benny across." I said the best way to accomplish this was for him to file an affidavit of support since he was a relative.

"Yeah, I know, perfesser, but you see I don't really think I'm close enough related."

"You're his uncle. That's close enough."

"Not really, perfesser. It's more like second or third cousin. You know how these Sicilians are. Everybody's an uncle."

"Aren't you Italian born?" I asked.

The American uncle drew himself up indignantly. "I'm an American, perfesser. Born and raised there."

"Then how are you Benny's cousin?"

"You see, perfesser, my wife's a cousin with his folks. That's how it is."

"Then your wife is Sicilian."

"No, sir, she ain't. She's American, too. Her people came from Italy. The north someplace. About getting Benny across, perfesser, I'll pay the tab, no matter how much it is."

"If your wife is Benny's cousin, she should sign the affidavit," I said.

"Don't think she will, perfesser. You know how women are—always worrying about signing things."

Across the table Benny was scowling at the way things were going. The conversation had stalemated. Frank and I were finished eating so we excused ourselves.

"See you in three days," Uncle Sam called after us.

Frank muttered. "The Sicilians have been trying for secession from Italy as long as I can remember. Why don't we give it to them? They are not Italians. We should be glad to be rid of them."

Three mornings later when we went down to breakfast, we found Uncle Sam sitting alone in the dining room. He got up to greet us. "How're you, perfesser. Been waiting here, figuring you'd be in. That Agrigento was a bust. Wouldn't you know it, those almond blossoms were *kaputt*. Just my luck. Too late for the flowers, too early for the nuts.

"Have a cigarette, perfesser! Sorry they ain't American. You can't tell what they put into these Eyetalian ones. Benny will be back with Luckies in a shake or two. He gets 'em black market for two hundred and fifty lire. If you go to a tobacco store, they soak you four hundred. It's robbery, but that's the way these Sicilians are. You can't trust them. Cheat you every time.

"That's how Benny's different from other Sicilians. You can trust him. I'll bet you wouldn't believe, perfesser, that I just gave Benny a ten-thousand-lire note to get me a pack of cigarettes. 'Uncle Sam, you can trust me,' he says. Wouldn't think the kid's never been more than thirty miles from Palermo, would you?

"Perfesser, I'm going to tell you straight out why I sent the kid out for cigarettes. I've been wanting to talk to you, and I figure this is my chance if I get rid of the kid for ten minutes.

"You see, perfesser, I'm not really the kid's uncle. I told Benny yesterday he ought to stop calling me 'uncle.' 'This perfesser's a smart guy,' I said, 'and he's going to think it is peculiar.' But then you know how they are over here. They're not like us Americans. They call everyone 'uncle.' Since I enjoy doing things for boys, I guess I'd say I *am* a sort of uncle to them. An American Uncle Sam!

"I got 'nephews' like Benny in Paris and Marse-ayse and Genoa and Rome and Tunis. In fact, I got 'em all over. They're not really my nephews, but just poor, unfortunate kids I like to give a helpin' hand to. Kids behind the eight ball. It's real gratifying to have the boys appreciate what you do for them.

"Of course, I don't do it for gratitude. You see, I was lucky. But it hasn't all been clover. When I got married in thirty-five I didn't have a pot—well, you know what I mean, per-fesser. I got into deep freeze on the ground floor and things've been hay ever since. I made my pile, I admit. That's why I like doing my good deeds.

"So I make this cruise every year to see my nephews. Usually start out right after January inventory. I tell you, perfesser, if I didn't have my cruise every year, it'd be a nervous break-down for me. My wife is understanding. It was she started calling my trips 'Sam's nervous-breakdown-prevention cruises.' I figure I owe my wife a trip, and one of these times I'm going to take her. We'll drop in on Palermo to see Benny, though my wife couldn't stand the town for very long. Too unsanitary. A lady likes soap in the bathroom and some of the comforts.

"Perfesser, it's my boy William that's responsible for my nervous condition. Tried to get him to go to college. Wanted to send him to Princeton, and, would you believe it, he didn't wanna go. Can't make him do a thing. Extravagant, too. Give him fifty dollars and in two hours it's gone. Trouble is, he's drinking a lot, which no eighteen-year-old boy should do. He just can't seem to keep his mind on nothing. Don't seem to have no sense of responsibility. I keep telling him he ought to have it like my nephews over here. Just one week of that is all I wish him.

"The ironic thing is, perfesser, here's this kid Benny, exactly the same age as my son and the difference is remarkable. Calls me 'Uncle Sam' real respectful. Why, he'd call me 'Mister' if I'd let him! That kid thinks the world of me. All my nephews do. Didn't know, perfesser, did you, that I had my plane tickets for Paris yesterday? When I told it to Benny, he started to cry. Well, sir, I'm not chicken, but seeing those tears on that boy's face fixed me. I changed my reservation for tomorrow just to spend two more days with the kid.

"Did I ever tell you how I met Benny, perfesser? Well, it was on my cruise two years ago. When I got off the boat, there he was on the dock. Asked me to carry my bag in perfect English. Just a kid—sixteen. I tell you, perfesser, he touched my heart. I hired him as a guide and kept him right in the hotel with me. Imagine what it meant to him, a kid that never had a lousy lira of his own, living in the Villa Igea? In case you don't know it, the Villa Igea's a classy joint. Charge you five thousand lire a night and don't give you no soap.

"Well, sir, I'm telling you, we had a time. I planned to stay three days and he had me here more than a week. Took me to his house for dinner, Benny did, to meet his family. You shoulda been there, perfesser. Made you glad you were an American. There they was in two rooms—you know how these Eyetalians live—the mother and father and five kids and an old grandmother thrown in.

"I expect you're wondering why I'm talking to you like this. Naturally I ain't quite in your class. But one thing you can always say about me, perfesser, I'm honest. So I'm going to come right out with it and tell you I'd like to impose on you for a favor. Not actually for me, perfesser, but for Benny.

"You see, I figure Benny's American material. He's got the stuff that distinguishes us from the rest of the world. You know what I mean? After all, I always say, we were all foreigners once. My own people came from Germany and Ireland and yours must'a come from someplace too. Naturally it makes you think.

"You know how it is with the quota and all them laws. It's just about impossible for an Eyetalian to get to the States these days. Well, I'm working on this scheme to get Benny to America. I got a way figured out to pull it off. I'll get him registered in some college, and that way he can get a student's visa for three years. In three years I can find him a little *signorina* from one of those Eyetalian families on Mayfield Road, and get him married. Then there he'll be—married and in America—and no one's going to send a man with an American wife back to Italy.

"The way I figure, it can't miss. And here's where you come in, perfesser. With your connections and my money—I'm not Rockefeller, you understand, but I admit I don't have to worry none—why, together we can pull it off. I figure with a letter from you saying what an exceptional kid Benny is, we can get Benny into a good college. Don't spare the expense, perfesser. I'm good for it.

"I don't anticipate any trouble at all getting him married to an Eyetalian girl. I'm telling you, perfesser, he's got a way with him. Why, with his charm, perfesser, I'd marry him myself—I mean, of course, if I were a little Eyetalian girl looking for someone who can ring the bell. D'ye get it? Here he comes with the cigarettes now.

"I'm sure glad I didn't go to Paris yesterday, perfesser, now that I've had a talk with you. Does a man good to get things off his chest. You're going to write that letter, ain't you, perfesser?"

I did not write the letter for Uncle Sam but I did arrange a job interview for Benny at the American business firm. I told him about it while the two of us were sitting in a little bar across from the opera house. I spoke candidly, reminding him that in the ten days we had known each other he hadn't always told me the truth. Immediately that crushing how-can-you-mistrust-me look crossed his face, but I went on. "I think I understand why you have told me lies," I said. "It is because you need your dreams to escape the hard reality of life. It is not wrong to dream, but one must also face the world realistically and learn the difference between dreams and reality. If you don't learn this you will never be able to work for Americans."

He interrupted me. "I am your dear, true friend who has never told you an untruth."

"You are lying now," I said angrily. "Unless you admit to me that you have lied I will not consider that you were ever my friend."

He was silent for a moment. Then I saw tears well up in his eyes and roll down his cheeks. His lips were trembling. "You are right," he said. "I am ashamed. So ashamed I can no longer look at you. How could I have made these lies to you—you who is like a god to me, the best friend I have ever had? May God punish me for my dishonesty. I am a bad boy, *brutto, cattivo*, unworthy of the friendship of one like you. You must not forgive me. I do not deserve it."

I began to feel I had truly touched his heart. I said he need not apologize, that I understood how poverty and frustration brought out the worst in people. I ordered some wine, and we drank to our friendship.

"Because I have been such a bad person I am always a sorrow to my mother," Benny went on. "My mother is a good woman whose whole life has been nothing but sorrows. She eats and drinks sorrows. Is tomorrow her birthday and I will get her something, some little thing, to let her know I love her. Is not necessary much, only a flower perhaps. Understand?"

Immediately I was suspicious, wondering if this were another assault on my sympathy and purse. But his obvious sincerity made me feel guilty for continuing to mistrust him.

"She will be forty-three years old and she has never in her life had a pair of nylon stockings. It would make her very happy to have a pair of nylon stockings for her birthday."

I said I would buy some nylons. Since I was still not entirely free of suspicion I suggested that we go together to buy them.

"They must be American nylons," he said. "Italian nylons are lousy." He seemed very happy.

"Okay," I said. "American nylons." He led me through a jumble of winding streets to a shop where he importantly asked for "nailon Americano." Several pairs were brought out. He discarded them quickly as not being of high quality. More were brought and he finally found a pair that seemed to suit him. He asked the clerk to remove them from the cellophane package so that he might examine the weave and the seams. To me he said in English, "Is often discards, these American nylons, and is necessary to be very careful." I watched him run his arm inside the stockings and spread his fingers like a Saks Fifth Avenue buyer considering a purchase of fifty thousand pairs. He found a flaw and asked for another pair. He pronounced the second pair perfect and asked the price.

"Two thousand lire," the clerk said.

"Two thousand lire," echoed Benny. "Too much. Is ridiculous!" Benny argued with the clerk for a moment and then walked out in protest.

"Is because they see you are American," Benny explained

to me quickly. "They are robbers. Thieves! Understand? They think I am buying the stockings for you! They do not know Americans are their best friends. I know a place where the same stockings cost fifteen hundred lire."

I suggested we go to the shop where stockings sold for fifteen hundred lire.

"But you cannot go along," Benny said. "That is the trouble. When they see an American they add five hundred lire to the price, *subito!*" Since I had observed the tactics of Palermo shopkeepers with American sailors, I gave Benny the fifteen hundred lire. He thanked me "a thousand times" and said he would meet me later in the hotel.

In a half hour he was in our room. Yes, he had bought the stockings; they were perfect. He had left them in the room of the American uncle downstairs. "My mother will bless you for your kindness on her birthday," he said. "It will be the only present she will have." He had one more small favor to ask of me. "Will you be so kind as to say to my uncle that you think I would make a good husband for his daughter?" he asked. "Understand?"

When Frank and I went into the dining room the American uncle was there eating alone. "Benny just left for Bagheria," he said. "Had to go out there because his old lady's got her forty-third birthday tomorrow and the kid—you know he's got a heart of gold—wanted to get her something nice, like some nylon stockings. Didn't have any money so I helped him out. 'Sure,' I said, 'you ought to get your old lady something.' I gave him five thousand lire and he went out to buy the stockings before he went home. You know how the Sicilians are. Sentimental as hell about mothers and things. That's one of the things that appeals to me about Benny. They don't come more honest or with a bigger heart than Benny."

A TOUR AROUND A LEGEND

"I am shepherd to another man,
And do not shear the fleeces that I graze . . ."
—WILLIAM SHAKESPEARE, *As You Like It*

CHAPTER 1

DREAM

ONE DAY in the streets of Palermo I came across an Oxford student negotiating to buy a donkey. This sturdy-spirited young Sancho Panza was going to spend his academic holiday crossing Sicily from Palermo to Syracuse in the classic fashion —on foot. The donkey was to serve as a companion and a conveyance for supplies. With a donkey companion he had successfully crossed Crete on an earlier holiday.

In Sicily, he soon discovered, donkeys were more expensive than in Crete. Nevertheless he purchased a gray, elderly beast which the Sicilian owner assured him would make a steadfast and loyal companion. The donkey, after a lifetime of heavy cargoes over Palermo's cobblestones, would be grateful for a holiday in the country. The student paid for the animal, which subsequently refused under any circumstances to depart from Palermo. The student consulted with the donkey's ex-owner, who said that naturally the donkey would not leave without his mascot. A donkey with a dog mascot would have been more convenient, but unfortunately this donkey's friend was a goat. The goat would cost another twenty-five thousand lire and would provide fresh milk on the trip.

Like the student, I wanted to cross to the east and see as

much as possible en route, but I did not want to do it with a goat. Sicily, which is about the size of Vermont, presents formidable problems of transportation. Not that it should, since it has been well traveled for over twenty-five centuries. The island, the first European soil won by the Allies from the enemy in the second World War, is a bridge between Europe and Africa, blocking the western gateway to Greece, Turkey, Egypt, and the oil fields of the Middle East.

Frank and I consulted a travel agent and learned that by rail it would be possible to puff at a snail's pace through the middle of the island, changing not only from train to train but from one width of track to another. The agent, an exuberant man, told us of a bus line which that very week was inaugurating a six-day, round-the-island tour with daily departures from Palermo. He showed us diagrams of an "automotive luxury liner" with a glass top, individual reading lights, controlled heat, a radio, washroom, a "sanitation," and a bar. In addition to the two drivers he promised "a uniformed hostess as charming as your American air-line hostesses." A map of the tour showed a clockwise route, clinging for the most part to the coast. The schedule, made out like a railroad timetable, provided a half hour for the temple of Segeste, thirty-five minutes for the ancient city of Selinunte, and twenty minutes for the important industrial town of Ragusa.

It seemed an appalling whirl and certainly no way to see Sicily. "Ah," said the agent, "it is exactly for discriminating travelers like you that we have inaugurated a daily service. You can leave your bus whenever you like, stay as long as you wish, and join up with another bus when you are ready."

This seemed reasonable, so we bought tickets to Taormina on the northeast corner of the island. "You will see the mountain lair of bandits," the agent said, offering his most persuasive selling point. "Before the death of Giuliano the bus was escorted by three police motorcycles and a jeep with tommy guns." I was sorry we were four years late. A glass-topped, air-conditioned, Sicilian version of the great train robbery appealed to me.

Early on Friday morning—the second day of the new daily schedule—the sleek bus collected us at our hotel. There were three passengers already aboard: a large, sullen, blond young man and a middle-aged couple from Zurich behind whom we found our numbered seats. I assumed other people were to be picked up but soon we were driving through the dreary outskirts of the city and it was obvious there were to be no more passengers. This dismal situation did not dampen the agonizingly high spirits of our hostess, a sprucely tailored girlish brunette who, it turned out, was also on her first tour of Sicily.

Shortly after getting under way she clapped her hands together sharply and said, "Ladies and gentlemen, we are starting now on our glorious tour of eternal spring. A happy journey to you all. I am Miss Provoloni, but to you I will be known as Carla, for we are all going to be friends." Carla repeated her well-rehearsed introduction three times—in Italian, in perfect French, and in charming, adequate English. "I introduce to you the other members of our holiday family. This is Enzo . . ." The driver at the wheel turned and waved. "And this is Tullio." The tall auxiliary seated at his side bowed stiffly. Carla told us the radio was out of commission, a blessed stroke of luck as we were to learn by experience with subsequent busses. The bar, an ice chest filled mostly with Coca-Cola, also was a dubious blessing. Otherwise everything seemed to be as promised.

Sicilians say nature covers their island with wild flowers to celebrate Persephone, who was gathering them when Pluto abducted her. We drove through fields of daisies, anemones, marigolds, meadows of red poppies, valleys of iris bluer than the heavens, and rows of ripening orange groves. There were

also flaming spikes which I didn't recognize and a tiny lilac
blossom that looked like heather. It was the time of the spring
harvest and the farmers were gathering peas, piling the green
pods high on their gay donkey carts. Cart painters are Sicily's
popular historians; they treat legend and fact with equal
spontaneity. Sicily's history is long and tumultuous. The ancient tribes of Sicani and Siculi were conquered by, and in
turn absorbed, Phoenicians, Greeks, Romans, Vandals, Byzantines, Saracens, Normans, and Spaniards. In addition to the
blood of their conquerors, the Sicilians also absorbed their
legends. Venus rises from her shell, the Virgin is assumed into
heaven. Charlemagne commissions his knights, and the cross-
eyed Orlando duels with Saracens; Garibaldi unites Italy and
Salvatore Giuliano is martyred by an assassin's bullet. It was
all on the carts.

As we moved farther into the hills, the villages became
meaner and poorer. Each town was an island of despair, as if
nature, lavishing her beauty on the fields, reserved all her
ugliness for the habitations of men. Barren little houses were
clustered together, their only sewage disposal being a street
gutter slimy with filth. Children and goats sunned themselves
in the mud.

"*Das ist schrecklich!*" said the woman in front of us in Swiss
to her husband.

"*Schrecklich!*" he said.

Towns had only two colors—the yellow-brown of stone and
the black of death. Finding comfort in mourning, the Sicilian
seems to long for death. Only children and unmarried women
do not wear black. Doors are hung with black rectangles of
cloth to indicate mourning. Some houses don't bother with
the cloth but simply paint a black streak across the doors,
permanently marking the home for sorrow. "*Per mia madre,*"
the words say, "*nostri parenti,*" or simply "*bambini.*" Breeding is the diversion of the poor; birth and death the pre-

occupations of the underprivileged; sorrowing their perverse joy. What with large families and high infant mortality, hardly a family exists that doesn't face death each year. Looking down a village street it seemed as if a whole people were mourning the death of their country.

Black is also appropriate to the hopelessness of a feudalism of slaves and land barons. Sicily has sixty princes, two hundred marquises, eighty counts, and two hundred barons, many still clinging to huge ancestral estates, draining the wealth from the land to support their sybaritic lives. One can see them, overdressed, with faces of ice, at the opera and the night clubs of Milan, Rome, and Palermo. Once the friends of kings, later the supporters of Mussolini, and now courtiers of democrats, they are bejeweled chameleons who learned generations ago to take on the protective coloring of their environment. Their cloaks are of many colors. But the peasants, whom they consider lower than beasts, wear the everlasting black.

For our bus the villages were filled with hazards. It measured fifty feet long and fourteen feet wide, hardly a foot less than the width of some of the streets. Occasionally we scraped against a building, but for the most part our drivers proved themselves highly skilled. At difficult corners Enzo painstakingly shunted the bus backward and forward while Tullio gave him signals from the outside.

Country hazards were of a different sort. Most numerous were the hitched donkeys and mules with their inevitable dog or goat mascots. Carla said the beasts of burden often become unmanageable without their mascots trotting beside them. Mules prefer goats, donkeys are partial to dogs. Other obstructions to our progress included funerals, a herd of buffaloes, and, on twisting mountain roads, other busses. We stopped for a cow, calmly suckling her calf while a farmer, holding the cow's rope in his hand, prayed at a wayside prayer station.

The first shrine pointed out to us by Carla was the village

of Montelepre. We drew up on the highway to look at it in the distance, a cluster of ocher-colored buildings on a hill. The atmosphere in the bus was one of hushed reverence.

"There was born Salvatore Giuliano," said Carla. "The name 'Salvatore,' " she added, "means 'savior.' "

All eyes were fixed on the birthplace of Sicily's newest god.

Giuliano's story belongs to the history of Sicily. It is inconceivable that he could have sprung from any other soil. Turridu, as he was known to his mother and friends, was nourished by the American dream; it drove him to self-conscious heroics and acts of foolhardy daring. The Sicilian hardly exists who doesn't claim American connections—a relative in Brooklyn, Rochester, Chicago, or any of a hundred other American towns. Turridu was more rooted than most; he could boast that he had been conceived in America and just missed being born there. His parents had emigrated. In America the hoped-for success had not materialized; the Giulianos were hardly better off than they had been in Sicily. Frustrated and probably homesick, they returned to Sicily in 1922 with their three children. The fourth the mother carried home in her womb.

She was a small, powerfully willed peasant woman who, from the moment of his birth, loved her youngest and most handsome child with a mystic fierceness, as if she sensed some unique destiny for him. The strong attachment of Sicilian mothers for their sons is in some way related to the Madonna and Child of the churches. The mother of Turridu, like the mother of Jesus, was named Maria.

Giuliano's parents nurtured him with fantastic tales of the riches and grandeur of America. He grew up thinking himself to be in some mysterious way an American. He was a good if somewhat spoiled child. During his adolescence he was known for piety in church. He read tales of knighthood and brooded about the injustices of the poor at the hands of authority. He liked hunting and became an excellent marksman.

He was sixteen when he went to work for the telephone company in Palermo. In the city he saw Hollywood crime and gang films; the fact that gangsters were often portrayed as Sicilian types must have impressed him. When the war came, he dreamed of being an Army flier, but Allied landings ended the fighting in Sicily too soon. It was a time of chaos. In Montelepre there were his mother and sisters. To help feed them, Turridu, like many others, became a black-marketeer. One night in a brawl over a sack of contraband wheat, he killed a policeman. It was a casual incident; to Sicilians, who so hate policemen that a family is ashamed if a son becomes one, it may even have been an act of bravado. Until the excitement died down, Turridu took to the caves of Calcelrama, the mountain which hovers over Montelepre in the east. From here he could look down on the house that was his home and the black dots of his family moving about the fields and the streets. He spent his time, as he later said, thinking about justice and "meditating on my future." As he brooded on the poverty of his people, on the oppression of landlord and church, he did not forget the religion of his boyhood. No doubt he dwelled on Jesus' forty decisive days in the wilderness. As he worked out his future course, his Robin Hood–Messiah complex was born. Never, he said later, did he think of himself as a criminal.

When the savior finally came down from the hills, secession was in the air. He became a mercenary for the Separatist Volunteer Army for Sicilian Independence. Another policeman was slaughtered in a civil uprising and the Separatists disbanded. It was the moment of crystallization. The fate-forces were moving ahead and Turridu couldn't turn back. He became his own political leader with his own army, consisting largely of hero-worshiping Monarchists and young followers of the Mafia. He organized an underground of agents and spies with hide-outs throughout western Sicily. His strategist was a brainy Italo-American named Frank Mannino. Turri-

du's own cousin, Gaspare Pisciotta, was his confidant. Pisciotta was the only one Turridu trusted. Toward the end he
would not be parted from him even while he slept. They
shared a Homeric blood pact, piercing their fingers and, with
sticky hands, swearing their fidelity unto death.

In the reign of terror, murder, ransom, and robbery that
followed, the victims almost always were the rich. Once when
some of his ruffians ransacked a poor town, Turridu had
them shot. He shared his loot with poor villages like Montelepre; how much it is not known, but it was enough to rally
the people to him. In the rise of the oppressed against the
oppressor he was to be their leader.

He read translations of American books, especially those
of John Steinbeck. Linking his American dream with his Messiah complex, he expounded the plan for Sicily to secede from
Italy and become the forty-ninth American state. He wrote
to Truman and was piqued that the President did not reply,
a courtesy he felt the head of one state deserved from another.
The plan was supported by American gangsters who saw in
Sicily an island base for European operations.

He became a romantic figure. Producers announced film
biographies of his life, and magazines described his "virile
beauty." Because of the powerful Mafia's protection, harassed
police could not track down Turridu even though he was
accessible to foreign journalists and cameramen who sought
him out. A Swedish newspaperwoman who came from the
north to share his life in the hills reported later that he told
her he would not "soil myself" with women. Turridu could
love no mortal other than himself, his cousin Pisciotta, and
his *cara mamma*. Now that he was a god and, like all gods, a
lonely being, he must have loved *her* more than ever, for was
she not a Demeter-Mary who, by the mysterious ties of blood,
was deeply involved in his maniacal fate?

His enemies were the organized police, the organized Communists, the reorganized Separatists, and, most of all, the gov-

ernment in Rome. In Turridu's hatred, Rome was now personified by Mario Scelba, a fellow Sicilian who was Minister of the Interior. Turridu considered Scelba a traitor to Sicily. When Scelba offered a reward of five million lire for the capture of Giuliano, Giuliano offered a higher reward for the capture of Scelba.

The death struggle between them was set off when Scelba ordered an army of more than a thousand hand-picked northern Italy soldiers to flush out and destroy Giuliano. To command the troops Scelba appointed Colonel Ugo Luca, a romantic military figure known as "the Italian Lawrence." His aid was Captain Antonio Perenze, a veteran of the war in North Africa. Giuliano tried to kill Colonel Luca and almost succeeded.

Giuliano was accustomed to addressing the people through articulate and forceful letters published in Palermo's newspapers. One of the colonel's first moves was to close the newspaper columns to Giuliano. Giuliano responded with hundreds of posters which appeared on the streets of Palermo.

When Maria—along with other relatives—was imprisoned in Palermo, Turridu's hatred turned into an obsession for revenge. "*Mamma*" became his battle cry. One dawn the Palermo posters addressed Luca and his men. Giuliano wrote: "I feel what 'Mother' means and I shall never surrender, for I consider you to be against motherhood. It is not only experience that helps me in my fight but God himself, whose aim is to protect the cherished love of our life, the Mother, from destruction."

Maria was finally released, for "reasons of health," it was announced, but more likely because the soldiers hoped her son would establish contact with her.

With the arrival of the soldiers from the north, Montelepre and the silent gray hills encircling it became a battlefield. The six thousand inhabitants lived under military rule; there were times when the curfew allowed them to leave their houses only for an hour in the afternoon. Shock troops, parachutists, and reconnaissance aircraft provided the necessary show for Rome. Tear gas, noisy machine-gun fire, and third-degree grillings became everyday occurrences in the daily lives of the people. Despite their suffering, they never wavered in their loyalty to Turridu. The monarchical Sicilians who hated their union with kingless Italy now called him the King of Montelepre and were proud to be his subjects.

It was a humble kingdom, this small town baking silently in the sun, even meaner and poorer than the others.

CHAPTER 2

BIRTH

THE BUS GEARS GROUND and we climbed a hill so slowly I could count the petals on the roadside daisies. In front of us the Swiss were discussing the other passengers with brutal candor. Since Swiss was the language of my childhood and Frank had picked up a considerable amount in his northern travels, we listened with interest. They had learned that the blond and bored youth was a Copenhagen travel clerk sent by his employers to see if the Sicilian roundabout would appeal to Danes. This was why Carla was giving him special attention. As for Frank and me, the Swiss wondered whether we were American or Italian. The possibility that we might be one of each had not occurred to them. When the woman said that we were "*gwiss cinque* [certainly wops]," Frank pointed to a goat leering from a doorway of a house. "*Ist das nicht schrecklich?*" he said loudly.

Mr. and Mrs. Swiss froze, but only for a moment. The wife greeted us into the fraternity of Zurich and some miles later made us a peace offering of chocolate. "*Schwyzer schokolade,*" she said, now that we were all chauvinists together. "You do not get chocolate like this in Italy."

We climbed up another hill and suddenly, from the summit, there it was before us, the vision of Segeste. I had seen the lonely temple to Demeter twice before and each time my heart had soared. For Goethe it was a melancholy sight. "A shrill wind whistled through the columns as if through a wood, and screaming birds of prey hovered around the pediments." Now swallows darted in and out of their mud nests in the cornices and in the valley below tiny sheep bells tinkled sweetly. The morning sun turned the soft-colored stone to gold. The floor of the temple was carpeted with flowers, and insects buzzed over the blossoming turf.

The temple is all that remains of a proud and prosperous Doric metropolis which faced the northern sea. Segestans were ambitious: they battled hard against their enemies of the even more powerful and ambitious Ionic city of Selinunte to the south. Both cities were fraught with intrigue. Eventually Segeste was overrun by the tyrant Agathocles of Syracuse, and, about the year 900, was completely destroyed. The temple which was under construction when Agathocles devastated the city was never finished. It still stands on a gently rising slope, a perfectly preserved quadrangle of thirty-six massive columns without a roof.

Carla was reading from an English guidebook. "The statue of Minerva was a beacon to sailors on the seas. . . ." I looked for the sea; a fragment of it was visible two or three kilometers away. "You have heard of the Punic wars?" The Swiss had gone off to write post cards and Carla was directing her discourse to the Dane.

"No," the Dane replied, indifferently.

"Threatened by the Carthaginians, the city confided her fortunes into the hands of Dionysius," Carla read.

I looked over her shoulder. The wind had turned the pages of her guidebook and she was reading, as I had feared, about Syracuse. She continued to read to the disinterested Dane.

"During the second Punic war Archimedes was killed. . . ."

From below came the blast of Tullio's horn; the twenty-seven minutes scheduled for Segeste were up. The temple had stood for twenty-five centuries and it would doubtlessly stand for twenty-five more, perhaps long after man has wiped himself from the earth. Frank and I suddenly had the same idea: twenty-seven minutes were not enough. We remembered that the *padrone* of a small *trattoria* below the temple had a room for rent so we decided to make our first stop of the tour.

Carla was depressed by our decision. The trio that remained to her was certainly a dismal group. "It is not a happy outlook," said Frank as we watched the bus leave. "Before the trip is over Carla and the Dane will either sleep together or kill each other. Either would be very tragic."

We were left in a lifeless place. Green lizards darted in and out of the porous rock, and clumps of greenery sprouted from the tops of the columns like mold on cheese. The roots cracked the soft rock; the columns were crumbling like rotten trees. The temple seemed to be dying before our eyes.

Still there was life in the silence. From a deep gorge behind the temple came the roar of water; cawing jackdaws swooped in and out of the canyon. The air was rank with the aroma of some pungent plant, probably wild onion. From hidden canyons came the sweet tinkle of the sheep bells. At the *trattoria* we bought some salami, cheese, bread, and wine. Sicilians say March is "*il mese pazzo* [the crazy month]," and as we started to climb the hill where the ancient city stood, a black cloud rolled over the mountain and brushed us with rain. We returned to borrow a large shepherd's umbrella. As we trudged up the muddy path, wet asphodel pollen speckled our clothes with orange. A lean shepherd's hound followed us, led on by the scent of the meat in our sack.

Of the four of Sicily's great classic theaters, Segeste's is the most awe-inspiring. Not as romantic as Taormina's, nor as grand as Syracuse's, its serenity is pure. Protected by a wall from the wind and rain, we watched a quick-moving Wagnerian drama of weather: alternating scenes of darkness and light rolled over the mountains and valleys and out to the sea beyond. A shepherd who was gathering herbs in the hills joined us in our seclusion. With him and the amiable dog we shared our lunch. As we ate the shepherd told us a legend.

"Sicily was the Garden of Eden, the place God created for man before man offended Him. Ever since then God in His anger has visited all His sorrows on Sicily."

"How did the men of Sicily offend God?" I asked.

"With the sin of avarice," he said. "The avarice of a few and the faint, weak heart of many."

So it was. Here was a medieval system of landowners and sharecroppers which, in a land of eternal spring and abundance, keeps nearly five million people in poverty and despair. Once the hills had been dark with trees and the valleys rich and fertile. Man in his greed had taken the trees from the hills. The soil had washed into the sea and the valleys became barren.

Suddenly in the late afternoon a shaft of sunlight broke through the dark ceiling of the world. It fell on the brooding valley, illuminating the temple like a house in heaven. A string of sheep in single file encircled the temple like a necklace. On the rocks about us golden daisies, red poppies, and flowers I did not recognize opened their faces to the sun. It was an apocalyptic vision begging for the brush of El Greco.

That night the moon rose early and large. The temple golden by day, gleamed with silver. Water cascaded in the gorge and somewhere in a paddock the sheep bells tinkled fretfully. Two shepherds rustled through fennel and parsley looking for a lost ewe. They found her on the temple floor beside twin black lambs newly born. The mother was still prostrate from birth; the lambs rose, tottering unsteadily on spread legs. Glistening wetly in the moonlight and shivering in the night wind, they cried like new infants.

"Da due minuti," a shepherd boasted proudly. "But two minutes old." He made a covering of his cloak for the lambs. Two minutes old! Here in the midst of a crumbling ruin was a renewal of life; in an eternal place, eternity was reaffirmed. It was spring at the temple of Demeter.

CHAPTER 3

SILENCE

FROM DEMETER to Aphrodite is a short trip. In less than an hour a diesel train took us to the noisy seaport of Trapani where, in a hired car, we began the climb up Monte San Giuliano. The town on the summit, where Aphrodite was worshiped, was known to the Greeks as Eryx; today it is called Erice. To ascend it is a gamble, for the mountain's attractions are its views, and they are cloud-covered more often than not. The everlasting mists must have provided a certain seclusion for the sacred rites to Aphrodite performed there by the active priestesses.

The shrine seems to have been especially popular with seamen. As our overheated hired car chugged up the sixteen steep kilometers of the massive rampart it occurred to me that the priestesses of the temple must have favored sturdy worshipers. "No wonder the cult died out before modern transportation," said Frank. "After scaling the mountain how could they still have the strength to worship at the temple?"

The vistas of Sicily are not as grand as those in the Alps of the north. Northern mountains are spectacles of granite and ice that are formidable and impersonal. The mountains of Sicily are related to the men who live with them and in whose hearts they stir awe, fear, love, and hate.

We arrived in a glorious burst of sunlight which lit up the landscape like a rainbow. The town rested above a pine forest which grew like a tonsure around the mountain. Below us, surrounded by the mirrors of her salt marshes, Trapani glistened like a holy city. Out in the sea three fishing islands rose darkly up through water and clouds looking as if they had just been created.

Erice is a silent place where only the conifers sigh. The town was thatched with turf like a grave. The everlasting moisture had sprouted grass from between the cobblestones of the streets and the old gray stones of the houses; the Norman cathedral was spotted with green mold. The high places of Sicily are cold. Whenever a cloud shaded the sun, we rattled like corpses. It may have been this cold feeling of death that hushed the voices of Erice. Cloaked old men padded silently through the streets; even the children whispered.

We lunched at the hotel on *triglia*, a delicious little pink fish cooked with olive oil and capers, and a fine dry wine that was particularly refreshing after the sirups of the towns below. While we were eating, several men came over to greet us. They shook our hands silently and then watched us eat. When we were finished, one of them, a heavy man with a shining black toupee, guided us through a museum and library and then took us into a basement café for some coffee. In the dark room the polished *espresso* machine glistened like an altar. Behind it a bent old grandmother manipulated the steaming valves. Two children, brothers about five and seven, watched her. Bright-eyed and smiling shyly above their shining white collars, they looked like a pair of misplaced angels. Like everyone else in Erice, they did not speak. When I addressed them, they stared questioningly.

Our host (we called him The Wheel because he seemed to be a sort of community greeter) began to laugh. It was a good joke on us, he said, that the children were deaf mutes. They came from a family of five children, three of whom were deaf and dumb. At a signal from the old woman the boys moved their lips. The older one managed an inarticulate grunt, the younger only panted loudly, forming a foam at the mouth. They smiled, proud of their accomplishment, and were rewarded by the grandmother with a sweet. They were beautiful children, smiling and silent, like Erice herself. "I hope that they never leave this mountain," said Frank. "Then they will live quite happily. Here no one needs to talk."

The Wheel took us by car to a thirteenth-century church. We drove through a forest as quiet and sun-dappled as a Bavarian wood. Inside the old chapel The Wheel sank ecstatically to his knees and wept over the beauty of a grisly blood-flecked waxen saint in a glass coffin. Outside we heard a hum in the forest. A single file of black-robed, chanting women approached the church, an endless procession weaving through the wood like a black serpent.

At dusk we descended in our hired car through the clouds toward Trapani. "I am thinking of those poor old ancient seamen," said Frank, "and how wonderful is modern transportation." In the sunset the three fishing islands, named Favignana, Levanzo, and Marittimo, seemed to be rising from a sea of blood.

"This is nothing," said our driver. "You must come to see it at the time of the *mattanza*—the spearing of the tuna. Then the water boils with blood. It is like a bullfight in the sea."

As we entered the city on the plain the din of the street seemed almost unbearable.

CHAPTER 4

DEATH

N THE MORNING we picked up a tour bus in Trapani. This
ne was almost full, and Frank and I had the last available
eats, the ones next to the sanitation. The location turned
ut to be both advantageous and disadvantageous. One ad-
antage was that it was a good point from which to appraise
ur fellow passengers. The drivers were named Giuseppe and
Rodolfo; the hostess, an elfish girl with nasturtium-colored
air, was named Olivia. She was an extrovert who in no time
t all was telling Frank and me this was her second season as
 hostess and that she was on the road every day, leaving
Palermo the morning after returning from her previous trip.
The new daily schedule required a minimum of seven host-
sses and, as Olivia put it, "it is not a work many girls can do."
Olivia was a Roman of Sicilian descent and she had some-
hing to be sad about. "I have been in Messina with the bus
wenty times," she said. "But not once have I had the time to
visit the graves of my grandparents."

We were driving along the seaside lowlands, a flat agricul-
ural landscape flecked with windmills and sheep munching
yellow oxalis under the olive trees. "The first tourists of the
eason are usually English," said Olivia. "The English come

early because they have to get home in time to plant their gar
dens. Next come the Germans and then the Dutch and th
Scandinavians. Of course, Americans we have all the time.'

In accordance with Olivia's schedule, many of the passen
gers did seem to be British. There was a tall and bombasti
dentist from Canada whom his timid, quivering, younge
wife, Selma, called "The Doctor"; and two elderly Eng
lish ladies in felt picture hats, named Sarah and Cissie
Frank and I took them to be a pair of pensioned school
teachers. There were also two Americans. One of them, a
old widow, wore an ill-fitting trench coat and talked to n
one. Olivia said she was an alcoholic who hadn't been sobe
since Palermo. The other was a young artist from Michiga
named Blake who had become chummy with a Swedish med
cal student. Olivia said they were one of the "tour friend
ships" in which the company took such a proud interes
Sometimes these friendships turned sour, however, as in th
case, two weeks earlier, of an Oklahoma student architec
and a New York interior decorator who had insisted on sha
ing a room up to Agrigento and after that refused even t
sleep in the same hotel. "I have found," said Olivia, "tha
Americans are nervous people."

We stopped at the white-hot town of Marsala for lunc
Our drivers delivered us to a restaurant where white-jackete
waiters bowed us from the bus. I mistrusted the flourish c
the greeting, and my suspicions turned out to have been we
founded. On the bus we had been sold meal tickets for nin
hundred and fifty lire. The meal included some veal, mashe
potatoes, cheese, fruit, and wine. At the end of this undistir
guished repast everyone was handed an additional check fo
five hundred lire for the cheese and wine. Usually in suc
cases travelers pay to avoid a scene. Not so the doctor. In Ol
Testament rage he stalked from the restaurant, leaving i
staff to scream after him in hysterical Sicilian. The deed ha
taken courage and won for the doctor the respect of his fello

passengers. With equal wrath he turned on a small boy whom he caught urinating on a wheel of the bus.

Inside the restaurant Sarah and Cissie were having a crisis of their own. Sarah had lost her meal ticket and the cashier was demanding that she not only pay the additional five hundred lire but the original nine hundred and fifty a second time.

After all this it took some time for the passengers to calm down. I pitied Olivia, who, trapped between duty to her employers and loyalty to her passengers, was trying to cope with an insoluble moral problem.

We had turned inland toward the wild highlands, the turbulent landscape in which Salvatore Giuliano lived when his mother's home in Montelepre became too dangerous. The mountain flowers, being closer to heaven, were paler and more gently colored. Also, it was cooler. Men wore tentlike black shawls which even covered the donkeys they rode. Sewage from a village drained into a field of vegetables; the peas and lettuce grew richest along its course. Lovely young girls peered from dark doorways at the passing bus. The inevitable swatches of black were on the doors.

Our next stop was Castelvetrano. This agricultural town of twenty-five thousand citizens, the largest in the area, was unknown to the world until a July night in 1950 when the body of a young man, seven bullet holes in its flesh, was found in a courtyard. The last weeks of Turridu's life had been fantastic, judged even by his standards. The fates had moved with awesome momentum. Murder had become as necessary for him as breathing; the score credited to him for seven years was slightly more than a hundred persons, most of them *carabinieri*. It was a damning record for one who wished to be known in America as a democratic leader. To the press, he had given the kind of policy statements that ordinarily come from ministers of world powers. The concept of atomic control he found unworkable; the Atlantic Pact had his approval. He sent communications to the Prime Minister, hoping to bring about a truce with Rome. But he wasn't the power he had deluded himself into thinking. In the end he must have known it. He wanted to escape to America, the *paradiso* of his life's odyssey. Two days before the end there was rejoicing in western Sicily when word spread that he was on his way by secret plane. It wasn't true, they discovered quickly enough, when they found the body in the courtyard.

No one would tell how the King of Montelepre came to his humiliating death. Stories swept over the hills like shrub fires. One had it that he had been caught in the arms of a woman, another that he had been duped by vanity into meeting a trumped-up Hollywood producer with a scheme to star him in a film of his own life. However he had come to it, the Roman soldiers took the credit. In Castelvetrano's Hotel Selinus, Colonel Luca entertained at a victory celebration; in Rome, the Minister of the Interior, Scelba, received the congratulations of Prime Minister Alcide de Gasperi.

Through that first morning the body lay in the hot courtyard. The journalists who saw it were shocked at its youth. Expecting a bloodthirsty Macbeth, they saw a troubled Hamlet, almost a Romeo, whom they described as "a handsome boy asleep." When the body was finally picked up from the paving stones to be moved to the mortuary, it was found that the bloodstains on the clothing had no relationship to the wounds made by bullets that had ended Turridu's life.

We went to see the spot where he was found. The walls of the buildings were the color of earth. It was an operatic setting not unlike the village courtyard of Mascagni's Sicilian opera, *Cavalleria Rusticana*. Indeed, the end of Giuliano was incredibly like the final scene of the opera. Mascagni's fictional Mamma Lucia sobbing off stage, "*Turiddu! Che vuoi dire?*" is no match for the benedictive act of the real *cara mamma* of Giuliano. "*Sangue mio!* Oh, my blood!" she shrieked, and then she went to the courtyard to lick the red pavements where her son had lain. The opera has not been written to match that curtain.

"They betrayed him," she sobbed to the crowds and named Gaspare Pisciotta, the inseparable friend. From his hideaway, Pisciotta denied it and vowed he would devote his life to avenging his cousin's death.

During months of investigation and the trial of thirty-two of Giuliano's men in the courthouse of Viterbo near Rome, the story kept changing, and the official version of the death by the police was many times discredited. It became known that when the machine-gun bullets were pumped into his body, Giuliano was already dead. The police shots had been a blind to protect the real executioner and to save the face of the law. The blood which had stained the body had not flowed from it.

Six months after the death of Giuliano, Pisciotta was finally captured and brought to Viterbo. "For me there are only three things," he called out in court. "*La mamma*, Sicily, and Jesus Christ." His confession was published.

"I, Gaspare Pisciotta, assassinated Giuliano in his sleep. This was done by personal arrangement with Signor Scelba, Minister of the Interior."

He had, according to one version, given his cousin a sleeping potion in their room on the courtyard and then fired the death shot while Giuliano lay in the bed which they shared. In another version Pisciotta, when Giuliano was asleep, had signaled Colonel Luca's aide, Captain Perenze, who then fired the fatal shot. In either case, it would seem, as Abraham Lincoln said, "Brutus was created to murder Caesar and Caesar to be murdered by Brutus."

Of one thing there was no doubt. The end of Salvatore Giuliano's American dream had added a new hero to the gallery on the donkey carts. In the door of a shop I saw his photograph, a familiar late one in which the face was round, almost fat, in the way Sicilian men fill out while they are still young. The fiercely flashing eyes set too close together looked straight out of the photograph. There was in their challenging stare, in the strong line of the mouth, in the powerful thrust of the neck, much hatred, but none of the psychopathic cruelty of a killer. There was also in the eyes, I think, the fear of a beast cornered at last. Above all, I felt the hostile isolation of a lonely man.

CHAPTER 5

TEA

FROM CASTELVETRANO we rode to Selinunte, the short-lived city of splendor and ancient enemy of Segeste. The sight of the desolate plain and the ruins of the temples excited the two old English ladies. "Cissie! Look!" said Sarah. "They've destroyed the whole place. It's a terrible thing. The whole city. They've torn it right down." Sarah turned to Frank and demanded, "Young man! Do you know what happened?"

Frank did. He explained that Selinunte was a small city of twenty-five thousand, but its eight temples were the most lavish in the ancient world. Her glory aroused the hostility of the Segestans to the north and stirred the envy of roving Carthaginians. In 409 B.C., when Selinunte was hardly two centuries old, the Carthaginians destroyed it, killing two thirds of its citizens and selling the rest into slavery. Three thousand escaped.

"Young man," said Sarah sternly. "Where do you learn such awful things? Do you read them in books?"

As a ruin Selinunte couldn't have been less like Segeste. Of the northern city nothing remains but a pure and beautiful temple standing like the tombstone of a city on a green and quiet mountain. Selinunte's broad expanse of rock-strewn ruins is on a plateau over the sea where it is swept by warm African winds which eat into the fallen columns like the sun into ice, except that a thousand years is an hour. Perhaps an earthquake finished the Carthaginian destruction. The stones, occasionally preserving the shape of a temple but more often seeming as disorderly as an abandoned quarry, lie in fields of high-growing wild parsley—the *selinon* from which the city took its name. It is a place of unfathomable desolation.

A sad-looking Sicilian tried to sell me a Greek coin that he had doubtless hammered out that morning. On the fallen columns lizards flicked their tongues at the sun. Below, the anxious horn blared and I could hear the voice of Olivia. As usual I was going to be the last one on the bus.

Throughout the afternoon, we followed the coast, winding along a ledge over the sea. While most of the passengers slept, Olivia entertained Frank and me with gossip. She told us the driver Rodolfo, a Bolognese, was a thirty-five-year-old bachelor who, two months before, had fallen in love with a rich American passenger. She had returned to America to divorce her husband, after which she would come back to marry Rodolfo in Switzerland. Giuseppe, a chubby fellow, had a wife and several children at home and "a *fidanzata* in every town where we stop."

While we talked we could hear behind us the snoring of the two gray ladies who were sleeping with their mouths open. One of the impediments to our progress was the bus's "sanitation." Each time a passenger entered it, Olivia pressed a buzzer to signal the driver to slacken speed. "When someone is in," she explained, "we must go slow-slow, otherwise it shake him just like a cocktail." An even greater hurdle was the donkeys. We came upon one suddenly on a curve above the sea. He was going in the same direction, pulling a cart painted with the Virgin and the Resurrection and loaded with freshly harvested purple cauliflowers, on top of which rode the farmer. The machine monster startled the beast, and he galloped down the road scattering cauliflowers over the landscape. At a corner he turned too quickly, throwing the cart off the road and tumbling himself, the farmer, and cauliflowers pell-mell into the sea below. Fortunately the water was shallow and in no time at all Rodolfo and Giuseppe and several male passengers rescued the man, beast, and cart, gathered up the cauliflowers, and set it all up behind the bus. The dripping peasant scolded everyone and bewailed the loss of some cauliflowers that had floated too far toward Africa to be saved.

In the squares of the towns, men stood by for the bus watch. This was a ritual, an exciting break in the unexciting village day. Since the bus was seldom more than a half hour off schedule, the men gathered early and waited to greet it. Sarah was disturbed by their idleness.

"Why are they all standing there?" she asked. "Why don't they work?"

"Perhaps there is unemployment," said Frank. "They have no work."

"Well, why doesn't someone employ them?" Sarah was indignant. "Why don't they pay them to clean up their towns?"

Women did not go to the square; they peered stealthily from behind curtains or the shadows of their doors as if we were creatures from another world. Southern villages have a special color, a bleached gray-white upon which the sun beats with a blinding glare. The houses are square, thick-walled and windowless, and huddled together for protection from bandits and inter-village feuds. In the larger towns there was an occasional cinema, frequently showing films with Gianni and Pinotto (Abbott and Costello) or Stanlio and Olio (Laurel and Hardy). Votive niches over the doorways were filled with wax flowers and a burning candle. Under one of them a child held a brown loaf of bread as lovingly as if it were a doll.

"You'd think they'd at least wrap up their bread," Cissie said.

In the course of the trip, the ladies had taken a strong dislike toward me. I suspected it was because I was American. On the other hand, Frank seemed to have won their confidence. They chatted freely with him of their travels.

"Sarah can't bear trains," said Cissie.

"Cissie won't get into an airplane," said Sarah. "Ever since she's been a little girl she's been that timid."

"I suffer from vertigo," said Cissie.

"Vertigo's all in the mind," said Sarah. "One doesn't need to suffer from vertigo if one doesn't wish to."

"Mother has a very strong will," said Cissie.

I looked at the two gray ladies in astonishment. So alike were they it hardly seemed possible they should be mother and daughter. They were, it turned out, colonial widows from India. Cissie was born in India and in her time married a young man who came out from England to join her father's business. When both men died, Sarah and Cissie returned to Sarah's old home in Manchester.

"Cissie's name is really Constance. Cissie is what her daddy called her when she was a little girl," said Sarah.

"I left Manchester on Tuesday by train," said Cissie.

"I left Manchester on Friday morning," Sarah said. "I think nasty train soot is far worse for one's health than a little vertigo."

"I can't make mother understand that trains don't soot any more," said Cissie.

"I got to Palermo before she did," said Sarah. "I had to wait three hours for her train."

"That's because I stayed in Rome one day to visit St Peter's," said Cissie. "Much too high church for my tastes."

"We're going back to England the same way," Sarah said. "I'm taking the plane and Cissie's coming by train."

Frank was, for once, speechless.

In the town of Sciacca the bus stopped at a small seaside café for tea. The two ladies, seated at a table next to ours, found the tea most unsatisfactory.

"I don't know what's worse when you are traveling," Sarah said loudly, looking straight at me. "Cold tea or that disgusting Yankee accent you hear everywhere."

Outside the café a funeral procession crossed the piazza. A caravan of chanting priests, nuns, and children preceded the coffin; men and women followed it. As the black procession passed the parked bus, the mourners forgot the corpse for a moment, continuing their prayers mechanically as they stared.

The funeral had a saddening effect on Frank. "Life is tragic," he said. "So little time and so many important things to do. I am worried always that I will not have time for them all." He turned nostalgic and began to reminisce of his experiences at the international school the year before. His studies seemed to have been largely related to love.

"In May I have a French girl who is also a Jewess and was engaged to another student there," one fragment of the story began. "She was a virgin when she came, but she was no longer when she went. I find it very pleasant to possess virgins. The biggest love of the summer came in August. She was the wife of a mighty American lieutenant of the occupation forces. She was very pretty and, having much time with nothing to do, she came to the school to learn German. She was desperate because the mighty lieutenant is so jealous, so I think to cheer her. Every time I possess her it is very exciting. I think how the mighty lieutenant could make a sad sack out of me. I possessed her for the first time on the thirteenth of

August. I am superstitious on the number thirteen and I try always to make nothing on the date thirteen."

"That's very foolish of you," Sarah said from the next table. "Young people should know better than to be superstitious."

"I have never found the thirteenth to be different from any other day," said Cissie. "One might as well say that the seventh is unlucky, or the twentieth. It's quite the same thing."

I was surprised that the old girls should be eavesdropping, but Frank wasn't disturbed. He continued his reverie, lowering his voice only a trifle.

"So it was the first time I possessed a girl on date thirteen. I have a great hot for her before thirteen, for she was always fooling with strange things like doing belly dances when bathing in the lake. We had a terrible desire for each other. Her husband came for a visit. He could see when we looked that we had desire, and there was a big scene. But she told him she liked very much my conversation. Women can always fix those things very well with their husbands in bed."

"It's just what you'd expect," said Sarah, and Cissie added, "Nothing Americans do surprises us."

Frank, lost in his reverie, paid no attention to them. "One night the three of us are reading books in three corners of the library, all watching one another. You have no idea how baroque that library is. An old maid in the fourth corner was always playing the expressive music of Ravel. We sat sometimes looking one to the other. I felt violent. There were terrible difficulties. I was scared. I did not want trouble with that mighty lieutenant.

"So, on the date thirteen, the lieutenant had to go away. When he had went, the wife and I make a walk in the garden. I told her I am feeling dizzy for being with her. In such cases I always tell women the right things. I said, 'I'm scared of kissing your lips.' She said, 'Kiss them. You must.' So I pleased her. She never kept quiet with her body while I kissed her. Her body was always running around."

From the other table Cissie interrupted, "What do you mean, 'her body was running around'?"

"Young man," Sarah said, "I'm not really sure I like my daughter hearing these things."

"Never mind Mother," Cissie said to Frank. "She never would accept my growing up."

"We kissed us in every place," Frank went on. "In every part of the big park, and in places where there was hay. She wanted to possess me. 'We can't go on like this,' she said. In the garden there was a strange construction of wood where there were kept horses. The grass outside was too wet, and inside there was mud everywhere and only a small wooden bench. The moon was falling in through the boards and the half-destroyed construction was lighted in a terrible, tragic way. We were shaking with desire because both of us had much fear. There were shadows in the garden—some professors with their *own* wives. I realized the only way to possess her was on the hard wooden bench. She said I must pay attention to not make a baby. I said I would pay great attention. We leaned on the bench which was so small only one could lean at a time and there I possessed her. I tried greatly to keep her quiet. It was really deeply tragic. It is terribly sad how it happens, these things.

"After, there was some ambiguity between the lieutenant and me whenever he returned to the school. A Belgian journalist was also very fond of her, but he didn't succeed her. Only I succeeded her. She told me she would remain in Europe and return to Brazil with me. I discouraged her from doing that. When she and the lieutenant left for America it was very moving. Even the lieutenant was sad. He said, 'Frank, you are my good friend. I hope we meet again!' He was a good man."

Frank sighed. After a moment of silence he said, "It was a

beautiful experience. Very, very sad. I get very tragic thoughts thinking how these good men always get involved with these women that are not so good as they."

"A man only gets what he deserves," said Sarah.

"Do you think," asked Cissie softly, "it was really a great love?"

"She sent me one letter," Frank said. "She wrote, 'Since Charles and I have arrived home we have reached an understanding.' She asked me not to write to her or try to find her if ever I come to America."

"Never mind," said Sarah. "Who'd want to go to America anyhow."

"It is terribly upsetting to think about," Frank said, "and discourages me to marry."

We had hoped to reach the south in time for the almond blossoms, but the mild season had brought them out early and now the groves on the hills were green instead of pink. As we rode through the dusk toward Agrigento, Frank watched silently, absorbed by melancholy.

Cissie reached from behind to touch him on the shoulder. "Don't be sad, young man," she said. "I'm sure that American lady couldn't have been worth your heart."

"Come to England," Sarah said. "You'll find moral standards much more satisfactory there."

CHAPTER 6

HAPPINESS

SPREAD OUT below us in the evening were the lights of Porto Empedocle. The ancient port was one of the principal Allied beachheads of the war. Some rusted landing boats still lay there, almost buried in the sand. Braying goats and sheep trotted by us on their way home for the night. Here one of the best harbors in Sicily is sheltered by a sea wall built in the eighteenth century with stone from Agrigento's great temple of Zeus. "That was very naughty of the people," said Olivia over the bus's loudspeaker system.

"The most beautiful city of mortals," Pindar wrote of Acragas, the high city on a ridge facing the sea. Settled in 581 B.C., it grew second to Syracuse among Sicilian cities. It was during the reign of the great leader Empedocles that the somewhat ostentatious temples were built. According to a contemporary, the citizens of Acragas were pleasure-loving voluptuaries who cared for neither war nor athletics, but "delighted in feasts and dances and music, frequent changes of clothing and hot baths and love and sleep." After the death of Empedocles, the effete city was quickly plundered by Carthaginians and subsequently by Romans, Saracens, and Normans. The ravages continued into our time: Agrigento was bombed and shelled in 1943.

The modern city, birthplace of Pirandello, is a sorry ghost of Acragas. Its twenty-eight thousand citizens live in a crawling casbah perched on a steep hillside above the ancient site. The narrow, climbing streets always filled with shouting people and the combined odors of fish, cooking, and unidentifiable things remind one of Naples. There were impressive changes since my last visit four years before. The war wounds were almost healed. More than any town in Sicily, Agrigento was building. The changes were the outward signs of an effort by the Sicilian and Italian governments to make Agrigento a popular tourist town. The money came from the Cassa per Il Mezzogiorno (Southern Development Fund), which was financed by World Bank and American loans.

Streets were torn up for repaving. In the twilight I could see the severe lines and bright pastel colors of new apartments everywhere. Once the town had scarcely any hotels; now it seemed filled with posh hostelries. The old bombed hotel in which I had slept in a sagging room with only a shutter between me and the street was now a luxury house and a room cost three times as much.

The bus was going on to Syracuse the next day, but we were spending three days in Agrigento after which we planned an inland trip to Enna. Sarah and Cissie, the doctor and his wife were all staying in Agrigento. Olivia hoped to fill the empty seats with passengers waiting in the town.

That night I slept hard, not awakening until the morning street noises filled my room. It was a fair, crisp Sunday and the streets were packed. I read posters calling for "*Tutti monarchici uniti*" (All monarchists united) and, scrawled in chalk on a wall, "*Evviva il Duce.*" Women dressed in black wandered in and out of churches. Walking along the Salita Purgatorio, I came upon the Piazza Purgatorio, a square so small it looked like a stage setting for *Cavalleria Rusticana.* Two small baroque churches stood side by side, the Chiesa Purgatorio and the Chiesa dell' Adorazione Perpetua. I went inside Purgatory. It was as dark and narrow as a doll's church. A little priest was droning a mass. Eleven women in black shawls rocked on their knees, kneading their prayers like bread. An idiot twitched spastically, while an acne-covered, bespectacled youth pumped a wheezy organ and sang a reedy *Gloria*. There was a penetrating chill in the place. Fat cherubs hanging from the cornices grinned mockingly down at me until I departed from Purgatory and returned, like Persephone, to the sun.

A crowd of children quickly collected and followed me through the streets. Unlike the shouting *ragazzi* of other cities, they whispered their requests for money as if they were ashamed of what they were doing. Yet they could not be shaken off. One boy pushed aside the others as if I were his property and, walking close to my side, repeated his soft and never-ending *"Cinquanta lire, cinquanta lire."*

The fifty-lire boy did not give up until I arrived at the door of the museum. Inside, I found our doctor keenly enjoying an absurd neoclassic life-size male nude statue.

"Splendid, don't you think?" said the doctor.

I thought the arrogance and soft nakedness of the statue rather unpleasant.

"You don't see religious art like this very often," said the doctor.

To call a naked Pan-Apollo sitting on a log with vine leaves in his hair religious art struck me as a bit farfetched.

"Much pleasanter than those scrawny hair-shirt Baptists," said the doctor. I looked at the label on the statue. It was indeed "San Giovanni Battista."

His wife was upstairs looking at the paintings, the doctor said, so he led me into a basement room to see some Etruscan pottery he'd discovered.

"Shocking, don't you think?" His shock, however, seemed well under control as he lingered over the little domestic scenes. "Surprised they keep these things out where women

and children can see them. Of course, in these Catholic countries they're more careless about such things than we are."

He asked me if I were going to Taormina and I replied
that I was.

"Shan't be getting there. Have to get back to my patients,
you know," the doctor said. "But I wonder if I might ask
you to do me a favor?"

"You can ask."

"I'd like you to buy some photographs for me."

"Photographs?"

"Of boys. Ethnological types." The doctor seemed em-
barrassed. "Naturally they're nudes. They're not for me, you
understand. I have an anthropologist patient who asked me
to bring him some photographs for his research. Now I find
I'm not going to get to Taormina."

I knew to what he was referring. A bearded and earnest
German baron had spent a lifetime photographing the male
population of Taormina in grottoes and under olive trees.
Though the baron had been dead almost twenty-five years
and most of his subjects were either in their graves or had
emigrated to America, the nude photographs were still being
sold in Taormina. I remembered them being just as absurd
as the young John the Baptist upstairs. For the Sicilian subjects nudity seems to have been a casual thing. For the bearded
German baron and now the Canadian dentist's anthropological alter ego, it was somewhat more.

A network of ascending alleys brought me to the cathedral,
a curious hodgepodge of a building with renaissance walls, a
Norman ceiling, and a Spanish baroque altar. A herd of little
girls assailed me with outstretched hands and whispered
softly, "Carne, carne." Although they were using the Italian
word meat to mean food generally and money with which
to buy it, they didn't seem very hungry. All were neatly
dressed and had Sunday ribbons in their hair. Merrily they

ugued, "*Carne, carne, carne . . .*" turning begging into a
olly game.

A ragged old gnome smelling of sour wine and sour vestments shuffled from a door and invited me to see the *tesoro*
within. I went along. The treasures consisted of a shabby
Madonna by Guido Reni, a battered *bambino* attributed
to Caravaggio, walls covered with stiff portraits of dead
bishops, and a collection of ecclesiastical vestments embroidered with rubies and emeralds. "Worth at least sixty million
lire," the sacristan boasted.

I had enough of the dark, stale room and I started out. My
guide thumped after me on his old legs. "*Vuole pagare,
vuole pagare,*" he screamed. In gratitude for the tip he came
with me into the transept to show me still another treasure.
In a small, illuminated chapel was a grisly mummy in medieval dress glistening in a gold casket. Kneeling in prayer
before it were two young girls in brightly colored dresses.

"San Felice," the sacristan murmured humbly.

St. Happiness was a grisly sight. The lips were gone and
his teeth were set in a gruesome grin.

"The teeth are original," said the sacristan. "The rest of
the body was turned to dust and has been restored."

It was the only time I expected to be face to face with the
saint of happiness so I smiled as it smiled at me with its
horrid mouth of death. The two girls looked up without in-
terrupting their chants.

"More than a thousand years old, more than a thousand
years old," the sacristan droned. Happiness was dressed in a
warrior's armor of mail. His halo, tarnished by the years, lay at
his side. His head was resting on a hand wearing a delicately
tapered white glove.

"The gloves will be laundered for Easter," the sacristan
said.

As I stood before Happiness, a bishop, old and shrunken

but appearing tall in his miter, tottered across the empty church. Two white-faced acolytes carried his long, jeweled train. The bishop's old face was empty and bland; his pudgy, folded hands rode piously on his stomach. The two young girls continued to pray for I wondered what secret happiness and the little beggars whispered, "*Carne, carne, carne.*"

CHAPTER 7

HORSES AND DOGS

WE WANTED to begin our exploration of Agrigento's temples with Demeter, the oldest of them all. Our map showed it to be far from the other temples beyond a distant hill. We hired a carriage to take us there. The driver, named Fernando, was young and enterprising; his horse, Stella, was old and tired. We told Fernando where we wanted to go.

"It is a very long way," he protested. "No one goes there. I will take you first to the temple of Juno."

The temple of Demeter, we insisted.

"There is nothing to see. No temple at all. Only a hole in the ground."

Very well, we would see the hole in the ground.

"*Signori*, Stella is old; the hill is high."

Then we would hire another carriage.

Fearful of losing his fare, Fernando grew amenable. "Naturally, if the gentlemen wish to go to the temple of Demeter . . ." He tipped his cap, swung himself onto his seat, and began to snap the whip over the old beast's hairless rump. Stella tried to run, but her ancient legs synchronized badly; the best she could manage was a fumbling sort of trot. She seemed also to have been badly shod, for her hoofs skidded on the volcanic cobbles. I thought of Robert Burton's observation that England was a paradise for women and a hell for horses, while Italy was paradise for horses and hell for women. It seemed to me that Mr. Burton had confused things, though Italy was not exactly a paradise for women either. As the hill steepened, Stella's struggles increased and we made less and less progress. Like a treadless tire on an icy hill, we began to lose ground. Fernando's method of dealing with this was to accompany the fury of his whip with oaths and obscenities. When we could bear it no longer, we leaped out of the hack and walked. Fernando also jumped from his perch. Soon Frank and I were pushing while Fernando walked alongside flashing his whip. In this way, we made it to the top of the hill. "It is the first time I have paid a horse for the privilege of carrying it," said Frank. "I am sure this is possible only in Sicily."

At the foot of some steep steps we were greeted by the caretaker, a small, eager man who was overjoyed that someone had come to see his temple. Life was lonely for him; we were his first visitors in three days. The shrine was hardly a temple at all, but a grotto dug into a cliff, the place, according to legend, for Persephone to enter and leave the underworld. The walls were encrusted with sea shells, a residue from the time when the cliff was under the sea. There were also water vats which provided irrigation, the caretaker said, since Demeter was patroness of crops. It was a crude, primitive place suggesting witchery and dark rites—a far cry from the golden temples which crowned the hills beyond.

We rolled so swiftly back downhill that I had to brace myself to keep from being catapulted out of the hack. The whip snapped like lightning, and Stella's hoofs struck sparks from the stones. Soon we arrived at the temple of Castor and Pollux, the four-columned fragment restored in the nineteenth century which has become a familiar symbol of Sicily. Near by, at the leveled temple of Zeus, a shabbily dressed

guide was addressing some tourists in English. In the group
I spotted the doctor and his wife as well as Sarah and Cissie.
The speaker was denouncing guidebooks.

"Do not believe that Carthaginians destroyed the temples!"
he raged. "Do not believe that earthquakes brought them to
the ground. Who did it? I'll tell you. It was the Christians!"
The doctor's Adam's apple popped above his collar as the
orator pointed a finger to undamaged columns still being
excavated. "See for yourself! The columns are perfect. Would
an earthquake have spared them? No! I tell you the destruction was in human hands." He paused a moment as if he
were waiting for the ancient gods to avenge themselves.
"Those devils, the Christians, committed the crime."

The doctor turned. "That man is insulting," he muttered,
and stalked away. His wife trotted at his heels.

Sarah watched them go. "I do think Americans are given
far too much to public demonstration," she said.

"The doctor and his wife are Canadian," I said. "British."

"All Canadians are *very* American," she said. "How can
they help it, being so close?"

The new city had spilled its population over the old for a
Sunday *festa* in Acragas. Never in its most hedonistic glory
could the old city have been so noisy. The motor speedway
past the temples roared with vehicles. On a straight stretch
between the temples of Zeus and Juno, scooters swayed from
side to side as their drivers raced one another and competed
in daredevil stunts. The old temples rattled with the vibra-
tions of motors and rang with the blasts of horns. "Nothing
but hooters and crazy people," Sarah said, and she and Cissie
clung to their hats. "One might as well be in Blackpool."

Midway in the *corso* was the temple of Concordia. It is the
only temple in Agrigento to survive in a more or less com-
plete state. For this the same Christians who were reviled by
the eccentric guide can take credit. During the Middle Ages
the Concordia was a church known as St. Gregory of the

Turnips. Standing in isolation on a rocky promontory of the Acragas plateau, it demonstrates once more the Greeks' dramatic flair for architecture in landscape. Glowing in the afternoon sun, it seemed to be pure gold. Actually, its columns are rotting away. Where earthquakes and vandals have failed, time and the eternal African winds are succeeding.

On the steps a half-dozen boys were playing with three blind puppies. The spotted dogs whimpered pathetically as they moved their pink nozzles exploratively, searching back and forth for their mother. "*Carini*," the boys said, playing with them like dolls. "Look at the little dears, the sweet ones." When the puppies squealed the boys laughed and dangled the tiny beasts by their napes, tickling their squirming stomachs. The doctor's wife ran up the steps.

"Selma," the doctor called sharply. "Come away! Don't get involved."

"Where is the puppies' mother?" Selma asked the boys, who were well dressed in Sunday knee pants.

"*Inglese*," one of them jeered, and all laughed.

"Selma! Come away!" The doctor spoke harshly, as if he were addressing the dogs. Selma ignored him and asked me to interpret for her.

"Where is the puppies' mother?" I asked the boys.

The mother was somewhere hunting, one boy said. She would return.

"Are you sure?" Selma asked.

The boy shrugged as if to say one can be sure of nothing. His companions giggled.

The doctor climbed the steps, grabbed his wife, and pulled her away. "Can't you remember you're in a foreign country?" he scolded. The boys roared with laughter at this domestic scene. To us the doctor explained, "She's crazy about animals. Not at all rational on the subject. We used to keep chickens but we had to quit because she could never bear to kill or sell one."

Behind us the boys held the squirming little pink faces to their lips. "Dear little ones," they cooed. "Look at the sweet things."

We had enough of human society for the moment, so Frank and I carried our wine, cheese, and salami to the valley below and found a quiet spot in an almond and olive grove by the Nerone tomb. Birds sang in the pale-green afternoon and the usual lean dog appeared, an uninvited but polite guest. There are always hungry dogs in Sicily and they are always respectful and well mannered. "It is not breeding but servility," Frank said. "It comes from a lifetime of beatings."

The temples stood silhouetted above us, golden columns in a fair and cloudless sky. As temples go, Acragas's are pedestrian. Their distinction lies in their noble situation on a long ridge between sea and hills. Looking up from below they appeared anything but immortal. Not only were their soft columns crumbling, but the soft ledge upon which they stood was gradually sliding away under them. They were temples of sand built on sand; gold that was fool's gold.

The day ended cloudy and cold. A turbulent El Greco sky rolled in from the sea—and the air turned damp. At the temple of Zeus crowds were queueing up for the bus into town. The doctor and Selma were in the line.

We waited. Suddenly I thought I heard the puppies whining. Selma thought so too. She darted from the line and up a hill.

"Come back!" the doctor shouted. He followed her for a distance. "Don't get involved!"

She paid no attention. I followed her to the edge of an ancient catacomb. Inside, we found the Sicilian boys. They were depositing the puppies in the pit, where they would surely die of the cold. The dogs were whining pathetically.

"Look at the little dears!" the boys shouted to one another. "See them squirm." They laughed like demons.

Selma took one of the boys and shook him. "Where did you get those dogs?" she demanded.

"We found them in the field," the boy said, frightened into a moment of sobriety. I suspected he was telling the truth. Obviously the puppies had not been abandoned by the mother, for they were fat and healthy. Someone had carried them away from her and left them in a field. No doubt it was a common solution on an island where dogs breed even more freely than men.

Selma picked up the puppies and wrapped them in her coat; they nuzzled against the wool. "You must find the mother," she ordered the boys.

They shrugged. In a land of homeless dogs what did three puppies matter?

"Were you going to leave them to die?" Selma asked.

The boys laughed. "*Inglese*," one of them repeated. "English." It was a good joke and they leaped up and down with the joy of it.

Selma and I started down the road. The puppies burrowed quietly and warmly inside her coat. The boys followed us, yelling like banshees. Two curious men caught up with us and stroked the puppies' heads.

"*Carini*," they said tenderly. "What fat little cherubs. *Senza madre* [without a mother], poor things." Then the men walked ahead, smiling wisely. At the bus stop they quickly lost themselves in the crowd. Sicilians waiting for the bus crowded around the crazy foreigners. It was struggle enough to feed one's babies, they said; it took English or Americans to fuss over dogs. The disturbance infuriated the doctor. "Put those dogs down," he ordered his wife.

She stood firm; the audience was her strength. "I'm going to find a veterinarian to put them to sleep," she said.

"A veterinarian! My dear Selma, where do you propose to find a veterinarian? This is not Toronto."

Selma's eyes brimmed with tears and the Sicilians looked

on, fascinated. A domestic explosion between a tourist and
his wife was a wonderful sight to see. A pair of hunters with
rifles arrived. The doctor asked them to shoot the dogs. Waste
expensive ammunition on dogs? They laughed. The doctor
offered to pay, but the hunters walked away, certain, like the
rest, that he was mad. A woman examined the puppies clini-
cally. *"Una femmina, due maschi,"* she reported to the crowd.

The bus arrived. It was one of those nightmarish rides. It
took ten minutes to squeeze the waiting line inside. The doctor angrily pushed himself on the bus, leaving Selma to fend
for herself. The Sicilians became angry. "No room for us on
the bus and the English bring dogs," they grumbled. The
puppies were whining again. Selma fought the crowd to
keep them from being suffocated. In the dim light of the
bus her eyes were shining pools of tears.

A quarter of an hour later she carried them under her
coat past the desk of her hotel. Once she reached her room,
she drowned them in the bathtub. We saw the doctor leave
the hotel carrying a newspaper parcel which he tossed over a
rampart.

CHAPTER 8

PLEASURE GIRLS

ONE DAY Frank met Sarah and Cissie in the post office. They were full of complaints about Agrigento. There was no hot water in their hotel, no heat, and, of course, no proper tea.

"We are going on to Syracuse," Sarah said. "We hear it's quite comfortable there. Why don't you come too?"

"I am going to Enna," Frank said.

"Where is that?" Cissie asked.

"In the navel of Sicily," said Frank.

"The what?" asked Sarah.

"The gates of hell."

"Why should anyone wish to go there?"

"To see ladies carry charcoal stoves under their skirts and men with icicles in their beards," Frank said.

"Young man, who tells you such awful things?" asked Sarah.

"I'm sure it's that Yankee," said Cissie.

So they went to Syracuse on the bus, and we took a tram car toward the gates of hell.

It was a wet morning, and at each stop passengers mounted dripping with moisture. The tram climbed steadily, and finally we saw the almond blossoms we had missed by the sea. Whole hillsides billowed with their pink flowers. At Dittaino we switched to a second tram, which smelled pungently of salami and garlic.

The engine pulled hard, and it was very cold. Passengers wrapped in black wool sat in muffled silence.

Across from us a young woman loosened a light-gray shawl, uncovering a wind-burned face and large, glazed eyes which roved wildly about the car. She could have been either a madwoman or a saint. She began to pray, fumble a rosary, and to weep. Frank thought she must be in labor, but this was impossible, for she did not even appear pregnant. Only her face was visible, but the tension on it was terrible. A cast in one eye gave her a maniacal intensity as she swayed her body from side to side and with her hands wove crosses in the air.

We were on barren heights now, and the passengers pulled their black scarves over their mouths. No one spoke. Except for the steam which froze on the windows, it was like a tram in Morocco, with only the darting eyes peering out. Suddenly the tram began to roll easily, and we were descending, passing through almond groves, puny and poor, but blossoming bravely. Soon we were in Piazza Amerina, where we were to spend the night. The town had only recently become known to tourists after the excavation of some mosaics. Its new, modern hotel, one of the Jolly chain, was a heart-warming oasis.

Stormy night fell quickly, and when the power capitulated to the tempest, the blacked-out town seemed swallowed by the earth. A few women were on the street carrying their glowing charcoal pots. They looked like fiery-eyed cyclopes. We could see into the open doors of homes, dark caves illuminated by the glowing red pots. Black-hooded women hovered over the pots, the red glow illuminating them like Halloween witches. Each room seemed to enclose some strange rite.

This was agricultural country in which the fear of banditry and loneliness brought workers hurrying into town at night on their donkeys. We could hear the *clop-clop* of the hoofs before we could feel their purgatorial presence brushing us in the street, the black capes of the riders billowing like bats' wings. It was utterly desolate. We felt like lost, doomed souls on a lonely journey. The wind raged so fiercely we had to cling to each other to keep from being knocked down.

As we pushed through the hotel door, the wind sent the wild, weird shadows of candle flames leaping across the freshly painted walls. The only other guests were a middle-aged American couple who had bought a Sicilian donkey cart to use as a flower box in the front yard of their Fairfield, Connecticut, home. The husband was absorbed in the problems of exporting the cart to America. The wild, unearthly night had unnerved his wife. She moved restlessly about the eerie lounge repeating over and over, "I love this place. It's the nicest place I've ever been. I want to stay here."

"Don't be a fool, Helen," the husband chastised her.

"One day I'll come back here and stay," she said.

"You're acting quite crazily," he said.

She would not be stopped. "I'd like to stay forever," she said. Someone put a rumba record on a phonograph, and the wife grabbed Frank and made him dance with her about the darkened room. They danced until the husband tore his wife away and led her, weeping like a child, up to bed.

The morning was clear and cold. The shivering town was full of activity. The donkey riders rode out to the fields; children with running noses and soiled black smocks struggled toward school. We took a quick look at the cathedral, the blue and white interior of which seemed to have been decorated by Josiah Wedgwood, and then drove in a taxi to see the mosaics.

About four miles from the town we arrived at a fenced-in enclosure. A guide at the gate was smiling perversely, waiting to tell us that 70 per cent of the mosaics were covered with sand to protect them from winter weather. "If the *signori* will come back in ten days . . ." We couldn't, and asked to see the uncovered mosaics.

In the fourth century, when they were created, much of Sicily was a forest wilderness rich in game. The villa, covering about two acres in a natural amphitheater in the lonely hills, was probably the hunting lodge of an aristocrat. Certainly the man who built it was a pleasure-loving sportsman. His richly mosaicked floors portray drinking and hunting scenes and athletic contests. The best known is that of the famous Bikini girls. There are nine of them—a tenth having disappeared. Since they are highly individualistic, it is not unreasonable to suspect they may be portraits of the master's favorites. They are as guilelessly playful as Marcel Proust's beach girls, except that Albertina and her friends would never have appeared so lightly covered. In dress and hair styles they are as modern as the entrants in an Atlantic City beauty contest. They wear what the French call *un minimum* at the hip and a twist of cloth over the breasts, less for modesty than protection of sensitive zones during games. For the girls seem immoderately athletic. They run and leap; two are playing handball and one blond amazon is exercising with bar bells. Another has just been awarded a palm leaf in a contest and a smugger young lady would be hard to find.

These exuberant girls bring tourists to Piazza Amerina from throughout the Western world. Bus lines have been routed through the hills and hotels built because of them. As I looked at them I wondered how many of the sorrow-ridden, black-robed dwellers of the town had ever seen them. Almost none, our guide said, and I was not surprised. The Bikinis had nothing in common with contemporary Sicily, where women are voiceless creatures confined to dark rooms, where innocence is rigorously supervised and a wife's infidelity is punishable by death at the hand of her husband.

What, indeed, could a Sicilian woman possibly think of them?

"If you will come back in ten days . . ." our guide murmured, and I thought of the line from one of Ruth Draper's travel sketches: "The next day it would have been lovely."

CHAPTER 9

ENCIRCLING GLOOM

THE BUS to Enna did not leave until late in the afternoon, so when our driver offered to taxi us there for a modest price we agreed at once. He was a dark, handsome peasant type, with curling gray locks falling from under a beret, a man you would pick from a crowd in Piccadilly or Broadway and say, "That's a Sicilian."

His name was Domenico Silenios. A sober, quiet man in his middle years, he surprised us by speaking perfect English, telling how he had gone to America with his family when he was eight, attended schools in West Virginia for several years, and returned to Sicily when he was sixteen. The return had been a fateful mistake; ever since he had been struggling to get back to America. Once it was almost arranged, but the year was 1939. For seven years Domenico Silenios was a British prisoner in North Africa. In 1948 a brother in Rochester filed an affidavit for Domenico with the immigration department. It had been approved only recently. Now the brother had sent him a boat ticket and he was leaving for America in four weeks. "In America there is democracy and it is good," he said. "In Italy we have a democracy that is bad. Because it is a bad democracy we have many Communists. We call our politicians marines because they sail their boat whichever way the wind blows."

As we moved nearer to Enna the landscape became more and more purgatorial. In the valley were the dusty green and yellow hollows of sulphur mines. The mines, after killing generations with their poisons, had ceased to be profitable and were no longer operating. Their fumes, however, still fouled the air. In one of the valleys we saw an oval saucer of dark water.

"Pergusa," announced Domenico Silenios.

Persephone's lake! On its shores the young daughter of Demeter was gathering lilies and anemones when she was abducted into the underworld by Pluto, lord of death. The sorrowing mother vowed no corn would sprout until her daughter was returned to her. A scorched earth was the result, and the people would have starved if Zeus had not commanded Pluto to release his bride for two thirds of every year, allowing him to keep her below the earth the rest of the year. Persephone was returned to the sunlight and in her joy Demeter restored the fields to fertility and the earth turned green with corn. This myth of Demeter and Persephone is the same as the Assyrian one of Aphrodite and Adonis and the Egyptian of Isis and Osiris, except that in the Oriental versions, the lost one is a dead lover or husband mourned by a wife.

I looked down on the famous lake. Once it had been beautiful enough, surrounded as it was with forest and flowers to become a symbol of spring and rebirth. Now it was barren and drab, with only a small grove of eucalyptus growing at a farther end. The water was brackish and weed clogged.

What had happened?

Man, of course, was the villain. He had cut down the trees without replacing them, and scraped the surface of the earth for sulphur without closing the wounds. Soon enough, erosion and drought turned a garden into desert. Now, as a final outrage, he had built an auto race track around Persephone's lake, a black band of macadam hugging the oval shores. Soon there would be the roar of motors and the thunder of Sunday-afternoon crowds.

Now the valley was quiet as death. On a low cliff not far from the water was a dark cavern, its entrance overgrown with weeds. It was a small, insignificant break in the crust of the earth, a dismal hole hardly worth inspecting. This was the cave through which Sicilians believe Pluto, overtaking Persephone among her flowers, abducted her into the underworld.

There was nothing to detain us at Pergusa so we sat on its shores only as long as it took to eat our lunch, which we shared with Domenico Silenios. When we had finished he drove us up the side of a massive rock. Huddled on the top was the frosty, cloud-swept citadel of Enna, the geographic and classic center of Sicily. Like Erice, Enna is one of the oldest and highest towns on the island. For tourists it has one attraction, an incomparable view for which it has been called the "belvedere" of Sicily. It also induces vertigo. No matter where you look—it is all down—it is a sight to make head and stomach reel.

Safely protected by a granite railing, we stood on the little square, with its statue of Pluto wrestling with a hysterical Persephone, and looked across the chasm to Enna's hilltop sister, Calascibetta. The brown earth flecked with the first green of spring was luminous with afternoon light, making the village beyond look like a spiral of burnished nests of cliff swallows.

When we were adjusted to the thin air, the dizziness, and the cold, we walked to the top of the town. There, on a projection of rock covered by the remains of a medieval citadel, is the spiritual heart of ancient Sicily, the site of Demeter's temple. The ledge which leads to it is Enna's municipal dump. We climbed over mounds of steaming garbage and routed some rheumy chickens salvaging it. The temple is gone, but the tumultuous pinnacle, dropping perhaps five hundred feet on three of its sides, is awesome enough. We could see almost all the topographical convolutions of Sicily, and the corner of Pergusa where we had lunched lay below us like a pit.

The rock, which is shaped like a ship, points east toward the snowy cone of Etna. Demeter worshipers on the rock must have faced the god Vulcania with trembling. For a people living at the mercy of a volcano, the underworld is the greater reality; Hell has more meaning than Heaven. Enna's Demeter was not the kindly Greek corn goddess, but a dark, horse-headed virago of the underworld.

We sat until clouds covered the sun and a piercing wind drove us from the rock. A corona of pink cirrus settled over the white cone of Etna like a halo, and the world glowed in apocryphal grandeur. I did not wonder that in such a place gods were born.

I had come to Enna to search for the *bambina* Jesus. The English book in which I had read of the statue said it was somewhere in Castrogiovanni, which is what Enna used to be called. I went to the *turismo* office and asked the man in charge if he knew of a Madonna statue with a female Jesus. He reacted as if I were mad and indignantly denied that such a statue had ever existed. I, however, was not ready to give up so easily and went to the museum. It was locked. Ringing the bell a long time roused a decrepit old priest who lived somewhere in the building. He told me that the museum director had the key. Where was the director? In Palermo, the priest said. Since the director never permitted anyone else to open the museum, he probably had taken the key with him. When would the director be back? The priest did not know.

So I toured the churches, starting with the cathedral, a grand affair with Greek columns and wooden ceiling. Its classic beauty was all but hidden under a clutter of bad church art. The statue was not there—at least so far as I could see. In the church of San Giuseppe, women preparing for the saint's *festa* were hanging drapes of red, blue, and gold. In San Tommaso women were praying, their skirts spread over smoldering ember pots like hens covering eggs. San Cataldo, San Marco, the Carmine—so many churches for such a small town, some crumbling away and each as cold as a tomb. Finally it was too dark to see. The statue still eluded me. Perhaps the tourist official was right, and it didn't exist at all.

The streets had grown as dark as the churches. People moved like dark shadows through the dusk or sat in a trance-like state that seemed to verge on despair. It occurred to me that the people of Enna paid no more attention to their view than the people of Piazza Amerina did to their nymphs. Having lived with it all their lives, they did not see it.

Enna is a comfortless place. Our hotel was very nearly the worst I have come across. The tiny elevator rattled ominously every time it went up or down. The garish elegance of our room was so thickly encrusted with dirt and dead flies that we were afraid to unpack our bags. The lumpy beds had not been made since the last guests. The sheets were damp, and there was no heat in the radiator with which to dry them. We were thankful that there were no vermin.

The streets were silent.

Men huddling on benches in their voluminous black capes looked like rows of small tents; women in black-fringed shawls looked like squaws in mourning. I saw two women with beards and many with mustaches. Shopkeepers wrapped in blankets huddled around charcoal braziers which cast a red glow on the merchandise. In a dimly lit tailor shop four boy apprentices about ten years of age stitched away as if they had to clothe the world before dawn. I forgot for the moment that in the morning I could escape this purgatorial desolation. I felt doomed.

Suddenly from the valley below rose the song of a child, filling the night like the flute of an angel. I remembered reading in Seán O'Faoláin's beautiful book * that John Henry Newman had conceived in Enna the hymn which he wrote a month later in the Strait of Bonifacio. The child who was singing had probably never heard of Newman or his hymn, but his song brought to life Newman's words:

> Lead, Kindly Light, amid the encircling gloom,
>   Lead Thou me on!
> The night is dark, and I am far from home;
>   Lead Thou me on!

The full moon was rising over Demeter's rock, and Etna in the far blue sky was the pale ghost of a mountain. The villages of Sicily were spread below us like twinkling constellations. I seemed to be looking down on the heavens from a super paradise.

Indeed, what did it matter now if there was or was not a statue of a Madonna with a female Jesus? What conceit that one should seek the statue at all! There was no need to prove what was in evidence all about—that faith, not creed, rooted men to earth, to life, and to God. The child's gift of song covered Demeter's rock with hope as it filled the night with sweetness and swept aside the encircling gloom.

> Keep Thou my feet! I do not ask to see
> The distant scene; one step enough for me.

* *South to Sicily*. London: Collins, 1953.

CHAPTER 10

HOMESICKNESS

MY DEPRESSION in the hotel foreboded an unhappy departure. Our bill, delivered verbally by a rodent-faced little man, was much too high. I asked for the accounting required by law. The man quickly made some figures on a paper and totaled it to somewhat less than the sum he had originally demanded. Suspecting it was still too high, I asked that he let me see it. He refused. When I reached for the paper he tore it into bits. I picked the pieces out of a wastebasket while he reviled me hysterically from the other side of the room. Later, in Syracuse, I pieced the bits together and found we had, as I suspected, been outrageously overcharged.

I hasten to point out that this was the only dishonesty I encountered in a Sicilian—or, for that matter, an Italian—hotel. It was my last sad impression of Enna. We left Persephone's town as if we too were returning from a dismal limbo to the world of humanity.

We took a bus south, to the coastal city of Gela, to join up with our tour bus. Gela is near the scene of the Allied invasion where General George S. Patton's 1943 "Operation Husky" resulted in 21,643 Allied dead and wounded. Some

rusty American equipment slept in the sand; concrete pillboxes rose from the earth like the domes of an underground
mosque. The road was good, and we rolled rapidly into broad
agricultural plains. The wide valleys and beautiful farms for
which Sicily is known as "the granary of Italy" reminded me
of Pennsylvania. Rich, black volcanic soil, farmed for two
thousand years with a never-diminishing fertility, was producing two and three crops a year. Grain waved in the wind
as far as one could see. Yet even here the villages were mean
and poor. Overpopulation kept the agricultural workers'
daily pay down to five hundred lire—less than eighty-five
cents. Workers had to travel five or six miles by donkey or
bicycle from their villages to the fields. We could see them,
wearing faded American G.I. fatigues and sailor pants, harvesting peas and cultivating beans. They worked by hand, for
hand labor was better than reducing employment of men still
more with modern machinery. That men should be slaves
in a garden of abundance is the cruel and everlasting irony
of a medieval agrarian society in which absentee landlords
seldom see their land or know their workers.

It was from Gela, another ancient Greek town that survived to modern times, that Acragas was colonized and it was
back to Gela that the surviving Acragantines returned after
the Carthaginian deluge. It is a town in which the African
sun burns the eyeballs. Here, even the children wore black.
The only color in the landscape came from red bandannas
worn about the head pirate style by barefoot youths working
in the fields.

Our luxury pullman was waiting. "Some of you are already
very naughty," scolded the hostess. "Because of you we are a
half hour late." Her name was Apollonia. She was a tall,
dark girl, severely beautiful, three or four years older than
the others we had known. The drivers this time were named
Agusto and Filippo. The passengers were an international
assortment. There was a gay young French couple named

Marlot who wore bright-colored sports clothes, including matching plaid trousers for both husband and wife. There was a pair of beaming gentlemen in their late thirties with thinning blond hair and bland pink faces, both wearing gabardine coats, gray felt hats, and carrying Leica cameras. They were not twins, as we had first thought, but a Dane and a German who had met on the bus and formed a "tour friendship." There were a sour American tourist couple named Allen and a delightful elderly English couple named Robinson. Mr. Robinson was a tall, starched old specimen with pointed mustaches; his wife was large and dumpy. Her round face beamed with blood pressure, and her gray hair was rolled in buns under a pork-pie hat. She wore a brown tweed suit, brown lisle stockings, and low brown shoes. She thumped about carrying *Le Guide bleu* like a prayer book and looking for all the world like a *Punch* drawing of Mother Britannia. There was even an Italian couple from Tuscany. He had black eyes and a pointed beard and was the type usually selected for Judas Iscariot in a village passion play; she was a good-natured, brown-skinned housewife.

Frank and I, remembering the jovial Olivia from the last bus, were quickly put into our place by the more starchy lady Apollo. "Now you be good boys," she scolded, "and stop pulling my legs." I suspected she was an ex-schoolteacher.

Outside the city our drivers had to unload the baggage from the top of the bus in order to pass under a bridge. The agricultural plains were behind us. We began to climb, snaking back and forth across the face of mountains as steep as Switzerland's. We came to Vittoria and then Comiso, glaring white-hot towns over which rose the spires and domes of many churches. Cemeteries were crowded with burial chapels and tombs, baroque cities of the dead more luxurious than the towns of the living. We crawled up into a monolithic land of stone. As far as the eye could see there was nothing but gray stones looking as if they had been hurled from heaven. "*Na-*

tura fiera," Frank muttered. It was indeed a fierce, terrible nature. Yet men lived here. One could see how they battled the gray stones, making a harvest of them, building their houses and barns, their wayside crosses and shrines, and a fantastic network of fences, skillfully fitting the stones together without mortar. The stones that could not be usefully disposed of were piled into gray cones which dominated the landscape like gloomy gods. The work was staggering. It made the bodies and faces of the people, who were lean, brown, fiercely gnarled, as hard as the stone itself. Behind the stone fences were neat green patches of peas and beans, the edges bordered with blue daisies.

The capricious Italian sun disappeared and it quickly turned cold. We began a chilling descent, the motor and brakes laboring together to lower us slowly into a ravine in which we could see the peaks of great gray pyramids and tendrils of rising vapor. This was Ragusa, noted for its asphalt mines and more recently the center of an oil boom financed by American firms. The bus made a scheduled stop for tea. The square was filled with men wearing billowing black capes. They crowded the cathedral steps like a covey of giant bats in a purgatory fresco. As we stepped out of the bus, they crowded around us as if they wished to claw us with bony spines hidden under their black wings. But they grinned a warm welcome and waited with shy dignity for us to make the overture. When Madame Marlot stepped from the bus in her sleek blue-and-red checked trousers, their eyes popped. A few old men began to snicker, but most controlled themselves politely. On the edges of the square the young men were less controlled. Unaccustomed to seeing women in trousers, they reacted with a mixture of shock and ribaldry. "Oo-la-la!" one shouted like a caricature of a Frenchman. They all laughed until Madame Marlot returned to the bus and did not leave it again.

The cathedral had a baroque façade and gracious Renaissance lines. A splash of sunlight in the windows of the lovely dome lit up the inside with a spray of golden rays. A few women were praying, but they left by a side door when we entered.

Above us bells began to ring; outside they were peeling from every tower in the town. "It happens every day at five o'clock," one of the men said, hobbling up to me on a cane, surprising me with his English. "I was an American for twenty-seven years," he said proudly. "I came back to Ragusa because of my rheumatism. Now I wish I might go back to Rochester, but it is too late. I am an old man, a very foolish old man who never made himself into an American citizen. I am homesick for America."

All the men were speaking English. "I *was* an American citizen," a rugged old specimen said proudly. "But I make mistake and come back. Now I cannot return. I am American war veteran (World War I). Until the last war comes every month my war pension. Now it no longer comes. Why does Uncle Sam stop sending?"

I said I didn't know but I supposed it was because the second World War had made him an enemy. I took his name and promised to inquire when I returned to America.

"There are three hundred men in Ragusa who have been in America," the American veteran said. "Many of us come here every Tuesday. On the bus there are usually Americans to whom we can talk."

Apollonia was clapping us back into the bus, so I said good-by to these ex-Americans, gathered as if they were attending a Kiwanis meeting. As we drove away, they waved at us, spreading their capes as if they would follow us in flight. We descended deeper into the ravine, past cave dwellings dug out of cliffs, past gray mounds of rubble rising as high as Pittsburgh slag piles, past buildings painted with the legend "DDT 1948," or any other year that they might have been sprayed in the Marshall Plan anti-malaria drive. Except for a small orchard of pampered orange trees, it was a dead landscape. We had a long wait at a railroad crossing where the guardrail was down even though no trains passed. The attendant was probably at his supper or taking a nap, Apollonia explained, and as a general precaution lowered the rail until he was ready to return.

The sun dropped swiftly; by a quarter after seven it was night. Our progress was slow; we passed through the baroque towns of Modia and Noto, but of Noto we could see nothing. The towns were deserted, with only a few men slinking through the streets like furtive night animals. Occasionally we caught a glimpse of a lamplit room where the men ate their supper and the women stood in the doorways. Only the barbershops, the social centers of the towns, were brightly illuminated.

In the country, agricultural workers riding home on their donkeys were a hazard on the road. Somewhere between Noto and Syracuse the bus jolted to a quick stop. This happened frequently, but at night it always caused uneasiness among the passengers. Softly I whispered jokingly to Frank, "*Banditti!*" It was a mistake. Everyone was exhausted and on edge. The rumor of bandits spread like a wind to the front of the bus. Madame Marlot screamed and everyone began shuffling his belongings. Mrs. Robinson said to Mr. Robinson, "I do think this is going too far," as she stuffed her traveler's çhecks into her shoes.

Apollonia announced that the trouble was nothing but a mule on the road, but only when a spotlight was focused on the beast did the passengers relax. The mule was hitched to a cart loaded with oranges, and though a frantic peasant was lashing the animal with a whip, it would not budge. We started to pile out of the bus, but the peasant shouted for us to go back. The mule, he said, was a ferocious beast. "He will destroy you with his hoofs and his teeth," the man warned. A pair of *carabinieri* drove up in an American jeep, but they proved equally helpless. Farmers arrived on foot, attracted by the noise. One of them knew what to do in such an emergency. On his orders, the chattering mob began gathering twigs in the underbrush, piling them near the mule's belly. A match was set to the kindling, and in a moment a fire blazed under the mule. Everyone stood at a distance to watch developments. With a warning snort the mule leaped up and rattled down the road, peasants and police after him, oranges showering the highway.

We continued to Syracuse.

CHAPTER 11

SWEET AND SALT

AFTER OUR NIGHT in Enna, Syracuse was a sybaritic delight. We stayed at the Hotel degli Stranieri, which faced the sea and overlooked the ancient fountain of the nymph Arethusa. Cicero described it as "a fountain of sweet water, of incredible size, very full of fish, which would be entirely overwhelmed by the waves of the sea were it not protected by a rampart and dam of stone." So we found it, pouring forth water from an underground stream, filled with papyrus plants and stocked with fish, hedged by glowing hibiscus. But there was one difference: Cicero's sweet water was turned brackish by an earthquake in 1798 and has been salt ever since.

Frank and I dined with Apollonia in a seaside restaurant on the outer harbor. The food was the best I ever ate in Sicily. There was a wonderful soup of mushrooms and artichokes, dozens of tiny shrimps crisply fried, and Moscato, a sweet and deceptively bland wine for which Syracuse is famous. After several glasses Apollonia began to talk about herself. She told us she was not Sicilian at all but from Genoa, where she had, indeed, been a schoolteacher. During the war a bomb had killed her mother and sister and her father had died shortly afterward "of a broken heart." Schoolteachers being badly paid, Apollonia had gone to Rome to seek her fortune, becoming finally a bus hostess, working summers between Rome and Venice and in winters in Sicily.

With Apollonia's help we boned up on the history of Syracuse. A victory over Athens in 414 B.C. had made her the mistress of ancient Sicily and the richest and most powerful of all the Greek cities. When Carthage threatened Syracuse, the city brought the brilliant and ruthless Dionysius to power. The rise of Dionysius, from modest scribe to the most powerful dictator the Greek world had ever known, has parallels in our own time. Like all dictators, Dionysius had to keep his subjects at war in order to maintain and extend his own dominions. His people were slaves. Because he lived in neurotic fear of plots on his life, he imprisoned and slaughtered whomever he distrusted, including members of his own family. He remained in power for thirty-eight years. At his death he had, by victory over the Carthaginians, made Syracuse the mightiest city of Europe. He was succeeded by a series of lesser tyrants.

At this critical time, Plato attempted to intervene in Sicilian politics. The teacher from Athens had visited Sicily after the execution of Socrates thirty years before and, though disgusted at the gross sensuality of life there, he had found a sympathetic friend in Dion, brother-in-law of Dionysius. After the death of the ruler, Dion called upon Plato to come to Syracuse to educate Dionysius' son in government and train him for the position of constitutional king. Plato saw in the call an opportunity to put his theories for a republic into effect. The mission failed, largely because of the personal ambitions of the weak Dionysius II. The sorely tried people of Syracuse then appealed to Corinth for help, and the mother city sent the able soldier Timoleon to rule the desperate city.

Timoleon replaced conquest and human slavery with the pursuit of wisdom and democratic government. He cleared the island of Carthaginians, recolonized destroyed cities, and instituted new and liberal laws. But his humanitarian spirit did not long survive him. He was succeeded by more power-hungry tyrants, the most terrible being Agathocles, who made himself King of Syracuse. Agathocles plundered the island as ruthlessly as the hated Carthaginians before him. He destroyed Acragas and Segeste, butchering their adult populations and selling their youths. Finally he was burned alive by his own people. But it was too late; his reign had turned the tide of Syracuse's fortunes. In the end, like most of Sicily, she was ruled by Romans, by Saracens, and eventually by Normans. Today Syracuse is a small, sleepy, beautiful town of seventy-two thousand people. The ruins of the ancient city, once enclosed by a twenty-one-mile wall, are a silent monument to the capriciousness of riches, power, and human vanity.

During the night a wind of cyclonic force had felled trees and rolled waves right up to the door of the hotel. The next morning the city was clean and bright. Perhaps we were stimulated by the bracing salt wind or the beaming faces of the people. In any case, after the somber lethargy of the cold mountain villages, Syracuse was euphoric.

Our first stop that day was at Dionysius' underground fortress, known as the Castle of Euryalus. We splashed through muddy, water-soaked tunnels behind a Sicilian guide who, because he'd lived twenty-five years in America, spoke good English and bad Italian. The roof of the fort was a lonely, wind-swept field of flowers sloping to the sea. The wild weather stirred into song a chorus of larks and thrushes. After waiting out a shower in the bus, we continued to the Greek theater. Here, on a stage lowered and raised by controlled water levels, which were probably as effective as the electronic devices producing the same effect in Radio City Music Hall, Aeschylus saw the premières of his plays. They are still performed in the theater. Like all of Sicily's great classic theaters, Syracuse's faces the sea. But the setting has changed: a railroad

and two new *autostrade* pass by, and the industrial smoke-
stacks of modern Syracuse are in the background.

We walked to the Roman amphitheater and the Latomia
del Paradiso, a quarry from which the ancients carved their
building stone. Later it was used as a political prison. Here is
"the ear of Dionysius," a cave seventy-five feet high and two
hundred deep. "The cave's acoustical properties amplify every
sound a hundred times," said our guide, continuing the
legend said to have originated with the painter Caravaggio
and now part of the apocrypha of all guides and guidebooks.
"Dionysius used it to eavesdrop on the conversations of pris-
oners below." To demonstrate he puckered his lips in a
whistle. It returned in a few seconds like the wail of a siren.
We were invited to test it with our own voices. Frank and I
rendered a chorus of "My Darling Clementine." By far the
most impressive test was made by the English Mrs. Robinson.
Standing with legs stolidly apart, she waited until all was
quiet. Then, in a hearty baritone, she called out, *"Evviva
l'Italia."* The salute was returned in magnificent volume.
Then, turning her back to us and pushing her head against
the wall, she sang "Do re mi . . ." This time, alas, nothing
happened. Mrs. Robinson was deeply troubled. An hour later
I heard her say to Mr. Robinson, "I must not have done it
correctly. Could it be I was facing the wrong way?"

We returned to the town and the temple of Minerva. Unlike other ancient structures, this temple is no ruin. It is the
cathedral of Syracuse and very much alive with an architectural confusion that reflects its stormy history. For twenty-five
centuries, it has been a place of worship. In ancient days,
rising from the highest spot in the island, its statue of the
goddess was seen by sailors far out at sea. A resourceful bishop
saved it from destruction in the seventh century by converting it into a Christian church. The Saracens in their time
turned it into a mosque, and the Normans returned it again
to Christian worship. The last transformation, coming after

the earthquake of 1693, destroyed the cathedral's Norman façade. Like a carnival mask hiding the face of a beautiful woman, a baroque façade now covers the lovely Doric temple. Purists frequently raise aesthetic objections to the façade, and on an earlier visit I too had been unhappy over it. This time I found it handsome. There is, of course, an infallible argument in its defense. Because of the care given it by Christians, the temple of Minerva is perhaps the best-preserved Greek temple in the world today.

On the square outside I was greeted by a polite elderly gentleman who spoke in the manner of W. C. Fields. "Young man, I am sure you speak God's language," he said. "I was in America for twenty-three years and then I made the most lamentable error of my life by returning to Syracuse. Due to that regrettable mistake I am now reduced to begging in the streets. It is a humiliating situation for one who, as you can see, has known better days." He startled me out of a hundred lire and then bowed with a deep flourish. "Bless you. One can tell you are a citizen of the land of magnanimity," he said.

Nowhere was the time allotted bus passengers for sightseeing so frustratingly insufficient as in Syracuse. Before the bus departed in the afternoon Frank and I had agreed on another stopover. Our second day there dawned gloriously—so bright and fresh that the day itself seemed washed. Frank left me to pursue his own researches. During his rambles he ran into his friends Sarah and Cissie feeding the ducks in Arethusa's spring. "Though I don't know why, really," said Sarah. "They kept us awake all night." They complained that the sheets had been damp and there seemed to be no one in Sicily but a lot of dreadful Germans and Yanks, so they were making arrangements to return as quickly as possible to the dry sheets and hot tea of civilized England—Sarah by plane, Cissie by train.

I made a leisurely review of what we had seen the day before, going first to the Latomia del Paradiso. I climbed into the quarry behind a priest, who, stepping carefully, lifted his skirts high like an old woman. Though the day was brisk, the enchanted secret garden below the surface of the earth was steaming like a hothouse. Protected by its depth from the harsher elements above, it received only the sun and the rain to nourish its fertile soil. What an assault on the senses awaited me. For the nose there was the oversweet pungency of orange and lemon blossom; for the eye, glistening banana foliage, pink geraniums, purple bougainvillaea and white lilies; for the ear, the musical twitterings of thousands of birds darting about their nests in the cypress trees and under the cliffs. It is aptly named, this miniature *paradiso*. It might have been created by Fra Angelico.

The terrible fact, of course, is that this *paradiso* began as an inferno. To an army of seven thousand Athenians imprisoned here by Dionysius, the music was not bird chirpings but the groans of the dying; the odors were not citrus flowers but the stench of corpses. It seems to have been a hell hole as infamous as the Dachaus of our time. Today the ghost of Dionysius' prison still lingers in the ropemakers' canyon, a covered grotto dripping with dampness which serves to control the texture of hemp. Here I found a man spinning a fish line. At the other end of the cave his son, who looked about eight years old, was turning the winding wheel with one hand and smoking a cigarette with the other. As the child worked, he coughed deeply, shooting puffs of smoke from his mouth.

I walked to another quarry, the Latomia dei Cappuccini. It was smaller than the Paradiso; its walls were higher and cascaded with bougainvillaea. The tops of the cypresses inside were on a level with the surface of the earth. So lush was the vegetation and so frenzied the birds that it made me think of the jungle paradise of W. H. Hudson's romance *Green Mansions*.

The catacombs are near by. They extend for more than a kilometer of intricate tunneling through hard limestone and are wired with electric lights. The entrance is next to the ruins of the San Giovanni church, a gray-silver wall with a paneless rosette window standing against the blue sky. Here I met a little Franciscan named Fra Giovanni Battista. He was so fragile that it seemed as if he were already sainted, as if his soul were quite remote from his body. His eyes were nearly closed, like a sleepwalker's. He spoke in whispers. He took me to the subterranean church of San Marziano, the oldest Christian church in Sicily, which he said was founded by St. Paul. The grotto was shaped like a Greek cross, and faded Byzantine frescoes were visible. Fra Giovanni pointed to a spot at the front and reverently said, "Paul preached here." When I left he asked me to send him some postage stamps for his collection.

I did not see Frank until late that night. When he arrived at the hotel, I was asleep. He was in a philosophical mood and awakened me to talk about the night's adventure. After considerable frustration, he had taken his research problems to a *carabiniere*, who had been agreeably co-operative. Frank told me about the girl to whom the policeman introduced him.

"She is not Sicilian; she is from Parma. She says it will be twenty-five hundred lire, but I say I am hardly an American millionaire, so we talk until we arrive at an understanding of fifteen hundred lire. She says for once only and I say that is not fair. Maybe after once I am still hungry. So we arrive at an agreement for her services for one hour. We go to her room and she says she has worked hard all night and I am her last customer, so did I mind if she did her laundry first. Then I sat on the bed smoking cigarettes while she did her laundry and I make an interview to her about her life. I am thinking, of course, of a film about prostitutes. She works maybe five or six hours a night and makes perhaps eighty thousand lire a week, which is, I point out, less hours and considerably more money than a university professor. She says she has a fiancé and a boy friend. The fiancé works in a factory. He is thirty years old. He comes to see her once a week. Her boy friend is only eighteen and he comes five times a week. With him she does Oriental things, some very nice and refined. She asks me my advice about a very old man who is rich. He is about seventy and wants her to do Oriental things for him. What should she do, she asks me. I tell her, 'If you see that the old man is going to die very soon, then perhaps you should. If he is yet healthy, maybe you shouldn't!'

"Then I asked her how were her business going generally, and she said this is a low period since many people gives up sex for Lent. She was very *simpatica* to me, for she helped Partisans during the war. She never accepts any money from a Partisan. This makes me feel very fond of her, though for sex I would prefer a girl who isn't old enough to have helped Partisans during the war. She is now finished with the laundry and is hanging it on a rope over the bed, so that the water is still dropping on me while I am possessing her in ordinary, un-Oriental way. When it is finished she says she is very tired, and I said I am still hungry, meaning I am hungry for love. She says to me she is hungry too and would like something to eat, that she was very rushed at the eating hour and had not dined. So we rang for the waiter, and while we are sitting naked on the bed he takes our order for two cheese sandwiches and a banana. When it comes she asks do I wish for a cheese sandwich and I said no, so she eats them both, and while she eat, I make interview some more. While we are talking the smell of cheese is flying through the room. She says she will save the banana for later and if I am still hungry she will now satisfy me some more. She said she liked me very much; that I pleased her because I am greater cultured than her fiancé and would *I* like to be her fiancé. She said I was very kind and gentle and she would like a fiancé who was those things. She did for me some nice, refined Oriental things until I was no longer hungry.

"When I go, she said, 'Now I am sad because you are so cultured and I want you for my fiancé. If you will be engaged to me you may come to visit me whenever you like without any cost to you.' 'That's very nice from you,' I said, 'but I am very busy.' She cried because I would not be her fiancé. She said if I should change my think on the subject, I should come to see her at six o'clock tomorrow. It was all so sad and I am very depressed."

He sat on his bed lost in thought. "What is a young man to do when things are so confused in the world?" he said.

CHAPTER 12

SIROCCO

"AFRICA," said Stefano, pointing to the sky and trying to lure me into his boat.

Stefano was the fisherman I had hired to row me across the bay and up the Ciani stream to the spring of the nymph Cyane. But this was the season of the sirocco. For four days the sea had been high and foamed like milk. Each morning Stefano and I met at the harbor and each morning I looked at the silvery mists hanging over the sea and said, "Not today." The row of saints' medallions, including Syracuse's miraculous weeping Madonna, lining the inside of Stefano's little rowboat did not reassure me.

"I have made the trip three thousand times with never an accident," Stefano said. He was a patient man, but even patience has its limitations. "The King and Queen of Belgium and the President of France were my passengers."

So I finally relented, making sure as I settled in the bow that the little boat was sturdy. Stefano wrapped me in shawls, solicitous as a mother who is afraid her child may be chilled. At the same time he removed his shirt. Golden holy medals were tangled in the hairs of his chest. He pulled at the oars and said, "*Un mare forte.*" Indeed, the sea was strong and growing stronger as if to meet the challenge of his strength and defiance. Great swells rolled toward us. I could hear the thunder of the breakers crashing on the other shore.

"*Tranquillo, tranquillo . . .*" said Stefano.

His voice was the unique thing about Stefano. It was limpid and breathless, gentle and strong. It had in it all the subtle softness of the Sicilian male and also his proud virility. Stefano spoke each word reverently, as if he were reading Scripture or making love. He must have been outrageously successful with his lady passengers.

His appearance too was right. He was forty years old. His face had the fiery animation characteristic of intelligent Italians. Black curls covered his head. His lean body had the bronzed sheen of men who live on water.

He gave me a waterproof bag so my camera would not get wet when the waves splashed over us. They were growing more furious, tossing us up and down as if we were a bit of cork. We might still have turned back, but by this time it had become a matter of pride between us, neither boatman nor passenger wanting to lose face with the other. With my face green as the sea I could not have deceived Stefano. I began to sense that he too was nervous but was feigning confidence to save me from panic. I shivered, not from the cold but from nerves.

"*Tranquillo, tranquillo,*" he repeated, caressing me with his limpid voice as a mother would calm a child.

To distract me he talked of himself. He had three children. "Quite enough. I can't afford to make any more," he said. "My mother is eighty-five. A healthy, vivacious old lady who forgets nothing. Alas, I am the only one of her children left in Syracuse. My two brothers live in Cleveland. One of them is captain of a great ship on the Erie lake. The other is a shoemaker. My sister lives in Michigan. Her husband works in the automobile factory Ford. They have many children, my brothers and sister. In America one can afford to make many children. But my brothers and sister do not come back to Syracuse. So I must take care of our dear mother. We all live together—my wife, my mother, my children, and I—in two rooms for which I must pay twelve thousand lire a month. It is too much. During the summer when there are many tourists it is not bad. I go to the Cyane spring three times—in the morning, in the afternoon, and at night—sixteen kilometers each time. In the winter when there are no tourists, it is difficult to earn money. Then I am a fisherman."

As we approached the shore he stopped talking. He was waiting for a chance to outwit the huge breakers that crashed on the beach. Surreptitiously Stefano made the sign of the cross. If he did not meet each one head on, we would be doomed. I held my breath and, gripping the sides of the boat, tried to hide my fears. Suddenly in one terrifying moment we were lunged into the air and quickly came to rest in a pool of foam. We had broken through.

We began to laugh. Laughter eased the tension and was our tacit recognition of the fact that the three minutes just passed had made us friends.

Facing us were the mouths of three peaceful fresh-water streams. We entered the one in the center, which was Ciani. She was straight as a canal, with a strong current, so that Stefano, going against it, had to work hard. On one side was a row of tall eucalyptuses; their mottled barks were mirrored in the water like tigers' skins and their washed roots looked like dens of serpents tumbling over one another to get into the stream. On the second shore were groves of oranges and lemons. The stream was the same dark green as the leaves of the trees and utterly smooth. Yellow iris grew at the water's edge and willow catkins dropped their pollen on the water, covering it with gold.

Stefano began talking again. He had rowed his first tourists up the stream with his father twenty-seven years ago. "As far back as I know, my family has taken strangers to the spring," he said. "But now is the time to finish. My sons will not do it—I will see to that. The work is too hard. A sailor never rests. No *festas*; no Sundays. Sundays are the worst of all. My boys will make their life on the land and enjoy their Sundays." He took a drink of water from an orange-colored bottle which he kept under the stern. Then he pointed to the darkening sky. "Africa," he said.

I was thinking of the journey back.

A duck scolded from her nest on the bank, and ravens swooped and cried out at us. Several fishermen lined the shore; the stream, said Stefano, was alive with fish. We were entering the avenue of papyrus, an arch formed by the plant of the Nile which Arabs brought to the streams of Syracuse. These tall reeds were topped with graceful, brushlike blossoms. Over the papyrus hung the exquisite spring foliage of willows. The stream narrowed until the papyrus heads were so thick above us that we were moving through a tunnel. At the end of it we emerged into a dark, circular pool. This was our destination, the pool of Cyane, the nymph who tried to prevent Pluto's abduction of Persephone and whom Pluto, in his irritation, turned into a spring. "She weeps for the loss of Persephone's innocence," said Stefano. If the weeping seemed overexuberant to an American, it was something a Sicilian could understand, since the loss of a young woman's innocence is still the greatest of Sicilian tragedies. The pool was perhaps sixty feet across; its dark waters seemed bottomless. It was a place of pastoral peace, and Stefano, who by his own count had been there three thousand times, quietly and respectfully let the legend live.

Such was the stillness that we forgot, for the moment, the raging sea. With a knife, which he carried for the purpose, Stefano carefully sliced a stalk of papyrus. Using only the yellowed base of the stalk, he shaved it very thin and wove the strips like a basket, explaining how the woven square must be pressed and dried by heat for several hours. Then he produced from under his seat, like a magician bringing forth a rabbit, a piece of brown papyrus paper. It was painted with a water color of the Greek theater.

Drops of rain began to make circles on the surface of the pool. Stefano wrapped me in the blankets, apologizing as if it were his own shortcomings that had made the day a disaster. We entered the papyrus tunnel. When we came out the storm was lashing at the trees and the rain fell in sheets. Stefano oared silently while I worried about the sea voyage ahead. We moved quickly with the current and in less than half the time it had taken us to get to the pool we were approaching the sea. Long before we saw it I could hear its terrible roar. The soapy breakers crashing toward us were four or five times the size of the boat. Stefano was obviously worried. I made a quick decision and asked him to let me out of the boat.

I was prepared to lose face with my boatman. I was sure he would despise me for my lack of courage, but to my surprise he was relieved. The voyage back was going to be rough and he knew he would have no time to keep me *tranquillo*. I suggested that he wait out the storm with his boat. He would not consider it; being a man of the sea, he had to master its challenges. He fingered the Madonna hanging from his neck and said she would see him through. We said good-by and he pushed the boat into the surf. I caught a glimpse of him leaping in and out of the foam like a piece of driftwood. Then I saw him no longer.

I trudged through the storm around the bay to Syracuse. Since I arrived soaking wet, I did not go at once to find out if Stefano was back. Also I was afraid he might see me and be hurt by my doubts. Later in the day I sneaked down to the quay where he kept his boat. It was there.

The storm continued to rage. All that night the great sea

thundered. Huge white waves beat against the rocks, and th
spray lashed over the town. In the morning the newspaper
said it was the most severe Mediterranean storm of the season
I received a cable from an English friend caught in Malta
where it was even worse. It asked, "Are you all right?"

CHAPTER 13

THE MADONNA OF THE TEARS

ONE DAY while I was living at the American Academy in Rome there appeared on the bulletin board an English-language announcement with the following headline: "SCHEME PROCLAIMED FOR AN INTERNATIONAL COMPETITION FOR THE CONSTRUCTION OF THE SANCTUARY OF THE MADONNA DELLE LACRIME IN SYRACUSE."

The details, printed in Italian, English, French, German, and Spanish, invited architects from throughout the world to submit designs for a sanctuary with a nave large enough to hold twenty thousand people, plus a canonical house, parish hall, office building, pilgrims' hostel, first-aid station, schoolhouse and orphanage for at least two hundred children. The architect fortunate enough to submit the winning design would be paid a prize of eight million lire plus a substantial fee for supervising the construction.

It gave one cause for reflection, this announcement by Syracuse to the world that it was going into the pilgrim business and its implied warning to France that Lourdes would have to look to its laurels. One could brood too on the caprices of fame and fortune. Not even in the dream city of Hollywood or in the television citadels of Radio City has there been anything like this success story. Almost overnight a piece of doll-faced chalk had become the most famous icon in Sicily and one of the most prodigious miracle workers o the Mediterranean world.

She wept, the people said, and they called her La Madonnina —the Little Madonna—using the diminutive of familia affection as if they were speaking of a child. Long before I arrived in Syracuse I was thoroughly familiar with her pink puffy face. It confronted me on medallions and statues, or holy pictures and on jewelry all over Sicily. I had seen he in lucite and neon, in porcelain and plaster, in chromium and in glass.

It may have been one of her miracles that I ever got to the shrine of the Little Madonna at all. Saints have been credited with miraculous intervention in mishaps far less catastrophi than the one I survived. I took a taxi, a lofty old-timer which shimmied so violently I wondered about its safety even before I mounted it. The driver, a complacent fat man, had a lively company of saints on his instrument panel: Cristoforo, Lucia Giuseppe, Antonio, Francis, and naturally the Madonnina was going to visit. Blithely we started off down the wrong side of the road. After a block or so, a huge lorry bore down on us like a cat on a mouse. Wham! Bang! We were rammed against a telegraph pole.

The van went on without stopping, and my driver, glisten ing like a tomato, ran after it a stretch, shaking his fists and uttering a torrent of Sicilian profanity. When I descended from the ruin, he came running back, fearful that he might lose his fare. He made a quick survey of the damage, proclaimed it *niente*, and pushed me back inside. The motor started. A tire, alas, was flat and the axle was so bent that he had no control over the car. "*Calmo, calmo,*" he shouted at me over the motor's racket. "Nothing is wrong." We wove herringbone fashion, back and forth across the street, com manding a wide berth from all traffic. I arrived at my destination in a state of nerves but physically unharmed.

At first sight the temporary shrine on Piazza Euripide looked like a provincial Japanese railroad station. Trains passed on one side of the V-shaped plaza, which added to this impression. Two great sheds extended over the streets as if they were train platforms; the higher main building was topped by a cross which bore the words *Ave Maria*. The shrine was brand-new and appeared much too fragile to weather the Mediterranean storms. Once inside, however, I could see that it was strongly reinforced with steel beams.

Since it was siesta time, there were no more than thirty persons in the sanctuary. Policemen assigned to the Little Madonna yawned with boredom. A dozen women in black were kneeling before the altar; some were weeping. I followed the maze of iron railings staked out to guide crowds single file to the altar. It was hot; the sun beating on the roof roasted everything inside. Trees under the roof were wilted and dying; flowers drooped and candles sagged.

In the panoply of drapes, flowers, and flickering wax, the Little Madonna was almost invisible. She was a hollow plaster shell of the type known as the Immaculate Heart of Mary, and in her hand she held a flaming heart. The shell was colored blue, pink, and beige and was eleven inches high. It was fastened to a piece of black glass measuring thirteen by fourteen inches.

The Germans would have called it *kitsch*. There is no word in any other language which so well describes the type of tasteless, mass-produced religious bibelots which have smothered all Italy south of Rome. I have heard the church blamed for this terrible blight, but one must remember that in centuries past it was the church which stimulated the artists of this country to produce some of the greatest religious masterpieces in the world. Protestant England and America must take a good share of the blame. The mass production of industrialism has leveled the taste of Catholic Italy to the least common denominator. Only lately has the church taken action to cleanse its temples of some of these horrors.

Perhaps it's too late. The Pope, always a wise and sensitive man, refused to become embroiled in the Syracuse affair. It is doubtful he could have done much even if he had tried. The climate for hysteria was right; no one knew that better than the cynical priests of Syracuse. There was nothing to stop the saccharine little figure of chalk. She was Persephone, twentieth century.

She was not even a native of Sicily, but came out of the north, from a factory in Bagni di Lucca where she was machine-made for the mass market, along with thousands exactly like her. Looking at her, one could not help wondering why destiny laid its finger on one piece of plaster and not on thousands of others exactly like it. It is a question which the manufacturers must also have pondered. Since the famous tears in Syracuse there has been an avalanche of orders for replicas. One of the most striking miracles of Sicily's Little Madonna has been the prosperity it has brought to the little town in Tuscany where they are manufactured.

I stood before the bland, factory-made doll wondering at its powers. Around the shrine the afternoon was coming to life. People collected on the piazza, where workmen were crushing stones to pave a street. A train arrived from the north. Its passengers crowded to the windows to catch a glimpse of the shrine. When I had visited Syracuse two years earlier, it had been a sleepy, indolent town with an air of hopelessness. Now everything was flushed with Madonnina prosperity.

Houses on the Piazza Euripide were turned into shops selling *oggetti sacri* (sacred objects). Their windows were filled with all manner of junk, including plaster replicas of the Little Madonna in all sizes and colors, pink lucite models lit up by tiny batteries, necklaces, rings, watch fobs, and scarves. An incredible assortment of post cards showed the Little

Madonna weeping, scenes of miracles, with paralytics being carried in beds and invalids in chairs, and abandoned crutches and wooden legs. Each shop had an *Ave Maria* over the door or in the window to show it was a pious place. Post cards were expensive—forty lire each and up. On the picture stalls, the Little Madonna shared honors with Syracuse's famous Landolina Venus, a headless, thick-thighed statue over which I had watched some Germans snickering the day before in the museum. The weeping Mother of Jesus and a nude Venus side by side! When one understands that, one begins to penetrate the mysteries of Sicily.

Not only were the houses on the square turned into shops but houses on the side streets as well sold flowers to lay before the Little Madonna and candles to burn at her shrine. Old ladies, opening the water closets of their little dwellings for the comfort of pilgrims, sat at the doors like black sphinxes, collecting their tithe of the holy largess.

On a house behind the sanctuary I saw a sign: OFFICE OF THE SECRETARY. I climbed some steep stairs into a bedroom office. Inside, I found two nuns and a young girl, dark and pretty. I asked them the question which had been bothering me since I had first heard of the Little Madonna. *Why did she weep?*

One nun was large and fat. "It's a secret," she said. "We don't know. The Little Madonna didn't tell us. She only wept. She did not speak." The nun, obviously bored by the question, began to pick her nose. The other nun—small and nervous—offered the suggestion that the Little Madonna had wept for the suffering of humanity. She gave me a published article by a social scientist, Professor Francesco Carnelutti, which said that the Little Madonna had wept for man's intellectual sins and for the indifference of a materialistic scientific age to matters of the spirit. As I scanned through the article, the nose-picking nun repeated irritably, *"La Madonina non parla. Piange soltanto."*

I made some notes. The nuns, seeing me write with my lef
hand, were greatly amused. In order to keep me writing the
began to talk.

Had the Little Madonna wept continually for four day
or only at intervals? I asked.

"*Continuamente,*" said the nervous little one.

"*Ad intervale,*" said the fat one.

They started to argue and forgot about me. In the mear
time the pretty girl told me that the headquarters were ope
ated by volunteer religious workers and lay people. The wor
consisted largely of looking after pilgrims and answering th
great quantity of correspondence.

"The whole world knows about us," said the big nun, an
she showed me letters addressed to the Little Madonna fror
America, Indonesia, India, the Canary Islands, Urugua
Libya, Australia, and many other lands. The letters begge
for mercy, reported miracles, and enclosed contributions fc
the *Santuario Permanente* to be built on the Piazza del
Vittoria, a few blocks up the Corso Timoleonte.

I asked the way to the house where the miracle had take
place.

"Two blocks along the Via degli Orti at number eleven,
the big nun said. "It is known as *La Strada dell' Inferno.*"

"Why is it known as 'the street of hell'?" I asked.

"Because the people were against religion and against law,
the nun replied. "They hated the Holy Church and its Hol
Fathers. They were Communists and they went to a Prote
tant church on the street."

"It was like a street damned," said the little nun. "Onl
the tears of the Madonna could redeem it."

"Is the house of the miracle now occupied?" I asked.

"Certainly not," the big nun said. "The house is a shrin
and no one can live in a shrine."

Her sister added, "When all the pilgrims came, the famil
was moved to another house."

I bid the nuns *buon giorno*. Starting down the thickly populated Via degli Orti, I marveled how the Little Madonna, rising to fame on the street of hell, had also, following Persephone's pattern, her season in the underworld. The dirty street was in the crowded Santa Lucia quarter, one of the meanest in Syracuse. The row of undistinguishable box-like hovels was piled with rubbish and puddled with sewage. The inhabitants were factory workers, unemployed fishermen, and farm workers who rode to the fields each dawn on bicycles, Vespas, or donkeys and returned each night after nightfall. Now a noisy parade of fifty-odd boy priests marched toward me in the center of the road. I stepped aside. They passed silently, raising their hats in my direction.

How friendly of them to greet me, I thought, and waved back. Then I noticed that everyone who passed—children, chimney sweeps, policemen, and beggars—paused in front of me. Finally, when a donkey driver stopped his beast and genuflected in my direction I turned around. I was standing by the door of number eleven.

The hall I entered had placards reading *Silenzio* and *Preghiere*, and a table with a visitors book. The house was small, with stone floors. Although the day was warm and bright, the two rooms were cool and damp.

In these rooms, early in 1953, lived Signora Concetta Sgarlata with her two sons, agricultural worker Angelo Iannuso and harbor stevedore Giuseppe Iannuso, and Giuseppe's wife, Grazia. The house was a perfect setting for a popular miracle. The family was as poor as the poorest; the sons, hoping for a change in the dreary despair of their lives, were rumored to have been flirting with Communism. In March 1953, the bachelor brother married his twenty-year-old sweetheart, Antonietta Giusto. The marriage mass was read by the Reverend Giuseppe Bruno in the Pantheon, a memorial to the dead of World War I built during the Mussolini regime. It is a garish architectural monstrosity which, curiously, has become popular for marriage ceremonies. As a wedding gift, Grazia Iannuso gave to her new sister-in-law an image of the Immaculate Heart of Mary which she had purchased for twenty-five hundred lire. The back room of the house was turned over to the newlyweds and there, over the head of the nuptial bed, Antonietta Iannuso hung the holy figure.

The bride conceived quickly and her pregnancy was a difficult one. From the beginning she was seized by violent nervous disturbances of an almost epileptic nature during which she suffered agonizingly.* Naturally her household was disturbed and the whole neighborhood soon learned of her affliction. During her seizures the bride sought comfort and mercy from the Madonna hanging over her bed. On the morning of Saturday, August 29, Angelo arrived in the fields late and in a troubled frame of mind. He told his fellow workers that, following a violent spell which had continued for several hours, his wife was blind and in an almost unconscious state.

It is not easy, even after three years, to get an objective account of what happened in the street of hell on that hot August day. The best one can do is rely on the published account documented and approved by ecclesiastical authorities, a copy of which the nuns in the office had given me. The official story tells us that at eight-thirty in the morning Antonietta Iannuso was suddenly restored to consciousness; that she stood at the foot of the bed and fixed her empty gaze toward the head; that her sight was restored, and that she saw tears flowing down the face of the Little Madonna.

She cried out, "*La Madonnina piange* [the Little Madonna weeps]!" In the front room the mother and sister-in-law believed poor Antonietta was having one of her hallucinations and came to comfort her. When they also saw tears, they ran from the house, crying "*Miràcolo! Miràcolo! La Madonnina*

---

* An English doctor has told me that the symptoms are those of kidney poisoning, a not uncommon affliction in pregnancy.

piange!" Soon up and down the street of hell the cries rang out. "Miracle! Miracle! The Little Madonna weeps!"

The news spread through the city, and everyone who could ran to the Via degli Orti to see the miracle. Fifty policemen (all of them testified as witnesses later) were required to manage the mob which stampeded the Santa Lucia area. Women wept and prayed. It is said that the Little Madonna, whose face was ordinarily a smiling one, had turned sad and that two streams of tears, flowing freely from both eyes, joined under her chin and dripped into the hand that supported her Sacred Heart. Those few who could squeeze into the bedroom had the presence of mind to absorb the tears with cotton wool. "Even the most skeptical, among whom were Communists, Freemasons, and Protestants, felt tremors and made the sign of the cross," says the ecclesiastical report.

At noon, the official story continues, brother Giuseppe Iannuso, returning from the harbor for his meal, was so enraged by the crowd disturbing the peace of his family that he went into the back room to smash the image. He saw the tears and was too terrified to carry out his intention. In the evening when Angelo returned on his bicycle from the fields he could not get near the house. Fearing that something had happened to his wife, he became hysterical. The police took him to her, and all she could say, over and over, was "The Little Madonna is weeping for me."

No one went home, and crowds continued to arrive. Toward midnight the police took Angelo and the weeping Madonnina to police headquarters on the Via Roma. During the trip her tears are reported to have soaked into the clothes of the policeman carrying her. At headquarters the officers observed the Little Madonna most carefully. Convinced there was no trickery, they told Angelo to take her home. By this time Via Roma was so filled with people that Angelo had to leave through back streets. Ecclesiastical authorities maintained what they called "prudent reserve." The next day ten clergy and several nuns went to the Iannuso house to investigate the miracle. A chaplain from the Syracuse Hospital thought of photographing the Little Madonna with tears streaming down her face. Two professors tasted the tears and asserted their flavor was similar to that of human tears. This so impressed two priests, one of whom was the Father Bruno who had married the Iannusos, that they called on the Syracuse Office of Hygiene and asked for a commission to analyze the tears chemically.

At eleven o'clock on Tuesday, September 1, the commission, with some prominent clergy, went to the street of hell. A police escort helped them through the mob into the dark little bedroom. There they were shown the Little Madonna, now locked in a drawer and covered by a moist napkin. She was, according to the report, weeping only from her left eye, and as usual the drops settled on the hand over the heart. One cubic centimeter of the liquid was sucked into a glass pipette for laboratory analysis. A powerful magnifying glass held over the eyes showed no irregularities in the surface of the glaze. The Little Madonna was detached from her glass base; she was found to be rough and hollow inside and completely dry.

The scientific commission released a report which said the tears contained exactly the same chemical elements as the tears of (1) an adult and (2) a three-year-old child. On September 2, chemistry professor Aldo Carratore wrote in the Catania journal La Sicilia: "Face to face with these miraculous drops . . . even the most obstinate incredulity has been forced into submission. The phenomenon is in no way to be denied. It would be like denying the sun gives light and heat. . . ."

The Archbishop of Syracuse was waiting for the opinions of the clergy and the chemists. When he received them he made his first visit to the Little Madonna. He found her hanging on an outdoor wall. The crowds were praying and singing hymns. He told the people on the street of hell that their sinful lives were the real cause of the tears of the Little Madonna; that her message for them was to end their indifference to the laws of God. The day the archbishop spoke was the fourth and last day the Little Madonna is reported to have wept.

The archbishop hurried off to Rome to report to the Pope what was happening in Syracuse. In his country residence in Castel Gandolfo the Holy Father advised caution and said the Church would wait and see. With diplomatic reserve the Pope said, "We will investigate. I cannot say more. Let us take this event as an incentive to strengthen our faith in the Holy Virgin, avoiding all exaggeration which might harm the prestige of religion."

In the meantime pilgrims had begun to move on Syracuse from all over Sicily and even Italy. Word that the Little Madonna was working miracles brought thousands, many on foot. The first miracle was that of Antonietta Iannuso herself, who from the moment of witnessing the tears was cured of her fits and her blindness. The second accredited cure was that of a forty-nine-year-old arthritic cripple named Nunzio Vinci from the town of Augusta. For twenty-eight months, Nunzio's arm had pained him so severely he was begging doctors to amputate it. In Syracuse he absorbed some of the Little Madonna's tears on a bit of cotton wool and applied the wool to his arm. On September fourth, while praying at the home of a sister, he felt a twitch in his arm. Afterward he was able to pick up his small nephew and shave himself for the first time since his illness.

An eighteen-month-old child named Salvatore Aliffi di Aurelio, given up by four physicians as mortally ill from intestinal obstructions, was miraculously restored to good health after the parents prayed to the Little Madonna.

Each report of a miracle sent the crowds of pilgrims into a delirium of ecstasy. On the evening of September nineteenth the Little Madonna was moved from the street of hell to Piazza Euripide. More than twenty thousand people followed her, singing hymns and chanting prayers. Cries of *Viva Maria!* rang through the city.

By this time so many miracles of healing were being credited to the Little Madonna that a medical commission was formed to investigate them. Of the more than three hundred miracles reported within two months, the commission examined and prepared documents on seventy.

A three-year-old girl victim of poliomyelitis was able to move a paralyzed arm after it had been brushed with the blessed cotton wool. A thirty-eight-year-old woman, paralyzed and unable to speak after a cerebral thrombosis, was carried to the Little Madonna, and after an application of the cotton wool she was able to speak, though still unable to walk. A sixty-nine-year-old man suffering from arteriosclerosis, diabetes, and a stiff left leg hobbled to the Little Madonna on a cane; while the crowd sang, he bent his leg. A group of barefoot pilgrims walked twenty-five kilometers from Avola with a sixteen-year-old dumb boy named Paolino Amato. He began to speak, and the sound of his voice, according to the report, "caused an indescribable scene." Another group came from Ragusa with a blind child of four who, led to the altar by a nun, was able to see the Little Madonna.

Not all miracles took place in Syracuse. Down in Modica a seventy-seven-year-old woman, bedridden for four years, was reported to have gotten out of bed alone, knelt and prayed for two hours, and then climbed twenty-five stairs. A miracle widely publicized on continental Italy was that of Bernardo Tranchida, a thirty-eight-year-old chauffeur who had been paralyzed since a 1948 car crash in Belgium. In the streets of Leghorn a woman offered him a bit of the blessed cotton wool. The same day he wired his relatives in Sicily: "Completely cured. Walking. Miracle." His arrival with four brothers in Syracuse threw the city into a commotion. At eight o'clock in the evening after a rosary service on the Piazza Euripide, Tranchida ran up the steps to the altar and over amplifiers which could be heard over the town thanked the Little Madonna for her miracle.

The most spectacular cure of all was that of Marianna Vassallo, wife of Dr. Salvatore Vassallo of Francofonte. Signora Vassallo, forty-nine years old, had had surgery for cancer in Genoa; a few months later another tumor was discovered. This time, according to the commission's report, the best surgeons in Genoa, Rome, and Catania told her husband there could be no further hope for her life. In a letter which she later wrote to the *Corriere di Sicilia*, Signora Vassallo said, "With all hope gone, I came home to die, praying to God to give me the grace to endure with patience the torture I knew lay before me. . . . I was one condemned to death, by an unredeemable sentence." Hearing of the miracles, she went to Syracuse. For several hours she and her husband prayed before the Little Madonna "for the supreme gift of life." In the evening the doctor husband fastened with plaster tape a bit of the blessed cotton wool on the small of her back above the diagnosed malignancy. In the morning the *signora* reported she was feeling well. She no longer needed morphine. Later, the surgeons who had doomed her pronounced her tumor gone.

Standing now in the quiet, empty little house, I tried to imagine the noisy events that had taken place here. In the first room there was nothing but a sink. The small back room was turned into a tiny chapel. It was painted pink and dimly lit with pale light which filtered through a window with yellow panes. On an altar stood a copy of the original Little Madonna. Seven bouquets of flowers and eleven chairs gave the place a funereal air. A nun was on her knees praying fervently before a white cloth. She felt my presence after a moment and turned to say, "With this cloth the tears were wiped from the eyes of the Madonnina."

She told me that as a result of the miracle, Angelo Iannuso

and his neighbors had become devoutly Christian and vehe-
mently anti-Communist. The ex-farm worker now had a new
job as caretaker of his old home.

I looked for Angelo about the premises, but he was nowhere to be found. On the street outside a woman came up
and offered to take me to his new home beyond the Piazza
Euripide. She was middle-aged, dark-skinned, and barefoot.
Her hair was in a snarl, and she was swathed in several orange
shawls. A fitting companion, I thought, as we started down the
street of hell. Her sharp eye spotted the Swiss shoes I was
wearing; the result was a pitch in peculiar variance to that of
the countless American "expatriates" who beg in Sicilian
towns. She talked in a sort of wail and never halted for breath.
"I am a poor Swiss from Locarno," she began, shrewdly
picking a town in Italian Switzerland. "Eighteen years I have
been in a foreign land. It was a black day that I left my poor
mother in Switzerland, and now she has died and I am alone,
a poor woman unable to go home. It is all I wish for before
the end of my life, to kneel and pray at my dear mother's
grave." Her voice as we moved down the street rose and fell
like a primitive song. "I know you will help me, a fellow
Swiss, to go home. I will take you to Angelo Iannuso and you
will give me five hundred lire. Soon I will return to the most
happy country in the world and I will pray to the Holy
Mother for the peace of your soul."

I had only one hundred lire in change, which I offered her.
She refused. "It is worth more to be taken to the house of
Angelo Iannuso," she sang. "Every day of my life I will pray."
In that case, I said, I would seek out Angelo myself. When
she saw that I was serious, she took the hundred lire and we
continued down the road. Even before we had arrived at the
piazza of the shrine I was growing uneasy about her because
she was obviously demented. She was, I could see, well known
in the neighborhood. Everyone was interested in seeing what

she had snared. Children followed us and jeered. She was apparently a regular object of their persecution.

"*Sicuro, sicuro*," she sang. "With me you are safe. You belong to me. I will protect you." She had forgotten her mother's grave in Switzerland and now wailed, "*Cento lire per dormire* [a hundred lire for a bed]." She screamed at the pack of children like a witch. Everyone was laughing; the whole street became a bedlam. I saw some police guards at the door of a government building and ran to them for help. They ordered the woman to leave. Turning her wrath on them, she pointed to me and screamed, "He belongs to me! You can't have him!" Handling her roughly, the police sent her reeling down the street while the crowd shrieked. Among the laughing women the police pointed out Antonietta Iannuso, wife of Angelo.

She was dark and pretty and, though only twenty-three, already matronly in the Sicilian manner. She was reluctant to talk; her husband was the family spokesman, and to all my questions she replied, "I must ask him."

Down the street I heard cries of "Angelo, Angelo." There he was, hurrying toward us, having heard that an *Americano* was looking for him. I was surprised by both his small size and youthful appearance. Though thirty, he looked like a boy. He had a pleasant face, a mustache, and a mild and gentle manner. He seemed shy.

With pride he spoke in a soft voice of an aunt and some cousins in Brooklyn. He twisted a key ring and spoke a dialect difficult to understand. A boy of ten, one of those precocious, bright-eyed children that are forever popping out of the pavements of Naples and Sicily, translated what he said into Italian. Angelo told of the Little Madonna's four days of tears. His story corresponded with the official published account except for one variation: in Angelo's version it was he and not his brother who wanted to destroy the Little Madonna. He said, "When I returned at night from the fields and I couldn't get near my house I was certain a terrible disaster had befallen my wife. All she would say was 'The Little Madonna is weeping for me.' I thought it was some crazy thing and I became very angry. I took the Madonnina from the wall and was going to smash her. Then I felt her tears on my hands and I knew that she wept also for me."

He spoke fervently. The crowd that had hooted and laughed a quarter of an hour before now gathered around to listen.

"The way I was living was wrong," he said. "That was the Little Madonna's message for me. Now everything is changed."

"What has changed?" I asked.

"My life," he said.

The little boy said, "He has a new house."

"After the miracle it was *sempre pellegrini*," Angelo said. "Always pilgrims. My wife, who was expecting the baby, could no longer live here. So the *municipio* bought the house to make it a chapel."

A woman said, "When it was time to move, the Little Madonna communicated to Angelo that she did not want him to leave the house. So the *municipio* made Angelo custodian."

"On the anniversary of the miracle, the chapel was dedicated by the archbishop and the mayor," said Angelo. "Five thousand pilgrims were here that day."

"Ten thousand," the woman corrected him.

"What about Communism?" I asked.

"There is no more Communism here," the woman said.

"Communism is an evil," Angelo said. "It is against the Madonna."

"What has happened to the Protestant church?" I asked.

"Finished," said the woman. "There are no more Communists and no more Protestants."

From the crowd came stories of still more miracles.

"A boy paralyzed from birth was brought to the Little Madonna and now he plays football."

"The aunt of my friend had tuberculosis of the bone for twenty years and now she does her own housework."

"They say in Bari a girl was raised from the dead."

"In Messina a young girl put a bit of the blessed cotton into a bottle. In the morning, the bottle was half filled with the miraculous tears. . . ."

How did the girl know it was tears in the bottle? I asked.

"She tasted them and received the gift of prophecy."

What has the girl prophesied?

"She prophesied that one of two things would come to pass," said the woman. "Either the world would come to an end or the world would be blessed with everlasting peace."

I could appreciate the effect of such a prophecy on the people of Messina, a city of catastrophe, many times destroyed by earthquakes, tidal waves, and war. No doubt they must have expected the worst.

What happened? I asked, turning to the woman.

"On Christmas Day the baby, a boy, was born," she said.

I had forgotten about the child which Antonietta Iannuso was carrying at the time of the miracle.

"An extraordinary child, sitting up almost at once for the photographers," said the woman.

So Messina had been spared and the baby's arrival on the birthday of Jesus had given credence to the prophecy of peace. The circle surrounding me was silent now, as if no one in it dared even to whisper that the tears in the street of hell had been an annunciation and that little Mariano (for so he was named) was a prince of peace. I turned to ask Angelo if I might see the child, but the shy father had disappeared in the crowd and I did not see him again.

I stayed a week in Syracuse and was never out of reach of the Little Madonna. Every evening *"Ave Maria"* glowed in blue neon over Piazza Euripide, and the prayers of pilgrims were amplified over the town. The last rosary was read at eight o'clock, and the archbishop usually dropped around for it. "We are sinners," I could hear chanted over the loudspeakers. "But still Your children. Immaculate Virgin, take pity on us."

Even by leaving Syracuse I could not escape the Little Madonna. One day I backtracked to Noto, where the little green-eyed figure confronted me on every street. I looked up a young lawyer named Carlo Galato whose name had been given me by a professor in Rome. Carlo belonged to an old and cultured family which had lost its property. He had studied English because he believed his only hope for a happy life was to emigrate to the United States. Realizing that this was next to impossible under the quota system, he was awaiting an immigration visa to Canada, from where he hoped, eventually, to continue to the United States. Carlo was an intellectual, a proud Sicilian who said he hated Sicily.

Together we wandered over the most beautiful baroque town in the world. The graciousness of the architecture, however, seemed lost on the people. Spiritless ennui lay like a cloud over the squares; there was a remoteness from the world that one finds in isolated mountain villages. We passed some women praying at a Little Madonna shrine, and Carlo turned away with disgust.

"Do you understand that?" he asked.

"Not entirely," I said.

"Then perhaps I can assist you to understand," he said. "The Madonnina is a great hoax."

I let that pass and waited for him to continue.

"We Sicilians have some noble qualities, for we are sons of Greeks and Normans. But we are also African, and Tunisia and Algeria are in our blood. We are a corrupted, defeated people.

"We have no faith. We look on the economic side of everything. In our land only the rich have rights; the poor have duties. A golden key, we say, will open the gates of Heaven. The rich are Monarchists. I must confess it is the party for which I have voted, though personally I do not believe in a king. I would prefer democracy. But we are sheep; we have to follow. We do not want to worry about anything—we want it all done for us. That is why we welcome American aid and American money. We think it is our just due.

"We are dreamers. Having a bad life, our people dream of a better one. Poor women dream of heaven and are Christian Democrats; poor men dream of Communism because they are told there is a good life in Communism.

"I am of the middle class. About the existence of God I do not know. But when I, with my modest intelligence, listen to a priest, I know quite firmly that he is the biggest liar in the world and that he does not believe what he says. Our priests, who are friends to the rich, have in the last years lost their influence. They have also lost their security. There are too many priests and not enough rich to support them all. No doubt the priests have thought how pilgrims would bring money to Syracuse. Even priests look on the economic side of things.

"So now we have the Madonnina. They say there were tears. In August our weather is sometimes very humid and the little room on the Via degli Orti is damp and dark. They also say there are miracles. I believe they are all by suggestion. Here in Noto a woman who could not walk prayed for four days and then walked a little. Naturally she had a miracle, even though she has not walked since.

"The one miracle that is expected of the Madonnina is to perpetuate the priests and their rich friends and frighten the poor away from Communism and back into their influence. The Madonnina can do this for a little while of course, but she cannot do it forever. A hoax is always exposed in the end."

If there were people in Syracuse who agreed with Carlo,

I did not come across them. In a government office I met a professor who had studied economics at Oxford University. He told me of the miraculous cure of a janitor in his apartment house.

"The janitor was paralyzed for five years, and his wife did the work," said the professor. "The tenants of the house took up a collection to pay for his carriage to visit the Little Madonna. He went to pray for three days. When I returned home from my office on the third day the police stopped me. 'A miracle has been performed,' they said. They took me inside, and there was our janitor walking." The professor concluded, "The Little Madonna lifted us to a spiritual awareness of which all of us were in need."

My last day in Syracuse I walked through the Santa Lucia district to the church of the saint which gives the area its name and who is also the patroness of Syracuse. On the steps I was greeted by a Franciscan about twenty-two years old. I was struck at once by an intense spiritual excitement which seemed to burn in him like a fever. His lean young body trembled; his black eyes flashed. In his ecstasy his feet hardly seemed to touch the ground. I had felt the same power of levitation with the frail John the Baptist at the catacombs. It is a quality, this taking wing, that I have noted often in Franciscans and never in a member of any other order, and I believe it comes to them from their saint who could live with birds and sing to "sister moon" and "brother wind." This young brother seemed to reach heavenward like an elongated young Spanish saint in El Greco's "Vision of the Apocalypse."

He took me through an underground tunnel to a circular chapel to see the tomb of Santa Lucia. The tomb was empty. The brother explained that the saint's bones were taken by Constantine to Constantinople and had since been returned to Venice, where they now rested.

"They belong here," he said fervently. "One day they will come back."

We felt our way through some catacombs, empty except for a grinning skull in one of the niches. With a feeble flashlight the brother pointed out some pale ghosts of frescoes, Byzantine saints and angels still visible on the ceiling. It was here that I spoke of the Little Madonna.

"In Syracuse, men neglected the Holy Mother," the brother said. "So she has come to us! She has brought us her love and her tears!" His voice rose so high that he seemed almost to sing. "The Holy Mother's tears are like the blood of Jesus. They are given to save men from sorrow. She has chosen Syracuse! Syracuse, from all towns in the world, because Syracuse needed her most!"

I thought I felt the brother floating beside me.

"Do you believe?" he asked.

"It causes me to wonder," I said.

"You must believe! You must believe! It is because men don't believe that she has been made to weep. Believe! Believe! Pray that you will believe."

In the underground darkness his eyes gleamed like a cat's, and I realized that there were tears in them. He reached for my hand and held it. His hands were warm and moist. "Poor brother," he said softly. "You must believe. Believe the Holy Mother wept for you as she wept for all of us." Behind him the pale skull gaped and a moment later when I departed from the church his voice followed me, singing, "Believe, believe . . ."

In my hotel I found the following wry note from Carlo: "Here in Noto they say another Little Madonna has begun to weep. Come to Noto and we will dry her tears together." Since it was necessary for me to move on to Catania, I could not accept the invitation.

CHAPTER 14

THE THREE BEARS

FROM SYRACUSE Frank was called back to Rome to work as
page boy on a new motion picture, so I went on to Catania
alone. It took about two hours by bus across the plain of
Catania, over the battlefield of Allied and German armies.
Families had set up housekeeping in abandoned pillboxes,
some of which were painted with *"Evviva Giuliano!"* and
others with the Separatists' motto *"Sicilia o la morte!"* (Sicily
or death!). Some pillboxes were overgrown with cactus. Cactus cultivated in rows made miles of impenetrable fences.
This was also citrus country. Orange groves hung heavy with
fruit. Village children offered nosegays of orange blossoms
for fifty lire.

The commercial city of Sicily is a black city. After the earthquake of 1693 it was rebuilt with lava rock in the baroque
fashion of the times. Streets are black, buildings are black, and
most of its adults are dressed in black. Entering the town, we
met the inevitable funeral. The atmosphere of mourning is
normal to Catania, which has been several times destroyed
by the eruptions of Etna looming white-capped above it.

Being a town of little interest to tourists, Catania has inade-
quate hotels. Some new ones were being built, but at the
moment there were only two which seemed to offer any sort

of comforts, and both were filled. The porter of one suggested I try the Red Geranium.

The Red Geranium was a small hotel run by Herr and Frau Teufelberg from Appenzell, Switzerland. The office of the hotel was a large, square, glass cage in which three people pored over huge ledgers. Herr Teufelberg was a gruff, squat man with handlebar mustaches, a Prussian haircut, and a large gold fob and chain dangling from his brown suit. Frau Teufelberg was a dumpy, short-legged woman in a black alpaca dress. Her dingy gray hair was loosely pinned and her face, beaming from soap, had no make-up. The toes of her flat shoes pointed out. The third person, an anemic, bad-complexioned, thick-spectacled young man, was the fruit of their union. The three of them poring over the long ledgers made me think of Papa Bear, Mama Bear, and Baby Bear.

Hardly looking up, Papa Bear grumbled there were no rooms. Then I spoke German-Swiss. My gargling of that unlyrical language was music to their ears; all three bears looked up. Mama Bear rose and, like one of those mechanical toys, bobbed toward me.

"Sie sind Schweizer?" she asked.

"A sort of Swiss," I hedged, not willing to give up any franchise for a room. I went on to explain that I was an American of Swiss ancestry and had spoken the language as a child. "Den you are still Sviss." She spoke to me now in English. "Vun is never finished to be a Sviss." I could see what she meant. She and her husband had passed more than a quarter century in Catania and were still as Swiss as if they'd never left the Rosslital.

As for Baby Bear—he was called "Oogy," having been christened Hugo—he knew enough English to tell me in a toneless voice, "I was made in Catania." I do not know whether Oogy had ever been in Switzerland, but I had seen his kind poring myopically over ledgers in every town in Switzerland. Oogy would have gone far as a banker.

There were two rooms. The first, a tiny claustrophobic affair, was too near the *gabinetto* for comfort. The second was larger and had two beds. Its window looked out on the shell of a building, a relic of the war. Mama Bear explained, "Vun day de chip exploded in der vater. Denn it is boombing all over. De dings come down, de walls brrrroke op and it is knotzering all over."

Mama Bear must have thought I had spotted a bit of dust, for, she confided, as one Swiss to another, that Sicilians were irresponsible domestics. "Dese foreigners dey do not like to verk. Vun must always vatch vat dey do." If I were to take the large room, she said, I would have to pay for a double room even if I slept in only one of the two beds. I asked how much that would be, and Mama Bear immediately made a detailed calculation which came out to 1,276 lire a day.

"Make it a thousand and finish," said Papa Bear, shuffling silently behind us.

Mama Bear turned on her husband and growled to him in Swiss, "I have to live, you have to live, our son has to live. You want to give a double room for a thousand lire!"

It grew into a sort of fugue, she growling and he grumbling. "I don't know why you don't make it a thousand for such a nice young Swiss man," he said.

Mama Bear, angrily rechecking her figures, announced she'd made a mistake. The price would be 1,376 lire.

"Tsh, tsh," said Papa Bear, "she is terrible." Putting a finger to his head and making the sign of a wheel going around, he repeated, "Terrible."

My reason for stopping in Catania was the opera. The city is the home of Vincenzo Bellini, composer of *Norma* and *La Sonnambula.* There is a Bellini theater, a Bellini museum in the house where the composer was born, a Bellini monument with statues of opera characters, some gardens known as the Villa Bellini, and the composer's tomb in the cathedral. Scurrying from one to the other, I passed through markets heavy with the odors of fish and blood, crowded with carcasses of lambs and goats and tubs of black, snakelike eels. It was the atmosphere of Naples. Children searched like rats for discarded scraps and ate them raw. I photographed two small boys hunched together on the sidewalk dividing the tobacco from a day's collection of cigarette butts.

The Massimo Bellini opera theater is one of two great opera houses in Sicily. Palermo's Massimo is larger, but performances in Catania were among the best I heard in Italy. Both houses are too expensive to be popular theaters and both draw patrons from the well-heeled aristocracy. Sicilian opera patrons are Monarchist in their politics, being nostalgic for the court life which once gave society meaning. In both Palermo and Catania the *palco reale*, or royal box, is preserved as an empty monument to kingship. As a guest of the managements, I have watched opera from both royal boxes. But my presence was always kept secret. I entered the boxes after the house lights were lowered and left them before they were turned up. In both theaters I was asked to sit back in the shadows to make certain I would not be seen.

My first evening in Catania I went to a performance of *Norma*. In the royal box with me were a young music critic from Amsterdam and his wife. At intermission we milled through the galleries. Fashions, subdued compared to the ebullient San Carlo in Naples, were still dazzling. The atmosphere had the regality of Milan's La Scala.

We entered the restaurant, and there at a counter stood a caricature. I thought I recognized it, but it took several seconds until I was sure. It was Mama Bear changed from her black alpaca to a black-green velvet skirt, which fitted tight to the knees, where it flared roguishly and continued to an indecisive hem between calf and heel. Her rose-colored blouse had billowing sleeves. Her hair was decorated with black jet ornaments and a high Spanish comb, from which, in voluminous folds, dropped a Spanish shawl. She wore a black necklace, gold banglets on her wrist, and pointed satin shoes with square rhinestone buckles. A black beaded bag hung from an arm, and her cheeks were rouged like a pair of red apples.

It was Appenzell at its most elegant. Mama Bear thumped about shaking hands, pushing herself into one circle after another, as she delicately balanced a plate of ice cream in one hand. Finally the foyer bell rang and she clattered into the theater.

The opera was over at eleven o'clock. Forty-five minutes later I was fetching my key at the Red Geranium. In the mirror over the key board I saw Mama Bear in her office. Although it was still a quarter of an hour to midnight, the pumpkin coach and glass slippers had vanished. She was wearing her black alpaca dress with the buttons wrongly lined up. Her hair was tangled; only the rouge remained. Her nose, supporting gold-rimmed glasses, was in the ledger. Papa Bear and Baby Bear were there, too, all poring over accounts.

"Good night, Herr Kubly," said Papa Bear.

"Good night," I answered.

Mama Bear glowered; the exchange of greeting seemed to her a continuation of the alliance struck up by Papa Bear and myself in the morning.

"Did you enjoy the opera tonight, Frau Teufelberg?" I asked.

"Vas you at the opera?" she snapped.

"I saw you but you wouldn't look my way," I said.

"Vere did you sit?"

As casually as I could, I said, "In the royal box."

Mama Bear stared uncomprehendingly a moment and then said flatly, "Jah, you mean the *galleria*."

"No. I mean the *palco reale*. The box of the kings."

A cloud crossed her face. It might have been disbelief, or anger with me for mocking her. "How came it you vas in the *palco reale*?" she asked.

"I was a guest of the *Herr Direktor* of the theater," I said.

"Vat is his name?" she asked, triumphantly sure that my invention would be exposed. Papa and Baby Bear had their pencils poised and listened with interest.

"Maestro Giovanni," I said.

Mama Bear's face grew dark. "Maestro Giovanni," she repeated. "You mean Maestro Giovanni has put you in the *palco reale*? Does he not know that no one is to sit there but a king?"

So that was it! Mama Bear was a Monarchist. A peasant daughter of one of the oldest and sturdiest democracies in the world had a nostalgia for kings. Now I understood the struggle for attention at the opera house, the nudging and handshaking of Catanian nobility. Frau Teufelberg of Appenzell wanted to be Signora Teufelberg, the friend of *marchesi* and countesses, of dukes and princes.

The frown on her face melted and her face brightened with another thought. "You are a friend to Maestro Giovanni?" she asked, her voice turning to oil. A friend of Maestro Giovanni's was someone with whom to contend. She smiled triumphantly at her husband. She had been right in charging the extra lire after all; a friend of Maestro Giovanni's could well afford to pay. She beamed at me and got up from her desk.

"Herr Kubly. Let me take you to your room," she said, wrenching the key from my hand.

I followed her down the long corridor. At the end she opened the door for me.

"Did you understand the opera?" she asked.

I said I did.

"But it was in Italian," she said.

"I understand Italian," I said. "Furthermore, the story is an old Druid legend with which I am familiar. I have heard the opera many times. *Of course,* not often so good as tonight in Catania."

"It is so," Mama Bear said. "But, of course, I have heard *Norma* in the San Carlo of Naples. Dat vas better."

"You are right," I said. "I have heard *Norma* at San Carlo. From the *palco reale*."

Mama Bear was beginning to fret. "Die opera is very gut in Italy," she said. "But never is die opera so gut as in Bayreuth. Ven I vas a girl I vonce heard der die *Lohengrin*."

"You are quite right," I said. "I heard the *Ring* and *Parsifal* and *Tannhäuser* last summer."

"You vas at Bayreuth?"

"In the *lögen* of the *Familie* Wagner," I said.

Mama Bear was astonished. But she quickly recovered and with a step that was almost a curtsy she moved aside for me to pass into the room.

"*Buona notte*," she said.

"*Buona notte*," I said, and Mama Bear bowed and closed the door.

Before I was in bed there was a knock on the door. It was Papa Bear, who was carrying a half bottle of white wine. "You must be thirsty after the opera," he said gruffly in Swiss. "Young men should enjoy themselves." He deposited the bottle on my night table and started to shuffle off. Then he turned back and said apologetically, "I do not like the opera. I never go."

In the morning only Mama Bear was in the cage. I thanked her for the gift of wine and added, "Shall I see you tonight at the opera?"

"Not tonight," she said. "I do not go."

"You are not fond of *Rigoletto*?" I asked.

Mama Bear hitched her glasses firmly on her brow. "Herr Kubly, I go to every opera," she said in Swiss. "I have a ticket with a *P* on it."

"*P*?" I asked.

"Yes. *Permanente!* I was to *Rigoletto* last week."

The Dutch couple and I were invited to a party by one of the singers that night so I did not get back to the Red Gera-

nium until after three o'clock. It was the only time I passed
the glass cage that I did not see at least one of the three bears
in it. When I went out late the next morning Mama Bear was
not in the cage. Papa and Baby Bear, silently working, nodded
as I passed. There was no opera that night and I returned at
a reasonable hour. Mama Bear was in the cage as usual.

"Herr Kubly. Did you like *Rigoletto*?"

"Yes. *Wunderbar!*"

"It must have been very *wunderbar*. You did not come
home until almost four o'clock. We do not make reductions
if you stay away all night."

"The thought hadn't occurred to me," I said, and started
toward my room.

She thumped after me. "Ver you again sitting in the *palco
reale*?" she asked.

"I vas again," I said.

"It is a *skandal*," she said, and turned back.

An hour later the Dutch couple arrived in my room. They
were leaving for Amsterdam in the morning and had come to
say good-by. After a quarter hour there was a stern knock on
the door. It was Mama Bear.

"Herr Kubly. Because you do not sleep in your room one
night does not mean two can sleep in it another night."

Over Mama Bear's shoulder peered the walrus face of
Papa Bear.

"See, I told you," Papa Bear said to Mama Bear. "There
are three of them. Everything is all right."

Mama Bear was a study in frustration. Finally she said,
"Herr Kubly. You have not yet paid a deposit on your room.
If you will be so kind, I will take it now."

Such an unorthodox request at 10:00 P.M. was insulting. It
was also embarrassing, for I did not have any money. I had
planned to cash a check first thing in the morning.

I explained this to Mama Bear. She interpreted my explanation as proof of my perfidy. I showed her a book of

traveler's checks and offered her one. She took the book and examined it. With sudden fierceness Papa Bear tore it from her hands and handed it back to me. "This is nonsense," he said. To Mama Bear he said, "Go to bed."

"Nonsense!" said Mama Bear. "And who must make de nonsense in dis house? Do you? Does Oogy? No. It is me makes always de nonsense. Without nonsense we would starve." She thumped off. Papa Bear loitered a moment in the door. Then he shook his head sadly as if asking for pity and closed the door.

The Dutch couple were giving up their room in one of the good hotels. I asked them to reserve it for me. In the morning they telephoned to say the room was mine. As I passed the glass cage, I asked Mama Bear to prepare my bill.

"You haf de money?" she asked.

"I am getting it now," I said. When I returned a half hour later Mama Bear greeted me with a broad smile. On her desk was a back issue of the French magazine *Match*.

"I haf another room for you," she said, purring like honey. "It is a single room and vill be cheaper. Come, I vill show you."

"I am leaving," I said firmly. "Please give me my bill."

"Do you not like it here? We are proud to haf a distinguished guest like Herr Kubly."

"I should like you to call me a cab when I am packed," I said. Within a few minutes—so soon it must have been already prepared—Oogy brought the account to my room. It was an elaborately detailed and beautifully inscribed thing, looking, rather, I thought, like a Gothic sonnet. Going over it, I came across the following item: "Vino: 250 lire." The only wine I had drunk was the complimentary bottle after *Norma*.

Before paying the bill I told the three bears I had not ordered any wine.

"Vy does Herr Kubly haf to worry about a little money?" said Mama Bear expansively.

"What do you mean by that?" I asked.

"Herr Kubly has very famous friends," she said.

I tried to figure out what she meant by the remark. Was it my connection with Maestro Giovanni? The Dutch couple?

Then she added, "Such rich and distinguished banking friends."

She showed me the magazine, opened to a spread of Bayreuth photographs of the Wagner family with some of their festival guests. Among them was the Nazi banker Hjalmar Schacht.

"You know him?" she asked.

"No," I said. "I am sorry. I am a chess player,* not a financial player."

Mama Bear accepted payment—minus the two hundred and fifty lire—without comment. Then she looked up at me with hatred flashing in her eyes like lightning.

"The night you vent to *Rigoletto*," she said, "I haf a friend who looked. My friend could not see anyone in the *palco reale*." She lurched into the cage and, drawing her spectacles down on her nose, joined Baby Bear in the ledgers.

Papa Bear, who had been watching over the top of his ledger, slowly got up and carried my bags to the taxi. When he had helped me in he looked at me with his tragic eyes and said, "My wife, you know, she is mad."

* *Schach* is the German word for chess.

CHAPTER 15

DUSK

DURING THE RIDE to Taormina a storm blew up as fierce as the one a week before in Syracuse. It lashed against the bus and uprooted trees in our path. Several times men passengers joined together to heave branches of oak or locust out of the road. Our progress was slow, and before we were halfway there night had fallen. In the village of Mascali we were delayed an hour by debris in the street. Mascali is a modern town, having been destroyed by Etna's eruptions of November 1928, and immediately rebuilt. It is the home of Turiddu Bella, author of *Turi Giulianu*, a long biographical poem written in Sicilian dialect about Salvatore Giuliano.

I found a travel office and went in to inquire how I could find the poet. The young man behind the counter invited me to a near-by café for coffee. When I commented on the warmth of his hospitality, the young man said, "In Sicily three things are sacred: hospitality, love, and a man's honor." It was the romantic creed of donkey-cart paintings and puppet theaters.

My host was named Giuseppe. He was a graduate of Catania University and active in community affairs. He spoke with sensitivity and intelligence of the problems of his people, and with open and profound admiration of Salvatore Giuliano.

164

"*Un buon ragazzo*," Giuseppe said. "A man who loved his country and his people. No one who was not a Sicilian in those times could imagine the suffering of Sicily after the war. Like all popular leaders, Giuliano rose to the needs of his people in a time of crisis. He was our Zapata, a man very close in spirit to the Mexican hero. As long as there are Sicilians alive on earth he will be revered."

Signor Bella welcomed us into the dimly lit, neat little parlor of his home. He was a strong Sicilian Nationalist, and his hobby was the revival of the Sicilian language, which he believed more beautiful than Italian. He was one of three national poets who wrote in Sicilian. His poem on Giuliano had gone through three editions and more than twenty thousand copies. While we talked, the poet's handsome children climbed on his lap. I could see he was a gentle person with no stomach for violence or anarchy. Yet he had sympathy for the mission of Salvatore Giuliano and he felt the bandit had been misunderstood by the world. "Giuliano wanted to lead his people," the poet said. "The persecution of police drove him to excesses, and in the end he died as all brigands do, not nobly, but betrayed. He was not right. Only the most foolish of men would call him blameless. But he was a youth of action, and to people who have lost their courage, he was a hero. When he died, part of Sicily died with him. It is something only a Sicilian can understand."

I said that I had journeyed over the land and seen the people, and I was beginning to understand the legend. Signor Bella autographed a copy of his book for me, and we said good-by.

The road was cleared; our bus was ready to move on. In a half hour we were at the seaside town of Giardino, where we started the long, winding climb to Taormina. I heard a rumbling which I took to be thunder but which turned out to be

Etna stirring in her bowels. The sky over the volcano became red, and streaks like flame bombs lit up the heavens above Pluto's fiery portals to the underworld. On a ledge over Taormina a white cross of stone shone in the night; otherwise it was dark. The wild wind shrieked like Vulcan's bellows as we registered at a hotel called the Mediterraneo. I had the strange sensation of being very close to both Heaven and Hell.

HEAVEN AND HELL

"The nearest approach to seeing Eden."
—JOHN HENRY NEWMAN, on seeing the
view from Taormina's Greek theater

CHAPTER 1

HEAVEN

THE MEDITERRANEO STOOD on a ledge between the sea and the town. From the terrace I could look out on my left to the sea seven hundred feet below, on my right to Mount Venus two thousand feet above. Across a piazza was a roofed shrine covering an old, armless Madonna. The piazza was a busy crossroads opening on one side to the town's public gardens, and on the other to one of the steep and dangerous footpaths going down to the seaside railroad station of Giardino.

Each morning was like watching the Creation. First there was light, rising like a coral flame to warm the world; then the sea lashing against the ancient grottoes and turning into a thousand shades of turquoise. The earth followed, with the graceful profile of Etna wearing a nimbus halo and a snow mantle of glowing cerise. Soon it was light enough to see the lemons, almonds, cedars, palms, red poppies, white arum lilies, amaryllis, hibiscus, and paper-crisp purple azalea, all growing in jungle profusion. Animals came next—slinking cats winding up their nocturnal missions and dogs sniffing across the piazza. The birds in the garden heralded the day, cocks crowed in the town, and fantailed white doves made love.

Finally man appeared on the piazza in all his curious varia-tions. First the young blades of the town, in their pin-striped suits and camel's-hair coats, going wearily home from their night's assignations; then barefoot fishermen, returning with their catch in sacks on their backs. As the town awakened, the dairyman drove his goats to the piazza, where the animals bleated impatiently while he bowed for a morning prayer before the Madonna. Then he milked them into the pans and pails of the women of the neighborhood.

Women carried everything on their heads. On one a bundle of laundry bobbed like a fantastic headdress, on another a basket of greens. One wide old woman swayed like a camel as she balanced a crock on her head. She was old and lame and tackled each stair sideways, like a donkey, zigzagging up the whole long climb. The brown-skinned boy who sold jellyfish carried a basket of the nasty gray stuff in one hand and in the other a brass-chained scale to weigh it. Children were the last —wrestling little boys and girls who skipped rope and brought nosegays of daisies and violets to lay before the Madonna.

At eight o'clock the watchman unlocked the iron garden gates, and the children rushed in, followed by camera-laden tourists, Austrians in *Lederhosen*, Swiss in knit stockings, Swedes in embroidered blouses. New arrivals from the morn-ing train trudged arduously up the path, stopping for breath by the Madonna. Nuns held hands as if they were children; priests, their sandaled feet covered with dust, recited brevi-aries. If it was Sunday, the caravan was long, with carefree Sicilian families, the father and older children carrying bas-kets of food and wine, and musical instruments, and the mother following with the little ones. When the morning cravan had arrived, I considered the day well born.

Many have called Taormina the most beautiful place in the world. I know none more beautiful. The youngest of Sicily's Greek colonies, it rose from the ashes of the oldest, called Naxos. Naxos was founded in the eighth century B.C.

by Greek traders who landed their craft in a natural harbor and raised an altar to Apollo, laying the way for five centuries of Greek domination in Sicily. Only three years ago Taormina fishermen discovered at the bottom of the sea in the vicinity of ancient Naxos the remnants of a temple and a rich archaeological vein of vases and coins.

Dionysius destroyed Naxos; her survivors climbed to the ledge above the sea and founded Taormina, which flourished for three centuries as a Greek city. Today it is a village of less than five thousand citizens who live by serving tourists, mostly German, English, American, and Scandinavian. Northern visitors are drawn not only by its natural beauty but by its reputation for license. For this Taormina is largely indebted to the German baron with a camera who for forty years before his death in 1931 made and sold some four thousand nude photographs of the natives. These were the photographs which the Canadian had wanted for his anthropological alter ego. Taormina's greatest prosperity, however, came in the thirties, when Mussolini's luxury-loving Nazi admirers filled her hotels. During the war, Taormina held the historical spotlight for a brief moment when it was the headquarters for the German general staff.

The inevitable Allied bombings cost Taormina dearly in lives and property. Though the scars are evident—the destroyed San Domenico church probably never will be rebuilt —Taorminians, with their eyes on the tourist dollar, have worked hard to restore their town. But for some of the war's changes there is no restoration. Dwindling fortunes and higher taxes kept people away, and the expected postwar boom came slowly. What with fewer idle Americans and the English unable to export funds, there is no longer a distinguished foreign colony. Some of the villas are closed. A few are rented on short-term leases to Americans, and more have been converted into *pensioni*. It is from the *pensione* dwellers that Taorminians maintain a moderate and steady prosperity. Their town is the cleanest in Sicily. A strong civic organization encourages the people to keep the streets scrubbed, as in a Dutch village. Begging is illegal. Prices are moderate and the tradespeople, most of whom speak enough English and German to do business, are congenial.

The place affects each man in his own way. For me Taormina was an extravagant theater with a never-ending polyglot drama—exaggerated, grotesque, bizarre, and tragic—played against a setting of wondrous beauty, with the incidental music supplied by Etna's *Götterdämmerung* rumblings and the sweet melodies of shepherds' pipes. The Reverend John Henry Newman, of the Church of England, who eventually became a famous cardinal of the Roman Church, looking down from the hilltop ruins of Taormina's Greek theater in 1833, said: "I felt for the first time in my life that I should be a better and more religious man if I lived there." Taormina's impact on modern visitors would have disturbed the Reverend Newman. A lady painter who left Oslo and a Norwegian husband to settle in Taormina said, "The moral landscape here is as different as the physical landscape. I found when I came here that the light was entirely different from the light in Norway. I needed different colors to paint. It's the same in matters of morality. One has to accept the different light, the different colors. It is useless to fight them. If you did not accept them, you could not live here."

In matters of sex, the lights and colors were certainly confused. Italy's double standard, her age-old battle between pagan and Christian morality, is nowhere more apparent than in this Sicilian village. Every young male fancies himself to be a satyr. Every young girl must remain a virgin. Although much of the everlasting boasting of the men is fantasy, one seldom sees unmarried native girls on the streets. Their virtue, an educated young Sicilian explained, "is something to be preserved, to be carried to the altar on a satin pillow." No matter how profligate he is, the young man demands virginity of the girl he marries. A sister's honor is protected at any cost. A young man who boasted constantly of his sexual exploits had a lovely sister whom I had seen stitching behind drawn curtains in the family's embroidery shop. When I asked him if I might meet her, he became hostile; soon word reached me from friends that he was threatening to beat me if I dared to look at her through the window again.

With tourists, young Taorminians are purposefully earnest. Their concept of hospitality toward ladies is not only bedding and boarding them, but also bedding with them. With the compulsive polarity of the fair for the dark, Calvinist guilt for Latin innocence, unattached women flock from northern winters to the southern sun. A young Sicilian said, "Brünnehilde comes to Dionysius for the phallic cure."

Some generous visitors are men, and for them the youths of Taormina make an easy adjustment. In a book called *Sicily, the New Winter Resort*, published in London in 1905, Douglas Sladen writes with curious Victorian innocence:

> Boys are a feature of Sicily. There are always dozens around a stranger. I think the best-looking boys that have come into my experience have been at Girgenti [Agrigento]. In the province of Messina [including Taormina] especially, you constantly meet boys as beautiful as Greek statues. At Modica you get a superb, aquiline type of men, but not beautiful youths.

Young Sicilian males are narcissists, and their sexuality is their godhead. They also feel a strong attachment to their mothers. Later they may lavish their affection on their children, the proud fruit of the phallus. Because childlessness is a disgrace, marriage is necessary. A wife is as essential to a man as a donkey to a farmer, but she is not necessarily an object of sentiment. An American girl with a camera was asked by a proud young Sicilian father to take photographs of his new twins, about to be released from the hospital. He arrived for the occasion resplendent in new suit and flashy necktie, ignored his wife, and posed with the babies as proudly, said the girl, "as if he'd done all the work." When he called for the pictures several days later, he made amorous overtures, explaining that "my wife is only the mother of my children."

Though "Swedish women" (Taorminians use the term loosely to cover all Scandinavian women, including Norwegians and Danes) and German girls are in abundance, English and Americans are popular—especially Americans, who usually have the most money. Since most women come for no more than a fortnight, little time is lost. The young men meet tourist busses in the town square and trains at the Giardino station, surveying prospects as the cars unload, introducing themselves in working English or German, carrying bags, arranging for hotels and taxis. In the village the young men frequent cafés, bars, and night clubs, walking usually in twos and threes up the Corso Umberto, from the Messina gate to the Catania gate, and down again. Some of the more enterprising take waiters' jobs in the hotels, working for as little as thirty-two cents a day, for the opportunity to make advantageous contacts. The most exotic operations are down by the sea. Like a chorus of young Apollos, they sport their browned bodies, chase one another in games, and strike up acquaintances with strangers. A few, pretending to be fishermen, own boats with which to beguile visitors to the jutting promontory of rock known as Isola Bella. The beach boys put a high price on themselves. An Englishwoman complained that her twenty-one-year-old fisherman cost her more money than it took to send her son, of the same age, to Oxford. With the money she was giving the fisherman, however, he was supporting a wife and two children.

When a holiday is over, the visitor is gaily escorted back to the station. Unless she has learned in the meantime the cynical ease with which the word *amore* flows from her swain's tongue, unless she has discovered that sentiment is a northern

characteristic, she does not know that during the farewell
kisses an eye over her shoulder is watching new arrivals stepping off the train. She finds out quickly enough, however,
when she sees through a coach window her lover-unto-death
returning to the village with another girl.

Many young bucks have as their goal marriage to a *stra-
niera*. Their demand for virginity in a Sicilian bride, however,
does not extend to foreign girls. Here the qualifications are
that she be blond, if possible, and, more important, rich,
with a chariot of gold in which to whisk them from the poverty and monotony of Sicily to the paradises of New York,
London, or, as last choices, Copenhagen or Stockholm. When
they meet a likely candidate, young men may go to desperate
lengths to achieve their goal. Those who succeed are remembered as heroes. One, a slip of a fellow named Salvatore, succeeded in impregnating a very rich Dutch girl twice his size.
Within four weeks Salvatore was summoned to Rotterdam
with a generous remittance for first-class fare. After Salvatore's marriage, his harassed father-in-law put him in charge
of one of the family factories. Salvatore, an outdoorman, was
not happy, so the father bought him a dairy farm. Now, once
a year, Salvatore returns to Sicily in triumphant splendor with
his family. Between visits he remembers his friends with post
cards telling them of his good fortune. His example is a shining beacon to the young men. As they abundantly sow their
seed, they offer a prayer to the Blessed Virgin that it will fall
on fertile soil.

To further their cause, the young men are ardent corres-
pondents, maintaining four or five brisk letter romances at
one time in the hope that one will yield a life of luxury and
idleness. In his romantic eloquence, the young Sicilian has no
match in the world. He will simultaneously insist, to girls in
Chicago, London, Glasgow, Copenhagen, and Oslo, that each
is the only woman in his life, that he cannot live without her,
that he will die if she does not return to him at once. Quite

a number of these pen Lotharios are actually successful in their international letter campaigns. Taormina has a considerable number of women, aging and lonely, who have left homeland, husbands, and children to live with young Sicilian husbands or lovers. Most of them have a hard time, for once a Sicilian is married he thinks of himself as a pensioner free to enjoy the rewards. A rich Englishwoman married a beach boy thirty years ago when he was twenty. Through a long-suffering married life she has had to support his mistresses and illegitimate offspring.

One who survived a disastrous Sicilian marriage with strength and humor is a jovial blond Belgian woman of means whom I shall call Henrietta Nunziato. Henrietta, in her middle forties, was living with her dark-haired, adolescent son in a villa filled with Tudor furniture and cabinets of French linens and silver. She had met her Sicilian twenty years before on a tour. He was a guide in Syracuse. After the cruise he wrote her letters. "Those passionate Sicilian kind that overcome the most cautious resistance," said Henrietta. They were married in Brussels, and for a wedding present she gave him a schooner and a limousine with a chauffeur to meet him at the ports in which he landed. Meanwhile, he spent her money extravagantly on other women. "A Sicilian man," Henrietta said, "will tell you he thinks only of love. That is not quite true. All a Sicilian man thinks about is bed, which he calls love. Sicilians know all about bed and nothing about love. They're as sexy as rabbits and know just about as much as rabbits about love. They are completely polygamous. The more women they have, the greater lovers they feel they are. If a Sicilian doesn't have a different woman every night he fears for his masculinity. I quickly learned to live with *that*." When her fortune was nearly spent, Henrietta's husband returned to Syracuse. She sees him, she said, about once a year.

One evening I invited Henrietta to go with me to a night

club, but she refused. "I can't be seen with men," she said. "You see, my husband has several women in this town, and they take delight in spying on his foreign wife. A Sicilian insists that his wife be faithful to him, even if it doesn't occur to him to go to bed with her more than once a year." Nor would she permit me to come to see her after sundown. I could arrive only in the afternoon for tea. "Sicilian men are fascinating," she said one day over a steaming pot. "But one must be prepared to pay their price. In the end it wasn't his mistresses that disturbed me. It was his habit of upsetting the routine of my household by coming home late from one of them for dinner."

I made two good friends at the Mediterraneo—an English couple named Hegswith who occupied an adjoining room. Donald Hegswith was "in a bank" and wrote poetry. He was tall and blond and spoke with crisp diction; to an American like myself he seemed perfect casting for a stage Englishman. Estelle had been an actress and now was devoting herself to their small daughter and the care of a "cottage" in Surrey. She was dark-haired and pale. Since her health was frail, Donald was as solicitous as a mother. While we watched the sea at night, Estelle recited poetry. Keats and Browning were her favorites. The Sicilian holiday was their first away from England in the ten years of their marriage. Their marriage was one of the happiest I had ever seen.

The hotel was less than half full. There was a pair of elderly English spinsters named Birdie and Rosie who had taken a fancy to a Michigan youth with a lame leg who drank a great deal and claimed to be a poet. He greeted them heartily each evening in the dining room with "Well, girls, what did you do today?"

"We went to the Greek theater," Birdie would reply. "We liked it very much, didn't we, Rosie?"

"Yes, we liked it very much," Rosie would echo. "We think all theaters are beautiful since they all create art. Don't we think so, Birdie?"

There was also a French journalist and an elderly Italian widow who never spoke. Others came and went, such as two Swiss ladies named Emma and Ida. Emma was a flashy blonde with a husband in Zurich. Ida was a virginal Berne school-teacher in knit stockings, on her spring holiday. Within twenty-four hours Emma made friends with several young Sicilians and took an apartment across the alley from my veranda. Betrayed by her friend, Ida took everyone into her confidence. She and Emma had met on the train. They had agreed that one only received the full benefits of travel by mixing with natives. "But," Ida said in German-Swiss, "one can mix with the people and mix with the people. There is the difference."

Emma gained quick fame among the village bucks; word got around that she was insatiable and many of them accepted the challenge. Ida, meanwhile, became somewhat unhinged. She took long hikes. Each dawn she put on her knit stockings and a little sailor hat and climbed a mountain before break-fast. In the dining room she reported her excursions in detail. Every account had the same climax—she was always followed by a man and she always outwitted him. One night she re-turned in a hysterical condition and told the most harrowing story of all. "I was walking through the tunnel when I saw a train coming. I started to run, and the train chased me. I ran and ran, with the train following me closer and closer. Ahead of me I could see the end of the tunnel. I ran faster, and when I was almost outside, I fell. I rolled to the side of the track and the train roared past me. My pretty hat was crushed by the train," she said, weeping. The next morning Ida departed unexpectedly on the northbound train wearing the neat little sailor hat.

Emma continued her amours. From my room we could

look in on them if we wished. "By jove!" Donald Hegswith said one night, not without admiration. "These Swiss are remarkable people!"

Estelle wasn't so sure. "I do think she goes a little far," she said.

The somnambulant lethargy of the Mediterraneo came to an end with a telegram in German which the clerk asked me to translate. It came from Berlin and requested reservations for ten double beds and nine singles for one week. The news transformed the *padrone*, a round little man named Stefanino. He recalled for us the lush prosperity of the thirties when crowds of open-pursed German tourists made Taormina their playground, and the flush war years when Nazi officers filled the town with gold and good living, all of which came to an end when the less lusty Allies moved in. The hotel became a whirl of activity preparing for the triumphal return. Clerks, waiters, and chambermaids talked only of *tedeschi*. Stefanino diligently supervised cleaning operations. Germans were fussy, he said, and everything must be scrubbed and polished. New help was hired. Linens were changed and waiters' uniforms were starched. On the phonograph the eternal, wailing Neapolitan love songs were replaced with Viennese waltzes. The day the Germans were expected, *tapetti* of flowers were moved in, potted cyclamens and hydrangea, bouquets of carnations, roses, and freesia. The parlor looked like a setting for a gangster's funeral.

As soon as the Germans arrived they turned the hotel into a bedlam of *Gemütlichkeit*. The house rang with their "*Bitte schöns*" and "*Danke schöns*." At night they sang to accordions on the roof. In the mornings we were awakened by group calisthenics, also on the roof, and heavy shoes clomping on the stairs. The men wore *Lederhosen* with complicated braces which they kept adjusting. "I keep thinking they're going to hitch one another to donkey carts," Estelle said.

The most trying of them was the *reiseleiter*, or tour man-

ager, a ruddy young Siegfried to whom a moment of silence
was a sign that he was shirking his duty. He did tricks with
silver and glasses, led group singing, and made announce-
ments: "Today at three o'clock I have arranged for a Sicilian
donkey at the front door for anyone who wishes to ride. At
four o'clock we will all go to the Greek theater. Herr Schag-
wald will read to us from Goethe's *Iphigenie* and Frau Klein-
münster will sing Elsa's prayer from the *Lohengrin* of Wagner."

To escape the Germans, the Hegswiths and I began an exploration of Taormina's night life. It took us to The Club.
"There," the hotel clerk promised, "you will meet the famous
peoples of many lands." The Club was a converted *palazzo*.
American, British, and Italian sports cars were parked in the
yard. A doorman greeted us at the entrance. The rooms were
decorated in a rich Edwardian style and illuminated by soft
blue lights. There was an abundance of golden candelabra
and crystal chandeliers, overstuffed furniture, statues, supporting trays floating with hibiscus blossoms. The low lights
and scented flowers gave the place a mortuary air. In a small
inner room, designed for the gentle twittering of a virginal,
four young satyrs pumped a samba from four accordions.
They were barefooted and wore shirts with plunging neck-
lines, bright sashes, and red scarves. As they played, they
moved about the room, their sun-browned, black-curled
heads swaying with the music, their white teeth glistening.
Other young men were clicking castanets and shaking gourds.
It was wild and primitive.

"I say," Donald Hegswith said, "this does make you want
to shuffle a bit, doesn't it?"

At least two thirds of The Club's patrons were male. Many
were Scandinavians. Suave, well-dressed Sicilians were rumored to be princes and counts from Catania and Palermo.
There were also Americans, including a young Negro, English, a few Swiss, and some Germans. There were, of course,

no Sicilian women. An American college girl named Carolyn, who was spending her junior year abroad, entertained a circle of admiring young Sicilians with an abandoned jitterbug. Long-legged, northern blond women were vivacious, gay, and smartly dressed. Not all were young. There were older ones whose lives were engraved on their faces like crude jokes. They usually had burnished platinum hair; their eyes openly sought out the young men. One of them, very drunk, asked me if I were an American.

I said I was.

"I hate Americans," she said. From the way she spoke I gathered she was one herself. Her hair was fringed in ringlets around her face; she wore a short dress and platform shoes.

I asked what her country was.

"I'm international," she said. "Don't you know nationalism is passé? Everyone here is international. I hate Americans. My name's Adelaide. Everyone calls me Addie."

Addie pointed to a lean Englishman about thirty years old talking to a blond youth at the bar. "That's Henry," she said, pronouncing it "Onree." "He's an international type. He and I are living together. We love each other like brother and sister; it's terribly innocent. Onree and I go into the country to be with peasants. We drink wine and eat cheese with them."

I tried to imagine Onree, in his tweed jacket, ascot, and open sandals, eating cheese with the peasants.

"Onree has to wear those sandals," Addie said. "He has this infection of the toes and he's spent more than fifteen thousand lire trying to get rid of it. Darling," she called to Onree, "show the man your toes."

Onree continued to be absorbed in his friend.

"Is the car fixed?" Addie asked.

Without looking up, Onree said it wasn't.

"I can't walk home tonight," Addie wailed.

"It's only half a kilometer," Onree said. "You've already

danced five kilometers." He turned back to his companion, a square-jawed, blue-eyed triumph of Aryan breeding. About twenty years old, I decided.

"Onree can't resist good-looking boys," Addie said. "He thinks Gilg is gorgeous and of course he is, rather. His father was a Nazi. He manufactures chemicals in Stuttgart and is a millionaire."

A somewhat scholarly-looking woman with ascetic features joined Onree and Gilg. "That's Dr. Ashenberg, a German writer," Addie said. "She adores Gilg too." She introduced me to them. "We're going to take him into the interior tomorrow to see the peasants," Addie said to Onree, apparently meaning me.

Onree raised his wrist to my nose. "I've bought some new scent," he said. "Do smell it. Rather tarty, don't you think?"

I excused myself to dance with Estelle. She liked dancing, but it tired her quickly. When the musicians broke into the current Sicilian song hit, "That's My Weakness Now," we sat down to watch. The Scandinavians and Sicilians flailed into a feverish Charleston. "Like seeing the revelries of Babylon," Donald said. The most indefatigable dancers were two Danes, a puffing, round little man and a slim blond woman in a shimmering pink dress who was a head taller than he. Some other Danes at the next table were scornful. A woman leaned over and told us, "They are just married. He is an architect, very rich and famous, who is fifty-eight years old. She is twenty and, as you see, has been a girl in a bar."

Our informant looked like an aging film star. She was blond and thin. Her dry, wrinkled skin was heavy with make-up; her tight lips were frozen in a smile. She wore a tight purple and silver satin dress, a diamond-set comb in her hair, and many rings on her bony fingers. It was difficult to tell her age: she could have been anywhere from fifty to seventy.

She asked me to dance. In turnabout Taormina, where

women pursued men, this was not unusual. She folded her thin body about mine like an eel. Speaking English stiffly with an accent, she told me she was Countess Oestgaard of Copenhagen.

"I have there my castle where I spend five months each year," she said. "For the hot months I go north to Sweden. In the spring I am in Paris and Italy." She gossiped about other revelers. "Professor Ashenberg is a writer for the theater," she said. "She is now writing a sequel to *The Tempest* in which Caliban will rule the world. Caliban is her God." I looked over the countess' shoulder at the slight and tense blond woman talking with the German Gilg and wondered why she worshiped Caliban. "You dance divinely," the countess said. "You will come with me. I will show you Paris and Copenhagen and Sweden in the hot months. . . ."

The Germans finally left and the Mediterraneo returned to its quiet, slovenly ways. Though it was only March, a midsummer languor settled on the island. It was wisteria time. Pendulous purple clusters bloomed all over the town, choking it with their heavy perfume. I settled on my little terrace to work, but life on the piazza below was too distracting. There was usually a noisy caucus of wives around the armless Madonna. Inside the park a leathery old woman stood on a bench each day and made a speech. She was dressed in an expansive skirt of checked material and a floppy bonnet fashioned from a square of white cloth. She supported herself with a cane. The speech was always the same, and she made it over and over, whether she had an audience or not. It was an angry tirade against the government, which, she said, paid her a pension of a thousand lire a month and then taxed her eight hundred lire a month on her property. It was her opinion that the government might as well not bother with her at all. Things were different under *Il Duce*, she pointed out over and over. She was hooted at by the boys who came to the park to weave fresh flowers into the spokes of their bicycle wheels.

Later in the day when the sun was setting over Etna, the Hegswiths and I would go to the summit of the town and the ruins of the Teatro Greco. Here the Greeks built their theater on a rocky promontory surrounded on three sides by the blue sea. Later, Romans added the high-arched *scena* and Corinthian columns. Here the ancients watched comedies and tragedies, the bloody fights of gladiators, and the execution of criminals. Foreign ambassadors were received and affairs of government were deliberated. Today, except for an occasional week when a company comes from Rome to revive the ancient plays, it is a place of deep quiet, broken only by the whistle of a bird or the croak of a toad. From the best seats in the house, now grass-covered ledges, we watched the enthralling spectacle of the sunset. The *scena*, fallen in ruins, framed it with broken columns and moldering brick walls. Beyond the evening sea the tip of Calabria rose from the mists of the straits; in the glowing western sky was the snow-covered volcano. Goethe, who dreamed of dramatizing the *Odyssey* here, wrote, ". . . never did any audience in any theater have before it such a spectacle as you here behold."

Here in this ruin, a monument to the decline of Greece and Rome, we spoke of the remoteness of the troubled world to which we must return and the dearth of great and wise men to guide it. Why were there cycles of golden and dark ages; why did a people rise to greatness and then decline? What makes a culture die? Was it because greatness, like all things, must carry within itself the seeds of its death?

Below us a village of soft and faithless men and women, English, Germans, Scandinavians, and American sons of pioneers, played like idiots in the shadow of decay. "Perhaps nature with such uncontrolled beauty corrupts the spirit," said Estelle, gazing over the town and the sea. "There are times when it all seems too extravagant. I am beginning to long for the austerity of England. I shall be quite content to return."

"But doesn't it make one feel silly to be so happy here?" asked Donald.

"I'm so glad we're enjoying it," said Estelle. "It might be the last holiday of our lives."

Their holiday continued through the celebration of Easter. Our final day together was filled with rainbows. The wind came up like a typhoon, blowing rain from the sea and covering Etna with a swirl of snow. Through the storm the sun kept shining. Suddenly the rainbows appeared, a host of heavenly arches rising from the lagoons of the sea and cascading over us. The storm continued fitfully into the night, when the rainbows became lunar miracles of silver moonlight. By this time everyone in Taormina was somewhat crazed by the weather. Old fishermen watched it with devils glittering in their eyes.

The storm finally spent itself and the fishing boats went out, stringing their lights like a necklace of pearls across the sea. Nightingales sang in the trees and from The Club came the music of sambas and Charlestons. The white cross shone above the silver town; over Etna the crimson inferno glowed.

In the morning the Hegswiths left. Old Stefanino seemed genuinely moved at saying good-by to Estelle. Before the year was out both of them were to die—Stefanino of a stroke in July; Estelle of the English winter in December.

CHAPTER 2

HELL

FROM ANY POINT and at any season Etna is incomparably beautiful. It is at its best seen from Taormina in the spring. Then the snow-capped eastern slopes fall gradually to the sea in a rhythm of delicate white curves.

I wanted to examine such beauty at closer hand. Since the bus tour made a daily ascent, I arranged to go along. The bus turned out to be the one in which I had left Palermo; Carla was the hostess. It was her third time around since I had said good-by to her at Segeste. Mr. and Mrs. Robinson from England and the Belgian and German twins, staying, like myself, in Taormina, were also on the excursion. Among the others were an American couple named Travers and a New Haven archaeologist named Bosworth from the American Academy in Rome.

We embarked at nine o'clock to Carla's cheerful wish for "a good treep and pleasant journeys." The radio, so happily out of repair three weeks ago, was now functioning, and we rolled toward Etna to the lilt of a Neapolitan orchestra. The morning was gloriously blue and crisp. In the east the white cone rose as gracefully as Fujiyama, sending up a spiral of white steam. Etna, continuously active for three thousand years, has

186

erupted at least a hundred and fifty times since men started keeping score. The last eruption had been three months before, and the lava still lay hot on her sides. The sky was red at night.

Carla was spieling away on the microphone. "The Roman Emperor Hadrian climbed Etna on foot and Goethe climbed on a donkey." The Belgian and the German spread a large contour map over their combined laps. The Belgian told his friend that he had lived two years in the Congo on the Ruwenzori range, known as "The mountains on the moon."

Carla continued: "Now we have an auto road two thirds to the top. In summer it is possible to walk to the top, but now it is impossible because of the snow and ice. Mount Etna is ten thousand feet high. . . ."

"That is nothing," the Belgian interrupted. "The Ruwenzori are sixteen thousand feet high."

"Etna is the highest volcano in Europe and one of the highest in the world," Carla said.

"The Ruwenzori are higher mountains," the Belgian said. So it continued. Subdued during the trip around Sicily, the Belgian now blossomed on the subject of mountains. "Etna is really no mountain to speak of," he said. "Nothing at all. A pimple on the world's face, exaggerated, like everything by the Italians." His German friend agreed heartily.

Their condescension was too much for Mrs. Robinson. She turned to them and said, "I really don't understand why you gentlemen are making this trip at all."

"To make comparisons," the Belgian replied candidly.

We drove along the sea, backtracking toward Catania through a wide, fertile valley. Here one could see the complexities of life in the shadow of an active volcano. Volcanic ash is as rich as any soil on earth, and on Etna's slopes it is frequently replenished. In the low-lying, subtropical belt along the sea it grows bananas and sugar cane; away from the sea, lemons and oranges, and a variety of vegetables. But it is a fertility resting on a false security. Life here is lived literally between the devil and the deep blue sea. On our left was the sky-colored Mediterranean; on our right, great black fans of lava. The danger of a volcano is at its foot. Lava streams flow down in crevices and gullies, and not until they get to the flatlands do they spread out and do their evil. We passed through the rebuilt town of Mascali and a village that had been completely consumed. Only a mound of boulders like a black stone quarry remained.

At the town of Giarre we turned inland and began climbing upward into a black world. The soil was black lava; the buildings were made of black lava rock. This second agricultural belt of Etna, lying between one and four thousand feet, is one of the world's most thickly populated farming areas. Here, in the gently rising lower lap of Etna, nature generously produces as many as five crops of olives, wine, grain, fruits, and vegetables a year. To protect themselves against lawlessness and banditry, landowners lived in windowless fortresses with iron bolted gates and observation towers gloomy as prisons. Even the fields were protected against thieves by walls and locks. The peasants' huts outside the gates were thick-walled boxes, dark inside and cool in the heat of the day. The methods of farming and irrigation, probably as old as the Normans, were remarkable. Sloping vineyards and orchards were terraced with stone walls which retained every fragment of soil in ledges often only wide enough for one row of vines. Irrigation was supplied by stone aqueducts which branched over the land like veins and arteries. The only color in this dark world came from wild spring flowers and the red bandannas with which the workmen covered their heads in the vineyards. The men worked on their knees, building a mound of earth around each vine. The closely pruned vines, still without leaves, covered the black soil like the arthritic claws of buried witches.

The horizon was dominated by church spires. We stopped at the village of Trecastagni, which means "three chestnuts."

Trecastagni is near a lava stream. Her people hold the mountain mother, on whose breast they live, in awe and fear. Because their danger is greater than the other villages, they have three patron saints instead of the usual one: Alfio and his brothers Filadelfio and Cirino. When Etna erupts, the trio of saints is carried in a religious procession to the lava streams. For more than two centuries the village has escaped serious harm, and the people believe it is because the saints have been happy. To keep them that way, the community spends much energy and time in pampering them. In May they are celebrated with a *festa*. Alfio is the patron of, among others, deaf mutes and hernia sufferers; large numbers of both are brought to him for cures during the *festa*. For a week the saints are cajoled with praying and dancing, bonfires and processions, games and bell ringings. The *festa* climaxes with the *corso*, a race of hand-picked youths dressed in loincloths and carrying burning flares from Catania about twelve miles away. Crowds line the road to cheer the runners. When they arrive at Trecastagni, they present the flares of Olympus to the three saints and fall prostrate before them.

The saints are such cherished personalities that visitors can see them only by appointment. An interview had been prearranged for us with the sacred trio. A young priest came to the door of the baroque cathedral, greeted us in hushed tones, and led us inside. Black-gowned schoolboys filed in and sang a hymn. The priest said a prayer. Then he stepped to the wall and directed our attention over the altar, where a pair of classic columns framed a proscenium covered by a gold metal curtain. The priest pressed a hidden button, and the gold curtains rumbled apart. The schoolboys dropped to their knees, piping prayers. It was a dramatic moment. On a stage as richly burnished as an eighteenth-century opera theater, and dazzlingly bathed in light, sat the three saints on thrones of glistening gold. They were large-as-life enameled dolls with flesh-colored faces and hands. As richly dressed as the three kings of the

Nativity, they held long golden quills and wore golden boots. The saints seemed wondrously gay and happy. The center one held his legs farther apart than his companions. This one, the priest explained, was Alfio, the hernia saint. The priest told us the three saints were also patrons of the town of Lawrence, in Massachusetts, and showed us photographs taken there at a saints' *festa*.

The priest closed the curtains and took us into the sacristy, a large room in which the walls were covered with ex-voto paintings. These, depicting cures and rescues from catastrophes, had been presented to the saints credited with the miracles. Some were painted by the donors themselves; others by professional ex-voto painters. The three saints of Trecastagni are busy miracle workers if their accumulation of paintings is any indication. The melodramatic pictures, on metal or wood, range in size from ten inches square to a yard wide and are painted in a primitive style. Their subject matter includes all the tribulations of man. In addition to Etna's eruptions, there were roof cave-ins, auto accidents, collapsing scaffoldings, war bombings and ship sinkings donated by war veterans, men falling out of trees and children into wells. There was a variety of sickroom scenes with batteries of white-robed doctors performing hernia operations, and consumptives coughing into scarlet-stained handkerchiefs. There was even one of an operation on a horse who recovered by miraculous intercession, and there were several dental scenes. By far the liveliest paintings were those involving donkeys. The beasts threw riders, kicked passers-by, and dragged their carts over women and children. Pious sufferers with more than one disaster in their lives painted both on the same panel; one accident-prone man illustrated four miraculous escapes. In the corner of every painting the three saints Alfio, Filadelfio, and Cirino were shown dancing a joyful roundelay, so happy were they over the recovery. There was also a macabre assortment of other votive gifts. One wall was covered with pink wax images of legs, arms, hands, ears, and assorted internal organs; also several red-speckled doll faces indicating recovery from either measles or pox. These were hung with gifts of women's hair, musty with years of volcanic dust.

I asked the priest if I might take some photographs of the paintings. He reflected for a moment and asked me if my intentions were serious. "Americans often make frivolous jokes of the pictures," he said. When I convinced him I was *molto serio*, he helped remove the pictures from the walls so I might photograph them outdoors. A group of young boys crowded around to watch, recounting for me the details of the accidents portrayed.

"*Vedi*, Giuseppe!" they said. "He is drowning. The saints put a rock under his foot and he was able to save himself."

"There is Michele falling from an olive tree in his own garden. The saints put a pillow of cabbages under him so he wouldn't break his back."

"Here is Maria Lucia having her appendix out. The saints stopped her bleeding and she did not die."

So it went. Alfio, Filadelfio, and Cirino obviously were the most versatile healers since Hippocrates.

From Trecastagni the climb became steeper. The road followed the lava flow, a solid dark vein like a giant coal strip. Burned-out forests were a wilderness of dead tree stumps. The only signs of life and color were green lizards taking the sun on the great black stones. We passed a lava stone crudely carved by a morbid primitive artist. One half showing a newborn baby was captioned "Prelude," the other half showing a skull was called "Postlude." On the microphone Carla pointed out that Etna's white cone, facing in the other direction, was no longer visible to us.

"In the Congo we *never* see the tops of mountains," the Belgian said. "They are all the time in the clouds."

"What a pity," said Mrs. Robinson tartly.

The road crossed the lava stream, taking us out of the *regione coltivata* and into the *regione boscosa*, a cool highland area with a shorter growing season. It seemed to be newly settled, for the architecture of the villas was in the severe modernism of the Mussolini era. Cultivated crops included grapes, chestnuts, and grains. Not as abundant as below, life was nevertheless safer as one mounted closer to the crater where the lava flowed by in deep gullies like river beds. This section was narrow, and soon we passed into the *regione deserta*, a desolate area of lava and snow. Except for a few sub-Alpine shrubs, there was no plant life whatsoever. Our drivers stopped to put chains on the rear wheels, after which we climbed for another half hour to the end of the road. In this bleakness of black and white we passed several Madonnas under gabled roofs—prayer stations for mountaineers.

From the end of the road it was only a five-minute walk to the Alpine clubhouse. There was a whipping wind. Mrs. Robinson put on a trench coat and tied her pork-pie hat to her head with a green scarf. The clubhouse was filled with young skiers, mostly continental Italian university students on their spring holiday. The free camaraderie between these boys and girls would have shocked Sicilians. A large log fire was burning. The thin, cold air made us ravenous. We ate spaghetti and steaks and drank beakers of wine. Outside, there was little to look at. The top third of Etna rose above us, but it could not be seen from the level of the clubhouse.

We descended by another route, passing black canyons filled with lava still steaming from the recent eruptions. Alongside the hot streams orchards were blossoming prematurely. I saw a patch of blue violets. At one point flowing lava had destroyed the road, and a small detour was constructed. Here our drivers stopped so we might examine hot lava at close hand. It was smoking, and under the surface it glowed like a smithy's forge. The Belgian and the German screwed and unscrewed their photographic equipment. Mrs. Robinson held her husband at a safe distance while several men lay on their stomachs to light cigarettes from the smoldering ash. Mr. Travers, looking closely at the glowing coals, said, "I'll be god-damned." Thinking it over carefully, he reflected, "How do we know it's new lava? Probably last year's. We wouldn't know the difference. You can't believe what an Italian says." Then he got down and lit a cigarette with the others.

As we rolled smoothly toward the sea, I heard Mrs. Robinson say to her husband, "I'm really not so fond of Etna any more as I was when I looked at her snowy loveliness from the terrace. She does seem to me to be very wicked indeed."

In the dusk, men were still working their land of Eden so close to hell, drawing sustenance from the black earth in which they were as firmly rooted as the vines with the grasping claws.

CHAPTER 3

THE BLACK PRINCESS

ONE OF the mysterious legends of Sicily is that of the Black
Madonna of Tyndari. Tyndari was a Greek city high on a
promontory looking out to sea. Today it is a village with a
jet Madonna that is one of the most revered holy images in
the Mediterranean world. For centuries devout Sicilians have
made their pilgrimage to Tyndari. At the time of the Black
Madonna's feast in September many walk barefoot from their
homes to her shrine.

To anyone not so pious, Tyndari is almost inaccessible.
Occasionally when enough passengers can be enlisted a bus
tour is arranged. The day I went our leader was Tito Dosola,
one of the professional guides operating on Taormina's sight-
seeing circuits. Tito was a familiar figure in the cafés and on
the beach. A blond Norman-type Sicilian, son of a poor farmer
on Mount Venus, Tito was usually seen in the company of
an equally fair, unattached lady tourist. From tourists he had
learned an adequate English, one of the peculiarities of which
was making a separate syllable of the *ed* at the end of past-tense
verbs. Since legends are living things which grow and change
according to the imagination and the caprices of man, I venture to suggest that Tito is contributing more than his share to
the curious chimera of Sicilian fact and fancy.

"Look at the cute little almonds, just like baby peaches," he said as we turned inland from the sea, beginning our climb into the mountains. His sirupy, sibilant voice drew the ladies to hypnotic attention; he would, I thought, have done marvelously as a gynecologist. On the small bus—there were only twelve seats—ladies were in the majority and all were English-speaking. The day began wondrously bright. Narrow valleys were dark with the curious blue-black shadows of Sicily, but the sunlit slopes shimmered with plum and pear blossoms. Caressing the ladies with his liquid words, Tito said, "Look at the mountains all in *peers*. Isn't it lovely?"

The ladies agreed, and agreed among themselves that Tito was also lovely.

As we reached the heights we drove through a series of model villages, each a cluster of twelve to twenty identical boxlike houses grouped about a boxlike church. Each village was in a pastel color—pink, yellow, or blue. Roadside posters said the villages were built by funds from the *Cassa per Il Mezzogiorno* (Southern Development Fund), a special government relief agency operating with loans from the World Bank, in which the Bank of America plays a substantial part.

Tito said, "Look at the villages! Aren't they lovely! They are for the poor people who have such terrrr-ible homes. You have heard of how they are going to give land to the poor people. When the poor people have their land they will live in these lovely houses. This is what the Communists are doing for the poor people of Sicily."

No one questioned Tito's startling logic. Since Sicily's government is Christian Democrat, Communists were hardly in a position to accept credit for social reforms. I was wondering how many busloads of visitors—people from England and Switzerland, Sweden and Norway, Germany and Denmark, America and Italy—believed Tito's unique little legend.

He elaborated. "You see, there are many poor and homeless people in Sicily. The Communists take care of these people,

poor and homeless. They make land reform. You may hav
heard of this. The Communists take the land from the ric
people and give it to the poor and they have build-ed for th
people these houses."

The ladies sighed. Apollo was speaking of Elysium. Th
villages, so clean and neat, were lovely to look at. None of then
seemed to notice that they were uninhabited. The problem
of getting water and electricity to the mountaintop, whic
the builders had overlooked during construction, had yet t
be solved. It occurred to me that it might be good anti
Communist propaganda to be able to believe Tito and let th
Communists take credit for the bungled project.

The highland fields blazed with wild flowers. It alway
exasperates me that Sicilians, so accustomed to their dazzlin
spring season, never know the names of their wild flower
One of the ladies in the bus turned out to be a botanist from
an American college, and on this trip, at last, I had access t
some reliable information. There were whole fields of lovel
chartreuse-yellow oxalis, asphodel, daisies, anemone, iri
poppies, and meadows of a cultivated legume with great blood
scarlet pendants called *sulla*.

We snaked through an ugly volcanic fissure and suddenl
were deep in clouds as wet and dark as in an Austrian pass.

"The mountain is Mandrazzi," Tito told the ladies. "I an
sorry it is so dark here, for it is a very lovely sight."

"Do they have poison ivy in Sicily?" an American lady asked

Tito was stumped. He had never heard of poison ivy
The botanist lady volunteered that poison ivy did not grov
in Italy.

We emerged into a disheartening landscape of stone. Afte
Novara, a steep hillside town covered with green lichen, w
descended swiftly past wartime pillboxes so overgrown the
had become indigenous to the landscape; past palm trees an
olives and a barefoot woman with a basket on her head wh
carried her shoes in her armpits to save them the wear and tea

of the rough country roads. At the bottom we crossed a series of wide, dry stream beds known as *torrenti*, through which the topsoil of the lean mountains had long since washed into the sea. Tyndari was visible in the distance.

"Look how lovely she is up there in the sky," Tito purred. "She was once a beautiful Greek city, and then those wicked Arabs destroy-ed it. I am of course Norman. We Normans preserv-ed the beauties; we did not destroy them."

The ladies sighed and all but congratulated him.

We passed through Castroreale, a dismal, low-set town choked with purple wisteria and red and pink geraniums growing like weeds. The road to Tyndari wound through a beautifully terraced landscape of vines and olives. We arrived at the summit just as the monastery bells rang out the noon hour.

"Now where would you like to go first?" Tito asked. "To the Madonna or the ruins?"

The ladies argued.

"I think we will have our picnic in the lovely theater," Tito said, deciding for them, in favor of the ruins.

Carrying their *pensione* lunch packs, they trotted behind Tito through an old Arabic-style village of windowless little houses. Each house had an outdoor oven like a tiny charred cave. "Our *paisant* way of cooking bread," said Tito. "Listen to the birds. Aren't they lovely?" The ladies listened as if they'd never heard birds before.

We climbed into some excavations in which mosaicked floors were being uncovered six feet below the roots of olive trees. The ruins were shaped like a basilica and seemed to be an early place of Christian worship. Tito had other ideas. "It is a Roman gymnasium," he said. "Here is the bathroom."

Like all Sicily's classic theaters, Tyndari's is gorgeously located overlooking the sea. The Aeolian islands and the volcano Stromboli rise from the distant mists. The theater, however, is a curiously hybrid affair. Large and very deep, it has in the pit a small Roman amphitheater for games and gladiator contests; behind this is the *palcoscenico* of the Greek stage. It was overgrown with grass and served as a pasture for tethered goats. In the center of the pit was a glistening white block. "It is an altar to a pagan divinity," Tito told the ladies. "Isn't it lovely?"

The ladies gasped. I did not have the heart to tell them that the divine altar was a block of white salt put there by a farmer for his goats to lick.

In the top rows of the theater we munched our sandwiches. The dark, silvery landscape was lit here and there by spots of sunlight which broke through the clouds. Like Segeste, Erice and Enna, Tyndari was a mist-veiled, silent place.

Tito was briefing us on the Black Madonna. He said "There is a legend of a plague in the town of Tyndari and of a young black princess who help-ed the people and when they recover-ed they have made her into a Madonna."

How, I asked, did she get to Tyndari, this black princess?

"It is said that the Romans brought her from Africa. But that is only a legend. Now I will tell you what is maybe the real story. There was a Byzantine ship that was shipwreck-ed against the rocks. To get away from the rocks the sailors threw everything overboard. They had with them the dark princess and they threw her overboard."

"Just a minute," I interrupted. "Was it a lady or a statue that was thrown overboard?"

"A statue. And immediately the tempest ceas-ed. The Byzantines then found their way home and the black princess walk-ed up through the water to Tyndari, and the people saw she was a figure of the Holy Mother."

It was the legend of the watery birth of Aphrodite and not the first time I had encountered a Mother of God with marine origin. In western Sicily, the Madonna of Trapani, and in Sardinia, Cagliari's Madonna of Bonaria are both believed to have been washed up by the waters of the Mediterranean.

"I am inclin-ed more to believe still another legend which

is my own private one," Tito told the ladies. "The black princess was not the Holy Mother at all but simply a very beautiful African lady who was a slave in the Roman legion."

My head began to swim. It was still swimming a half hour later when, in the monastery chapel, I faced the jet Madonna holding her jet child. I would have been less surprised by her if I had found her in Venice. The influence, if not her origin, was certainly Byzantine. The black faces of mother and child had a Semitic leanness; their orientally slanted eyes were closed as if they were dreaming. The statue was set on a lavish altar; the figures wore gold-jeweled crowns and jeweled robes of ivory and gold. (On the Adriatic, in cities facing the East, one finds such regal richness.) In the dark chapel the splendor was enhanced by candles flickering among waxen arum lilies.

The pious among us knelt and made the sign of the cross. Tito's honeyed voice flowed. "There is another legend that the Madonna di-ed in childbirth."

I had, for the moment, enough of legends. In the sacristy I found a delightful gallery of ex-voto art. Here sternly mustachioed young Sicilians were being saved from scooter smash-ups; a small child was catapulted down Tyndari's terrifying precipice and then was found playing happily at its foot. This last, judging from the frequency of its occurrence in the paintings, seemed to be the Madonna's most popular miracle. Chapel frescoes showed still another variation of the Black Madonna's history. The Byzantine ship had a statue—not a lady—on board in a coffinlike box. During the storm sailors threw the casket overboard and the statue floated to the shore at the foot of the cliff like Cagliari's Bonaria Madonna with her candles burning. The paintings showed muscular fishermen pulling up the casket. The statue, having come to miraculous life, was standing above the box, and the fishermen were prostrate before the resurrected Madonna.

From a window I could look straight down the cliff to the spot where, according to the frescoes, the Madonna and Child were washed ashore. It was like looking at the sea from a plane, with multicolored whorls of water making a contour map below. Some of the infinite variations of greens, blues, and blacks were made by algae and the rest by changes in the depths of the sea. Far below, gulls swooped and screamed over a curled spit of sand. This, said Tito, was the Madonna's dry-sand miracle. Of it our lady botanist took a dim view. "Just a dry sand flat such as you see anywhere on the New England coast," she said. "Only here they make a miracle of it."

Our driver tooted us back to the bus. Outside, a tall, burly man who had made a pilgrimage to the Black Madonna was asking Tito for a ride back to Messina, through which we were returning. Tito consulted the ladies and it was agreed the pilgrim should ride with us. The man bowed to the ladies and was introduced by Tito as Cosimo Bramanto, a Messina policeman. As a fighting soldier in 1942 he had prayed to the Black Madonna before a battle and vowed to her he would make the pilgrimage on foot from Messina to Tyndari if she would spare his life. After the war the man had not until now found time to fulfill his vow. Prior to the foot pilgrimage he had explained to the Madonna that he suffered from the common policeman's affliction of fallen arches and she had permitted him to walk in his arch-supported shoes rather than barefoot. He had walked the eighty kilometers in sixteen hours with only two bananas to eat.

He was well dressed, neatly shaven, and polished. The monks who had fed and housed him overnight now waved him off. One of our ladies asked the pilgrim how he felt about having accomplished his vow. Tito translated, "He says he feels very, very happy to have dedicated himself to the Black Madonna." The pilgrim took a front seat in the bus and, like a triumphant hero, waved to people along the road, many of whom recognized him from his foot journey.

We passed through a town called Barcellona and over rich farm lands with Moorish castles to Milazzo, the embarkation

point for the Aeolian islands. The wharf of this picturesque
little port was piled with several thousand barrels of wine
awaiting shipment. The Communist hammer and sickle was
painted on the baroque façades of the quay. Here, as in every
town, crowds ran alongside the bus cheering our passenger,
shaking his hands through the window, for the pilgrimage
seemed to have transformed him into a sort of holy man.

We approached Messina from the hills, down through forest
slopes of eucalyptus trees planted and nurtured by the government. In this corner of Sicily the barren mountains have been
restored to their ancient verdure and the lives of the people
have been altered. Against the sun sinking into the sea, Messina seemed to rise from the waters like a heavenly city of gold.
Reggio Calabria was a rose-tinted cloud beyond.

We delivered our holy man to his family. A crowd gathered
quickly to greet him. He embraced his womenfolk and shook
the hands of neighbors as if he'd just won the Italian bicycle
race. We left him making a speech.

As we rolled through the dusk along the sea to Taormina,
Tito continued to weave his loom of words, unraveling with
each new version what he'd woven before. "Now I am going
to tell you the legend of the black princess expecting a child.
She was traveling on this Byzantine vessel fill-ed with beautiful
goods when she di-ed in childbirth. Immediately when she
di-ed there came up a *tempesta*. The sailors made a coffin for
the dead mother and child. The ship was wreck-ed and everything was thrown into the sea. The tempest was ended at once.
But everything was sunk-ed. Only the coffin was wash-ed up
to the shore of Tyndari, and there the fishermen found the
black princess and her child."

One of the ladies raised her hand like a little girl at school.
"How did the black princess get on the Byzantine ship in the
first place?" she asked.

Tito smiled a sweet smile of disarming modesty. He said,
"That is a secret I do not know."

SEVEN WORDS

"Sometimes it causes me to tremble, tremble, tremble."
—AMERICAN SPIRITUAL

CHAPTER 1

"Father, forgive them; for they know not what they do"

PALM SUNDAY dawned fair and warm. The bells rang early and the town glowed with sunlight on flowers. On window ledges clay pots sprouted delicate blades of young wheat, the symbol of fertility with which each home entered the holy season. In the cathedral the seeded floor of the Madonna's chapel had sprouted a fragile chartreuse carpet in the shape of a cross.

The monsignor archpriest of Taormina frowned at the imprints which the feet of a child had left in the tender wheat. The Monsignor was an excellent organizer and administrator, a practical man who ran the town's religious life like a successful business. The people of Taormina were proud of him. Still a young man, he had been dedicated to the church by his parents when he was a boy. He had grown up rather more worldly than spiritual, but this was more useful than spirituality in leading a worldly parish. As is the custom in Sicily, the Monsignor centered the social life of his flock in the church. The movie theater which he operated in the basement was a thriving venture. The priest's policy was to give his people the *divertimento* they loved, at the same time assuring them that they were preparing for eternal salvation.

The high point of the Monsignor's ecclesiastical year was Holy Week. Of all Sicily's pagan-Christian festivals the week of Easter is the most colorfully and spontaneously celebrated. Whole villages participate in the day-by-day re-enactment of the Passion of Jesus. In Taormina, to which an incomparable setting brings hordes of Easter tourists, the citizens, for all their religious fervor, never lose sight of the foreign gold.

The church was illuminated with candles and a lovely light was cast on the floor of the nave by rose windows. Otherwise it was a somber, brooding place, with all the religious figures and pictures covered by dark mourning cloth. From the cathedral piazza came the buzz of townspeople and tourists gathered for the procession of the palms. The Monsignor collected his assistants and went outside. Little boys in white sailor suits and little girls veiled like tiny brides waited with parents, grandparents, and chaperoning nuns. Both children and adults carried like icons their elaborately woven crosses of palmetto fronds, ribboned bouquets of palms for peace, olive branches for purity, wheat for fertility, and date palm buds called *riso delle palme* for brotherhood. Clusters of young men ogled the older girls, who hid behind their pale, waxen bouquets.

The people pushed forward for the blessing on their palms, but the hum of movement and whispering drowned the Monsignor's voice. The procession formed. First came the Monsignor with priests and acolytes carrying holy relics, and then the citizenry—groups of piping children, women in black, and finally the men. They all moved in a long line down the *corso*, through the Messina gate to the church of San Pancrazio, then back and forth through the town, to all the churches— Santa Maria di Gesù, Santa Caterina, San Michele—chanting and singing along the way.

In the church of San Giuseppe I found myself kneeling beside the young workman Ilario. Afterward I walked with him in the procession. Ilario was a fine-looking boy with curly hair and large, gentle eyes, but the eyes were a deception. During the war he had been an American prisoner in Africa. He was known as a reader of books and a conscienceless violator of women. We held our palms in prayerful attitudes, but he talked freely as we walked, only occasionally joining in the chanting. "As you can see today, the church is necessary to us Sicilians," he said. "That is why we are not a progressive people. The power of the church depends on things continuing as they are. You Americans speak of democracy, but how can a country be democratic when its people do whatever a reactionary clergy tells it to do? Democracy is not so much a form of government as it is education, and we are not educated to live in a democracy. It will take a long time—generations perhaps. Before it will happen, before this century of wars is over, free men are going to have to rise against the church and destroy the backward forces of reaction. In the meantime we will continue on holy days to march behind priests."

Ilario interrupted himself for a moment of prayer. Then he said, "Italy is what she has been for centuries, the bordello of Europe. You see, in the south we understand very well the respectability of northerners. They come to us under the pretense of looking at paintings and photographing ruins. But we know they come to the warm south for one thing alone, like people going to the baths for a cure, and as long as they pay for it with their money, we Italians are only too happy to serve them."

The day grew hot, wilting flowers and veils. The pious procession turned into a circus. Men sold balloons and sweets, peddlers shouted their wares, and shops were open for business. Ilario told me he corresponded with girls in Germany, Sweden, and Belgium. "Have you ever been in Japan?" he asked. I hadn't. "Lately I have been dreaming of Japanese girls," he said. "My ambition is to possess every girl in the world. Whenever I hear of a man having a girl, I am jealous whether I know the girl or not, because I want to have her too.

There are so many girls in the world. I should like to live a thousand years. It wouldn't be time enough."

In the doorway of a butcher shop stood a child dressed in the white rabbit fur which Sicilians so love for their *bambini*. The baby wandered under a freshly slaughtered veal and blood dripped on her. Ilario nudged me. His eye was on a pair of girls solemnly carrying their palms several rows ahead of us.

"*Straniere*," he said. They were indeed strangers to Taormina, for they were dressed with city chic and moved with a freedom and confidence unknown to village girls. Waving his palms and chanting, Ilario led me up through the procession until we were ahead of them. They were slim, extremely pretty, and quite un-Sicilian looking, even though Ilario assured me they were. How he could tell, I did not know. The older—she appeared to be in her early twenties—was a brown-blonde with brown eyes. She wore a tailored blue dress and a small hat that was little more than an arrangement of flowers. The younger was a captivating child. She had blue eyes, very fair skin, and long blond hair caught with a ribbon. She had the air of an upper-class American private-school girl. Ilario and I dropped back until we were in line with them.

"A blessed holy season to you," Ilario greeted the older.

"A blessed holy season to you," she replied.

The younger one spoke to me. "*Siete Inglese?*"

"*Americano.*"

"It's a pity," she said. "I do not speak English."

"I speak Italian."

"We will be friends," she said some steps later. "Perhaps you will fall in love with me?"

She said this with a captivating elfishness, laughing with a child's innocent confidence.

"Perhaps," I said.

"I like men falling in love with me," she said.

Ilario was progressing with the elder. We introduced ourselves. Their names were Serafina and Flavia and they lived in Catania.

"Sisters?" Ilario asked.

They laughed as if it were a private joke between them. "Yes, sisters," Serafina, the younger, said. We were back at the cathedral now. As we kneeled together I could see Ilario's hand move around the waist of Flavia; Serafina, watching, mischievously slipped her hand into mine. When the rites were finished we walked back over the *corso*, pushing through the palm-waving crowd. All around us were the little communion brides.

"You must have very modern parents," I said to Serafina. She laughed. Everything I said struck her as a wondrous joke. "My parents love me and I love them," she said, dancing about me like a sprite. "Do you have a wife in America? No? I am happy. You will fall in love with me, won't you?"

I said there was no doubt of it.

Suddenly she was off ahead with the doll vendor who had taken over a corner of the piazza. With picture hats covering their blond curls and flowing with ribbons, the stately dolls were walking back and forth on the pavement. "*Bellissima!*" Serafina cried, kneeling to let a doll walk stiffly into her arms. "*Come si chiama?*"

"Patrizia," the doll man said, and named the others. "Dolores, Teresa, Lidia, Concetta."

"I like Patrizia the best," Serafina said. "Flavia, can I have Patrizia?"

"Dolls! *Cara*, you have too many dolls," Flavia said. "You would only tire of her and we would have to carry her with us all the day." Flavia spoke with a sharp, staccato intensity.

"Flavia doesn't like me to be silly with a doll," Serafina said peevishly. "It is because she likes Ilario." She took my hand and we followed Ilario and Flavia. "I am glad you do not have a fiancée," she said coquettishly. "You will become my

fiancé, and when I am old enough we will be married." It was
children's make-believe, and I fell right in with it.

The four of us ate lunch at a flower-covered table in the
sunlight. The friendship between Ilario and Flavia was
progressing rapidly. Wine was making her volatile. She complained about the food, the flowers, the discomfort of the train
upon which they had traveled. She poured wine for herself and
thinned Serafina's with water. Serafina paid no attention; she
drew her chair close to mine and put her hand in my lap.

"Look, the little one sulks because I did not buy the doll,"
Flavia said.

"I shall have the doll," Serafina said. "Peppo will buy me
the doll when he comes."

Flavia's eyes flashed angrily at Serafina. "Peppo is my husband," she said to Ilario. "He is coming for Easter." She picked
up a long stick of bread. "My husband is good like this bread.
He is the staff of life," she said, waving the bread in the air.
"But he does not come till Friday."

Ilario looked pleased. The state of things suited him very
well. After lunch we walked down to the sea, where Ilario bor-
rowed a fisherman's boat to row Flavia to a grotto on the far
side of Isola Bella. "You will wait here with the *Americano*,"
Flavia said. "He will look after you. Tonight when we go
dancing at The Club you may come along."

They left in the boat.

I was drowsy with wine and lay on the beach. Serafina
continued her little game. "I do not think you will marry me,"
she said. "I do not think so because in America there are very
many beautiful women. I am not so beautiful as they."

"You will be as beautiful as they," I said.

"But I am not now. That's what you mean."

"How old are you, Serafina?"

"Flavia says I am too old to play with dolls. Will you dance
with me tonight?"

"I will try."

"I am mad at Flavia and I do not wish to go with her. I think I should rather go to the cinema. There is an American film. Will you take me to the cinema?"

"Whatever you wish, Serafina."

"You are a dear. When will you fall in love with me?"

"It would be very foolish of me to do so at any time."

"Why? I have already fallen in love with you." Suddenly she was beside me, her hair spread over the sand like golden seaweed.

"How old are you, Serafina?"

"I am so old," she said, bringing her face next to mine and kissing me. It was fresh and sweet, as if the sea had washed over me.

"Serafina, how many years do you have?"

"Flavia does not want me to tell. I am angry with her, that is why I will tell. I will have thirteen in June."

I knew she was telling the truth. "Why doesn't Flavia want you to tell?" I asked.

"She is my mother, that is why, and doesn't wish you and Ilario to know Peppo is my father, and when he comes here on Friday he will buy me the doll. I hope it is not sold before he comes. I have two brothers who are in school. Flavia was married when she had fourteen years and now she has twenty-eight years. In another year I shall be old enough to marry. If you love me, you may kiss me."

She was a doll herself, playing a game she did not understand.

"Serafina, do you really wish for the doll?"

"The one called Patrizia? Oh, yes, I want her very much. I have no doll so beautiful."

"Then let us go find the doll man," I said.

Serafina jumped to her feet, shook out her hair, and smoothed her dress. I told the fisherman whose boat Ilario had taken that we were returning to the village. We climbed fast, as if hurrying might save us the doll. We failed to find the doll man at his morning place; he had moved to the terrace of the Anglo-American bar in the main square where tourists sat out the siesta under gay umbrellas, with tea, yoghurt, vermouth, or beer.

"Look! She's there," Serafina cried, seeing Patrizia. The doll man released Patrizia and she walked straight to Serafina's arms. We set her between us under one of the candy-striped umbrellas, where we served her an almond cake while Serafina had some ice cream and I a Cinzano. Later we took Patrizia to the cathedral to see the movie. The Monsignor was showing an old American film: *Scarface* with Paul Muni.

CHAPTER 2

"Today thou shalt be with Me in Paradise"

MONDAY WAS the Feast of St. Joseph. This was a minor occasion, for Sicilians, having more confidence in female saints than male, had reservations about Jesus. "Jesus was not much of a man," a fisherman told me. "A sort of feminine intellectual who never got ahead. He was inconsiderate of his Mother, always making trouble for Her, who was the greatest saint of all. His miracles were little ones compared to those of Catherine, Cecilia, and Lucia, who saved Catania from Etna. What did Jesus do? Chase some fish into a net and get himself crucified because he wasn't man enough to prevent it!" A people with such an attitude about Jesus could not be expected to concern themselves much over the carpenter Joseph.

I spent the afternoon in the town of Giarre watching with an audience of children a holy week puppet performance. The *opera d'i pupi*, as the people call it, is the traditional theater of Sicily. Until the invasion of cheap motion pictures it was the most popular form of entertainment. Early in the century puppet theaters were as numerous as film houses in America. Today there are only four or five permanent companies operating in Palermo and a half-dozen itinerant companies which travel to smaller towns and cities. The subject matter

213

of Sicilian puppetry, like the heroic paintings on the donkey carts, deals almost entirely with the Saracen-Christian wars of Sicilian history. The plays, adapted by puppeteers more than a century ago from Ariosto's sixteenth-century classic *Orlando Furioso* and other historic accounts of the Crusades, can run for as long as fourteen months without repeating themselves. I had visited one of these theaters near the Palermo water front. It was a dark, smelly, dimly lit room full of men and children. The performance went on for almost three hours, thirty acts from three to ten minutes long, jumping in action from Palestine to Paris to Sicily. At least once every quarter hour there was a noisy, saber-rattling duel. The Saracen villains were thick-lipped, jet-black, heavily turbaned Negroid types; the knightly heroes were noble Norman blonds, always ready to sacrifice their lives for a woman's honor. The audience knew it all from memory. Throughout the performance men murmured to one another, "Now will come Charlemagne," "Orlando will wait in the forest to meet the traitor Gano di Maconza." By listening to my neighbors, I knew two or three minutes ahead what was going to happen. When the evening's show was over, the puppeteer announced the coming attractions: "Will Ruggero overcome the traitor Gano and will he meet his love Bradamante? Why is the beautiful Queen of Persia disguised as a knight? Will Rinaldo recognize her? Come tomorrow night . . ."

Puppet theaters are usually family affairs. Argento Giuseppe, the Palermo impresario, inherited his from his father; his oldest son, aged ten, was already helping him backstage. Emilio Sollima of Giarre inherited his theater and puppets from an uncle; he too was preparing his son to carry on. Sollima, a modest, quiet little man, was president of the Sicilian Puppeteers Guild and the best-known puppeteer in Sicily. Unlike other impresarios who buy new puppets from professional puppet builders, Sollima builds his himself. He has about two hundred. His pleasant, pert little wife makes their

costumes. The couple operated the theater with the boy
Agusto and one hired assistant. It was hard work. The metal
puppets, three feet tall and weighing from fifty to seventy
pounds each, were operated by steel poles from the top of the
stage; as many as five or six were often in action at one time.
The operators spoke the heated and eloquent dialogue.
Agusto played the women's roles.

Sollima's little theater was not so oppressive and dark as
the one in Palermo. The seats were boards laid on boxes.
Those of us who had come by hired bus from Taormina,
Sollima greeted like guests in his house. "I am not worthy to
have such a distinguished company in such humble surroundings," he said.

The stage was so perfectly proportioned to the puppets that
they appeared life sized. They moved through an ingenious
variety of movements and in their strong and colorful personalities they almost seemed human.

The play opened peaceably enough with a messenger bearing the terms of truce from the King of Vienna to the King
of France. The messenger's travail began when he met three
dragons in succession, all of which he slew. Then he was am-
bushed and slain by Gano di Maconza, a perennial puppet
villain. The result was war between the armies of France and
Vienna. Sabers clanked in rattling duels and knights leaped
on one another with ferocious intensity. The most heart-rend-
ing episode was that of a little white dog who, coming upon
his master wounded in the forest, ran barking across a country
or two to the king's palace for help and returned with two
knights, only to find his master dead. With a sorrowful yelp,
the little dog succumbed on the dead master's body. A more
confusing episode had to do with Angela, "the princess of
India" (related, no doubt, to Palermo's Queen of Persia), a
blond-haired, blue-eyed Norman maiden who wore a new
pink gown fresh from Signora Sollima's needle. Angela be-
guiled a Viennese knight who attempted to violate her; she

was saved by the timely appearance of the great knight Orlando. Orlando and the Viennese slashed noisily at each other, until it seemed certain that the two tin figures would shatter each other to smithereens. Children stood up and cheered. The battle ended with Orlando felling the Austrian and slicing him in half. At this point gentle Angela, worrying about the dying man's soul, had him baptized before he died. At the moment of anointment, Jesus, wearing a pink gown and a long golden wig (among dark Latin peoples heavenly personages are invariably portrayed as fair), dropped onto the stage from heaven. He expressed his sorrow at the evil of men and made a promise to the dying knight. "Today thou shalt be with Me in Paradise," Jesus said. Then, while cherubic angels and white doves fluttered over the stage, Jesus and the late Austrian knight wafted heavenward in each other's arms. The Easter play was over.

CHAPTER 3

"Woman, behold thy son"

BY DAY and by night the women of the town were busy embroidering. It was not the leisurely embroidering of women who have time to kill, but the frantic stitching of women doing piecework to help support their families. One saw them—grandmothers, mothers, daughters—on a good day catching the sunlight as early as seven o'clock in the morning; in the evenings they huddled in the doors of their houses harvesting the last rays of the sun; and, after dark, they clustered under a solitary bulb, stitching themselves into blindness putting maps of Sicily on luncheon cloths and donkey carts on women's blouses, all to be sold in the morning in the embroidery bazaars of the *corso*. Some mothers of the town earn as much embroidering as the fathers who fish and work the farms. Some are widows, for, as everywhere in Sicily, women outlive their men. As they stitch, they worry about the prospects of their marriageable daughters. It is a serious problem, for too many local youths have been spoiled for any life but the adventuresome one of entertaining tourists. The women have cause for worry since the young men on the beach and the *corso* are also their sons.

One of the stitching women had a son named Como. He was

a hotel waiter who worked ten hours a day for four hundred lire—approximately sixty-four cents. There were hotels in Taormina that paid less. Tips and the opportunity to meet the guests were considered sufficient compensation by unscrupulous managers. Como liked hotel life. In the months when no tourists came to Taormina he traveled north to Venice to work in a hotel there. He was blond, humorless, and of an ardently romantic nature. Women found Como appealing.

He had been taught to please them at a tender age. As a *bambino* Como had long golden curls, and his father, an unemployed laborer with a large brood, of which Como was the youngest, dressed him in a diminutive white American sailor's suit and took him to the fashionable San Domenico hotel to jig for the tourists, who gave him money. When foreigners asked him what he would be when he was grown up, he always replied, as his father had taught him, *"Un Americano!"* The answer never failed to draw some extra lire from the Americans. During the war, when there were no tourists, Como stole bags of coal from the railroad yards down by the sea and carried them up the steep donkey path on his back in order to sell them in the village. When there was no bread at home he stole fruit from orchards and occasionally a loaf from the baker. What he could not eat he hid under a ledge on the cliff. When he returned the next day to eat the bread, it would be hard as the rock and nibbled at by lizards and other small beasts. He held other brief jobs, once as a tailor's apprentice, once as a road worker; he pointed proudly to the cliff road known as Via Roma, which he said he helped build. He was seventeen when he rediscovered that being attractive to tourists could be made to pay. For four years he had specialized in English and American ladies.

"American ladies are sometimes very capricious but they are sentimental and always generous," Como said. "Swedish women are easy but they do not have as much money. English

ladies are the least passionate of all and not very sentimental.
I do not waste time with them. I am of a very hot nature."

Como was clinging, like every Sicilian male, to the legend
that no men on earth are as erotically gifted as the Sicilians.
"When a lady pretends that she doesn't mean business, I wait
for five minutes and say, 'Madame, you love. Otherwise,
good-by!' Usually she love." Nevertheless, Como had religious
qualms about his life. He had lately even considered turning
Protestant. "A Catholic is not supposed to have any love if
he is not married, and Protestants are allowed all the love
they wish, even if they are not married."

I asked how he'd come by such an interpretation of Prot-
estantism.

"It is easy to see," he said. "The women who come here for
love are Protestant." Reflectively, Como added, "It is impossible to live without love. One has the choice of breaking off
the *uccello* * or becoming a Protestant. I think I would rather
be a Protestant, even if it means believing there is no God."

In many ways Como was unlike the high-spirited lads of
the night clubs and the beach. He didn't like dancing, and he
thought there was something indecent about displaying one's
body to the public gaze. He was a proud and brooding lone
wolf whose childish desire to become an American had never
left him. So desperate was his drive to escape the poverty and
indignity of Sicilian life that he thought of England as a possibility and recently had even considered Scandinavia. He spent
long hours writing letters, maintaining painstaking and passionate correspondence in English (which he hardly spoke)
with women he had known as long as two or three years. "One
time one of them will send for me," he said. It was the sustain-
ing faith of his life.

It was the letter writing that brought us together. I was
typing one day on my terrace when a voice calling from the

* Literally "bird"; as used here a popular Italian designation for penis.

piazza below asked if my *macchina* was American. I replied
that it was, and the young man asked if he might come up
to see it. To peasant Italians a typed letter represents the
pinnacle of quality and elegance. Como carefully examined
my machine and asked if I would assist him with some of his
English correspondence. I said I would if I might make carbon
copies of the letters for myself. He agreed readily: the idea
that anything he wrote would interest me was pleasing to him.
We began that evening with two letters.

The first went to a girl named Jacqueline in Chicago.

It is now a month since I have received and answered your
last letter. The month that has passed has been one of terrible
anguish, and each day my heart has bled because I haven't
heard from you. The sun does not shine for me, and the weeks
are endless. Why haven't you written? Can it mean that some
one else has replaced me in your heart? Please write and tell
me at once that this is not so.

I long for a photograph of your beautiful face so that I can
look at it and remember it in my dreams the long nights
through. You are the only woman in my life. There can never
be room for another in my heart.

Your Como sends his heart wrapped in kisses. . . .

The second went to a girl named Dagmar in Stockholm.
"She is fat and not very pretty," Como said with a shrug. "But
perhaps she will get me a visa."

MY DEAREST DAGMAR [Como wrote]:
What a joy it was to get your letter and the lovely photo-
graph of yourself and the other of the beautiful little prince.
I have been thinking of you all the time, so you can imagine
what an answer to a thousand prayers before the Blessed
Virgin your letter was. Indeed, I think it was the Blessed
Virgin made you write to me.

For you I have only thoughts of love. The days since you
have left Taormina have been nights of sadness, for there is
no other whom I would hold in my arms. I dream only of the

time when you will be mine and we will be together forever, only you and me. I think always if only I could come to Stockholm, your beautiful city, to be with you. For that I shall wait until eternity, because for your Como there can never be another Dagmar. Even if it is wicked to say so, I must tell you, you are dearer to me than the Mother of God herself. I think only of love, nothing but love. In all my dreams you are my angel and I am,

YOUR COMO

There were no more letters that night, for Como had a rendezvous at the Anglo-American bar with a Mrs. Parson from St. Paul, Minnesota. The next evening there was time for two letters. The first went to a Miss Ivy Phipps of London. I quote in part:

DEAREST IVY:

You can't imagine how glad I was to read your sweet words and hear that I am your ideal, the man of your dreams. You are for me the same and I would like that our engagement should end in a true love and that this love soon could transform itself into our matrimony. From the moment I saw you I haven't had any peace, and I have no more desire to do anything because you are my true love and I hope to bind myself to you for all of my life. . . .

The second went to Christine Steensholm of Copenhagen:

MY BELOVED CHRISTINE:

You are the Ophelia of my soul. Your voice wraps around me like your smile. I shall hold to the ideal of you all my life. From sunrise to sunset I escape the hard material world by my memories and my dreams of you. . . .

For a week we wrote letters, one or two an evening, to Liverpool, Oslo, Memphis, Zurich, and Boston. We had hardly finished with the list before answers began to arrive. A housewife from Oslo wrote:

My husband does not wish to investigate possibilities of a visa for you, but I will do it myself without his knowledge.

Lovingly,

YOUR BERGIT

In ten days came a letter from Dagmar, the plain, fat girl in Stockholm. Como brought it running and shouted to me from the piazza. Dagmar had sent him a dozen snapshots of herself, of her mother (a large, plain-faced woman in a shapeless print dress), of a variety of sisters and brothers, and a collection of post-card photographs of the Swedish royal family. I examined the photographs of Dagmar. They showed her to be a big and not very pretty girl of obviously modest means, simple and trusting.

MY DARLING COMO [Dagmar had written]:

Your letter was the most beautiful I have ever received. I've read it over and over and I shall keep it to read forever. I have been to the Italian Consulate about a visa for you, but they say you must do it yourself by going to Messina. You will have to have a job, and if you send me your working papers, I will try to find a job, though I don't think I have much influence. I have no capital of my own. Since I am unmarried, I must work, for I cannot live off my parents.

Love and kisses,

YOUR DAGMAR

"No capital," Como said. "That is not good. But if I promise to marry her, I will get a visa." He was on his way to meet a lady from Strasbourg at the Anglo-American bar, so he gave Dagmar's letter to me. "You will answer it for me," he said. "Tell her I will go to arrange for my visa and come to marry her. Write her the usual stuff about love."

I looked at the photographs of Dagmar and her mother and father, her brothers and sisters and their children, all plain, middle-class, hard-working people, austere, Lutheran, frugal, devoted, living lives as predictable as the spokes of a wheel.

I looked at the picture of the prince, a blond little boy of about six years. He looked at me with such serious, childish innocence that I felt quite guilty over the destiny I was help- ing to spin around one of his loving subjects. After dinner I went upstairs and wrote my last letter for Como.

DEAR MISS:

I am an American writing for Como. He has asked me to tell you that he will come to Stockholm to marry you and that you should send him a letter agreeing to this. Such a letter will facilitate his getting a visa. Having conveyed his message, I should like to advise you to do quite the opposite and end at once a correspondence which I think will bring you only unhappiness and trouble. The magic of the Sicilian sun can- not be moved to the temperate north.

I signed it with my initials and took it to the post office.

CHAPTER 4

"My God, my God, why hast Thou forsaken me?"

SUSPENDED like an eagle's lair on a mountaintop is the village
of Castelmola. Though only eight hundred feet above Taormina, it is almost two miles by the serpentine road. It is a
dark, poor place of fifteen hundred inhabitants, a covey of
little houses crowded on the knob of a hill with foul, narrow
passages for streets. It smells unwashed, as indeed it is. Much
of the year there is no water supply. The men herd goats in
the hills or work on the land, and the women silently spin in
the sun with age-old wheels. As a compensation for its mean-
ness, Castelmola has one distinction—a superb view of the sea
and the hills of Taormina spreading out below. For this reason
it was a favorite gathering place for lair-loving German officers during the Nazi occupation. From its heights they operated a short-wave radio station.

Castelmola's patron is St. George, the dragon killer. There
is an image of him killing the dragon in his own church, San
Giorgio; he sits astride a white charger with gold harness. It
is a sort of beautifully oversized hobbyhorse. The only other
place of interest is the Café San Giorgio, hung on the edge
of the precipice, where tourists stop to drink wine, liqueurs,
or coffee and buy souvenirs and post cards. It is a small room

crowded with rustic furniture; the walls are covered with prewar German and Scandinavian travel posters. There are shelves of shepherds' pipes, wood carvings, and souvenir pottery; on the tables lie well-thumbed copies of German magazines. In one corner is a tiny bar over which the *padrone* presided. He was a man in his early fifties, good-natured, extroverted, pompous. He spoke several languages, but German was his favorite—had been ever since 1943. "The Germans were always gentlemen," he said. "Twelve officers, all of them my dear friends, lived in my house. I cooked for them myself; I would not trust my wife with their food. They asked me to broadcast for them to the Sicilians and Italians. Those were happy days in Castelmola. Then the entire village lived well." He showed me a letter from a Nazi soldier who had been one of his friends. The soldier reported returning to Austria after two years of wartime imprisonment in Texas. Of Texas the soldier wrote: "*Wie im Paradies.*"

It was a moody day in Castelmola. The sea was hidden by swift-moving clouds, and the town of Taormina kept appearing and disappearing in the Wagnerian mists. It was easy to see why the German militarists had liked it there.

Two long, black Chrysler sedans drew up outside, and four couples, rich, stolid, red-faced burghers, entered the San Giorgio. When he heard them speak German, the *padrone* rushed forward with open arms to greet them. They were Liechtensteiners and gave the name of a Munich German who had sent them. The *padrone* embraced the men warmly and set up drinks. In the confusion even I received a free glass of wine. It was superb and devilishly powerful. The *padrone* boasted of making it himself from grapes, oranges, and lemons. He gave us all a copy of a handbill, which told us in six languages that the *padrone* had seven albums containing more than 100,000 autographs of "nobility and gentry" who had visited him since 1907. The sheet quoted from articles appearing in *Stars and Stripes*, the *Deutsche Wochenschau*, and

Adler im Süden, the Nazi army equivalent of *Stars and Stripes*. The *padrone* brought out the volumes. In his older guest books I found signatures from many of the royal families of Europe—Austria, Denmark, Rumania, Holland—and the American names of Rockefeller, Morgan, Vanderbilt, and Henry Ford. In a later book devoted exclusively to Germans, the *padrone* pointed out his most prized signatures, those of Field Marshal Kesselring (whose 1943 headquarters were in Taormina's San Domenico Hotel), the composer Richard Strauss, and hundreds of autographed photographs of German officers and soldiers.

The Liechtensteiners clucked as excitedly as broody hens over the Nazi memorabilia and passed coldly over autographs of American and English soldiers which followed. "Uncivilized people, Americans," one said in German. He was short-necked and short-haired, like a George Grosz drawing, and he held a gold-headed cane between his knees. He bewailed the bombing of Nuremberg, where he owned property. "How they bombed our great German cities!" he exclaimed. "In twenty minutes Nuremberg was *kaputt!*" The *padrone* agreed with him; the English and the Americans stationed in Sicily had not been the gentlemen the Germans were.

The day was ebbing. Outside, a man rode from the fields on a black donkey, and a woman dressed in black followed with a herd of braying black goats; on her head was a bundle of kindling wood. They would use it to heat some supper on a chimneyless hearth and, as the night cooled, they would hole up for comfort with their beasts. The *padrone* told the Liechtensteiners how a donkey that had cost only two hundred lire before the war now cost fifty thousand. Somehow, the Americans were responsible for it. More wine was poured. The Liechtensteiners wrote greetings and signed their names in the German book.

Suddenly outside there was a terrible roar like an airplane motor. A bug-shaped German-model sports car careened up he winding road and came to a screeching halt on the little piazza. A blond figure leaped out, jumped to the stone wall on the edge of the piazza, and stood poised, scanning the view. I recognized him; it was Gilg, the golden boy from Stuttgart, the square-jawed German Apollo who had held court one night at The Club. He leaped off the wall and into the Café San Giorgio. The *padrone* greeted him respectfully, and we were introduced. His name was Gilg Mann. He drank some wine quickly and refused to sit down. He was tense with nervous energy; a young man in a terrible hurry with no place to go. His hair was the color of straw, his eyes were blue, his mouth heavy. His square face was wind-burned and flushed. In a purely physical sense he was certainly extraordinary. In fact, there was something shocking about him. When he smiled, his lips curled in contempt; his eyes narrowed cynically. It was a merciless face filled with hate, as cruel as it was handsome. The Liechtensteiners fawned on him like sycophantic courtiers, but he ignored them. To me he spoke in a neat and precise English with an accent that was partly Oxford, partly German. "What kind of a car do you drive?" he asked.

"I don't drive any," I said.

Such a possibility had obviously never occurred to him. "How did you come up here?"

"I walked."

This struck him as even more absurd. "Then you will ride down with me," he commanded.

I thanked him. The climb up had taken an hour and it was almost dark.

"We will go at once," he said, looking around with contempt. "Here there are only empty bottles." He charged out of the café and into the car. The *padrone* followed us with a farewell gift, some picture post cards of the Café San Giorgio, with a grinning photograph of Mussolini, under which, in bold letters, it said, "*Saluto al Duce,*" and another of Victor

Emmanuel, the late King of Italy, under which was printed
"*Evviva il Re d'Italia, Imperatore d'Etiopia.*"

"For souvenirs," the *padrone* said. "They were made before
the war. When they are gone there will be no more."

I promised to treasure the pictures. Gilg Mann, his motor
booming, waited impatiently with the car door open. He
looked like a jet-propelled superman from an American comic
strip about to soar off into the stratosphere. We reared like a
bronco, turned around, and plunged down the spiral road
spinning around its hairpin curves as fast as the car would go
I was terrified. I shouted to him to slow down, but I could
not make myself heard above the motor. So I hung on and
prayed. In no time at all we were in Taormina. Gilg Mann
put his foot on the brake so suddenly we almost flew out. The
motor was already off.

"When I am nervous this is how I relax," he said.

"It's no way to relax me," I said, getting out.

"Don't go!" he ordered. "I want to talk. We will drive down
to the sea and then we will have dinner."

"If you want to talk it will have to be outside the car," I
said. I refused to get in again, so he got out and we ordered
some Martinis in a bar.

"To relaxation," I toasted.

"I can't relax," he said. "I haven't relaxed since I left Germany two years ago."

"Where have you been?" I asked.

"In Greece, in Paris, in Capri. Everywhere it is the same
Life is rotten, people are hypocrites. The whole world is an
empty bottle. People are empty bottles. Empty bottles!" He
repeated the phrase maniacally and his mouth curled in
scorn. "Those Liechtensteiners pretending they are Germans
Empty bottles! That Sicilian with his love for Germans! An
empty bottle! All Italians are empty bottles. Decadent traitors
who welcome their conquerors and then betray them. The
minute they meet you they are your friend; the next day they

etray you. I hate Italians. Germans are the only people who
nderstand friendship. I wish I had stayed in Capri. More
;ermans and less Italians in Capri." He gulped down his
Iartini and ordered another pair.

"Better let me skip this one," I said. "I drink slower too."

"Do you work for a living?" he asked.

I confessed that I did.

"I have never had to work for anything," he said. "It is a
errible tragedy not to have to work for a living."

"It's a tragedy I don't anticipate in my life," I said.

"I envy you," he said. "You don't know how lucky you are.
Vork makes character and builds strong men. I've never had
) work in my life. Everything is given to me. All the money
can spend. All the women I want and more, begging me
) take them. Everything is too easy. People like me for my
ioney, for my car, or because I am handsome. They never
ke me for my insides." He pointed to his heart. "Do you
ke me because I am rich?"

"No," I said.

"Because of my car?"

"No."

"Because I am handsome?"

"I don't like you at all," I said.

But Gilg Mann didn't even hear me. "To have a good
:iend is the most important thing in life," he said. "Only a
;erman understands that. For two years I have searched for
friend. I have found nothing but empty bottles. The hu-
1an race is degenerate. Men no longer know how to be
:iends. Everyone is disloyal. Everyone is a traitor. Empty
ottles! I can tell you are not an empty bottle. I want you to
e my friend!"

"Sorry," I said.

"I know. It is because you do not like Germans. It is the
ime with everyone. No one likes Germans. The world has
>rgotten that only Germans understand the hungers of the

soul. Without Germans the world would be an empty bottle! To my horror I saw there were tears in his eyes. It was like watching a statue weep.

"All I want from life is one friend," he said.

"There are the women," I said.

"Women!" he repeated cynically. "One sleeps with women. But women are not men. One cannot talk to a woman. One cannot make a friend of a woman."

I got up to go. "I hope you will find a friend," I said.

For a moment he clung to me. "You are like the others," he said. "The world has forsaken me. The world has forsaken Germany. The world is an empty bottle."

I ran into him once more, the day before Easter. He told me he had rented a villa in Taormina. He was going to do his part toward improving the decadent non-Germanic race by enriching them with his own pure Aryan blood. In his villa he would attempt to sow his seed broadly and render pregnant as many non-German women, Italian and otherwise, as possible. It was, he said, the least he could do.

CHAPTER 5

"I thirst"

T NOON on Holy Thursday the Monsignor entertained the
welve disciples at the Last Supper and five hours later he
ashed their feet before the high altar.

The Monsignor, playing the role of Jesus, each year hand-
icks twelve apostles for their virtue, piety, and poverty. To
e selected is a high honor, worth being poor for a year. To
etain his seat the holy disciple will run ecclesiastical errands
nd perform menial chores. The last supper, held in an inner
hamber of the cathedral, is a private affair at which no towns-
eople are permitted. But foreign writers, especially if they
ave cameras, had no difficulty gaining admission. Gathered
watch the holy breaking of bread were a half-dozen Brit-
hers, including Donald and Estelle Hegswith, and myself. All
f us were Protestants.

The room was large, with dark beams. Incense and the smell
f cooking were heavy in the air. The table, set for thirteen,
as long and narrow, as in Leonardo's painting. The similarity
ent no further; the repast was far from the humble bread and
ine that Jesus served his disciples. There were both bread
nd wine, to be sure, with the wine in huge pitchers. There
as also a large, gaudy cake with colored icing. A dog waited

by the table. When we arrived, the Monsignor was bustlin
through last-minute details, giving orders to the womer
dressed in the inevitable black who were cooking in th
kitchen, angrily dispersing curious children from the doo⟩
and helping photographers set up their tripods. Finally, whe⟩
everything was ready, the twelve disciples were bidden to th
feast and made their humble entrance.

It was a startling company. The disciples were wrapped i⟩
togas of orange, red, blue, yellow and green, the familiar brigh
colors of "Last Supper" paintings. Ten of the twelve wer
elderly men, some so old they tottered. Two were boys; th
younger, the beloved St. John, grinned foolishly in a pin
tunic. A waiter at the Mediterraneo had told me at breakfa⟨
that his father was to play the role of Judas. This was probabl
a fantasy, for, other than St. John, the disciples are not usuall
identified. The father, whom I had met, was a merry littl
man and quite out of character as the betrayer. As a group, th⟩
disciples seemed ill at ease; a few of the older ones, howevei
managed to shuffle to the table and take their appointed plac⟨
with dignity. The dog settled under the table. A hush fell ove
the room while the Monsignor, corpulent and bald, blesse
the disciples and invited them to eat of his body and drink ⟨
his blood.

They started on the blood, great beakers of it, which, unde
order of the Monsignor, they held suspended in mid-air, whi⟩
one of the Englishmen made a color exposure. Then the
drank heartily and the women brought in the repa⟨
It started with copper kettles of *pasta*. Each disciple was serve
enough macaroni with meat and tomato sauce to feed a fan
ily. They ate noisily, washing it all down with plenty of win⟨
After this came the roast beef, huge cuts which covered th
plates, and a variety of vegetables, and cheeses. No one spok⟨
but the room echoed with the sounds of eating and drinkin⟨
While they ate, the disciples threw fat and gristle to the do⟨

ho gulped it silently. Protestant appetites began to react to
ne sights, sounds, and smells of the food, and one by one the
witnesses left. I stayed until the dessert, which included plat-
ers of fruit, the fancy cake, and cigars for all disciples. They
were refilling the wine pitchers as I walked out the door.

We were told there would be a crowd at the foot washing,
announced for five o'clock, so the Hegswiths and I went early
o find places. The cathedral was softly lighted; the altar was
barren of the Host, and the images were draped in mourning.
y a quarter to five the cathedral was filled with gossiping
icilians and tourists in a holiday mood. No one paid much
ttention when nothing happened at five. But by five-fifteen
eople began to be restless.

Finally, at a quarter to six, the Monsignor appeared, dressed
a vestments of gold and purple. Behind him came two assist-
nt priests in vestments of gold and ivory, and next in the
rocession, plodding uncertainly, the twelve disciples. They
aned on tall shepherds' crooks, to each of which was tied a
ag of pebbles, presumably from the River Jordan. Like a sad
iry they lined up on a raised platform covered with red
elvet. Cherubic acolytes wearing tomato-colored vestments
nd carrying lighted tapers attended them. One of the two
riests began the annual sermon on humility. It was a pas-
onately angry affair, a fierce denouncement of the sin of
ride. The Sicilians listened dutifully; obviously they had
eard it so many times that they knew it by heart. Through
all the Monsignor listened silently, occasionally interrupt-
ng the sermon to shush some children or order someone to
t down. His pudgy hands, heavy with ecclesiastical jewelry,
ere folded piously on his stomach.

When the sermon was finished, the Monsignor removed
is outer vestments and put on a white apron. The disciples
n the red platform began to struggle with the boot laces of
heir right feet. Some of the older ones, unable to bend far

enough to reach their heavy shoes, were assisted by acolyte
After the shoes came the socks. One saint had trouble with hi
garters.

"This would never do in the Church of England," sai
Estelle Hegswith.

Twelve right feet were finally bared and everything wa
ready. Almost, that is. The Monsignor, aware that Sicilia
houses were not equipped for personal hygiene, was takin
no chances. An acolyte brought to one of the priests a larg
silver tray on which were twelve white cotton puffs; to th
other priest an acolyte brought a silver chalice containing th
ablution water. The Monsignor and priests bowed to eac
other and to the first disciple on the platform, after whic
the Monsignor took a cotton puff from the tray, dipped
into the water, and brushed it over the disciple's foot. Di
carding the wet cotton, the Monsignor lay flat on his stomac
and kissed the foot. The kiss took no more than a second, afte
which the Monsignor stood up and repeated the whole routin
over and over until all twelve disciples were attended. Th
Sicilians in the church watched intently. This was what the
had come for—the spectacle of their priest touching his lips t
the gnarled feet of the poor and humble.

After it was finished with a benediction there was the nois
confusion of socks, garters, and shoes. When the shuffle wa
finally over, the disciples started their procession through th
town, the sad journey to Gethsemane, where, according to th
carpenter Ilario, "Peter will betray Jesus and the cook [si
will crow."

"I think a Martini would be in order," Donald Hegswit
sensibly suggested.

At the Café Nuovo, where they were excellent, we took
table by the window. We were on our second when the hol
procession passed tight against our window, first the Mor
signor and his assistants, then the acolytes and the disciple
leaning heavily on their staffs as on a third limb, and finall

the natives and the visitors. Toward the end, walking between a pair of gallants, her hands folded reverently and tears of holy passion streaming down her cheeks, was Emma, the Swiss wife from Zurich. "Blessed are the pure in heart," said Donald Hegswith solemnly.

When we went to the Mediterraneo for supper the town was dark and quiet. On the way, in a narrow *salita*, we came upon two old men mumbling incoherently as they tried to help each other up a flight of stairs. I recognized them as two elderly disciples. Though it was hardly the hour, somewhere above us a cook crowed.

CHAPTER 6

"It is finished"

ON GOOD FRIDAY the weather failed. A dark gloom covered the town and a damp, marrow-freezing chill blew up from the sea. In the cathedral the wheat had grown tall and turned dark green. Before the altar of the Church of St. Joseph in a glass and gold casket surrounded by burning tapers and arum lilies lay the prone image of Christ crucified, waiting. Farther up the hill in the Church of the Varo, *Mater Dolorosa,* the image of the sorrowing Virgin, also waited.

The procession was scheduled for after dark. At dusk I went to the Café Nuovo to watch it from indoors. Many tourists were already there, drinking the famous Martinis while they waited for the procession to start. The night had turned a purgatorial black. In deference to the crucified Jesus there were no street lights. The people moving slowly and mournfully through the streets were dressed in black.

We heard the timeless funereal wail of the village band. A drum corps beat out a death march. The length of the *corso* was lit with thousands of candles flickering in the wind. First came a procession of men bearing the flower-heaped glass coffin of Jesus down from St. Joseph's. From the hill sobs rent the air and we knew that the procession of women

236

was descending. It was led by thirteen black veiled matrons bearing on their shoulders the platform of the *Mater Dolorosa*, guiding her through the town in the sorrowful search for her son. Following her were the women of the town, also veiled, carrying candles, blending their keenings with the dirge of the musicians. The statue clothed in black was surrounded by a blanket of arum lilies. Everything was black except the lilies. The grieving white face of the Virgin was brought by the glow of candlelight to dramatic life.

At the cathedral the two processions, the male one of the dead Christ and the female of the sorrowing Mother, came together and welcomed the living Christ, riding on a box of green fertility wheat. The young men of the beach and boulevards carried it on their shoulders. They wore crowns of thorns and rope lassos around their necks. Among them was Como, the letter writer.

The musicians now played a slow, plaintive waltz tune. The processions merged into one, led by the Monsignor in a white ermine cape with a long train carried by small boys. After him under a lofty canopy escorted by priests, an acolyte carried the Eucharist; then came the youths with the risen Christ, the men with the dead Christ, and finally the women with the weeping Virgin. At the end came a group of little girls in white carrying toy ladders, symbols of the ladders used at the Crucifixion to mount the cross. As the procession crawled back and forth across the town, stopping at churches, the people began to sing. I could hear the shrill falsettos of the little girls and the chanting of the boys, but most of all I could hear the rich soprano voices of the women ringing out over the town like a chorus of Demeters wailing for their lost Persephone.

It came to an end, finally, at the cathedral. The narrow streets were dark, the voices silenced. Only the wind whistled in from the sea. The town was a tomb.

CHAPTER 7

"Father, into Thy hands I commend my spirit"

THE RESURRECTION of Jesus was celebrated on Saturday. My friends told me that Sicily, being so close to Palestine, received the news of the Resurrection a day early. Whatever the explanation, I suspect that the urge to get on with the celebration, to leave sorrow behind and enjoy the rites of Demeter and Persephone, also entered into it.

The town awakened to a cacophony of bells—bells in the cathedral towers, bells in the churches of San Pancrazio, bells in all the churches, proclaiming the end of Lent and the beginning of the cycle of the earth goddess. Powder charges were exploded from the Messina gate to the Catania gate. Up on the heights the people of Castelmola also joyfully proclaimed the end of wailing with bells and cannonades. There were great Easter masses planned for Sunday, but except for these, religious responsibilities were considered fulfilled. Three days of dancing, drinking, and feasting were about to begin. The mountainside, covered with blossoms, was bathed in warm sunlight and the scent of wisteria.

It was as if the town had suddenly changed genders. The religious observances had been women's affairs. Even such male rites as the last supper had women sewing costumes and preparing food. But the Saturday activities were distinctly male. Now, respecting the male urge for release, women faded into the background. Male laughter and music rang out over the town. On a flat roof in the upper part of the town a dozen workers in denims drank wine and danced with each other. From the hills above echoed the flutes of herdsmen. Down on the beach barefoot fishermen played guitars and the young bloods who had worn thorns a night ago danced sambas on the sand.

In the Danish-operated Hotel San Pietro, it was a Copenhagen Easter with Cherry Heering, pastries, eggs, and a songfest. The San Domenico was occupied with a holiday visit from the Prime Minister and his retinue. Even the Sicilians who disliked the government in Rome still felt their civic pride stirred by an event of such magnitude. The village was filled with visitors from near-by towns. They climbed the donkey path by my window, strumming guitars, rattling tambourines, and carrying string sacks bulging with wine bottles, loaves of bread, and cheese.

In the afternoon I went to call on Dr. Sieglinde Ashenberg, the German writer who was working on a sequel to Shakespeare's *The Tempest*. I scarcely knew her, but in the compact foreign colony news traveled swiftly; she had heard I also wrote plays and was, like herself, a teacher, so she invited me to Easter tea. She was thin and delicate looking, but her appearance was deceptive. She had boundless energy. She was quite beautiful, with northern blue eyes and blond hair. Her manner was formal, her clothes tasteful and simple. I could not guess her age. While she seemed young, her youthfulness was the kind that some women carry far into life. The Caliban play was only one of her projects. She was also a world authority on Hindu culture and was transcribing some ancient Asiatic scrolls into German. I asked her about the play.

"An American should find it very interesting," she said.

The tea was steaming; she poured it into delicate china cups
"You see, I make Caliban a symbol of your country. He uses
his supernatural powers to destroy the world."

I thought I might have heard wrong, for Dr. Ashenberg's
voice was low. She passed me lemon and sugar and some Sicil
ian cakes. "Have some. They're honey, nuts, and figs, terribly
sweet and filled with fertility." I took one and laid it on my
saucer. She continued, "America is the Caliban in the family
of nations. The uncultured primitive, the sensual materialist
Americans are destined to be the most hated people on earth.'

"For trying to preserve democracy in Europe?" I asked.

The doctor laughed softly. "There is no democracy in
Europe," she said.

I reminded her of Switzerland, an old, time-tested democ
racy.

She smiled. "The most unimaginative, uninteresting peo
ple in the world, running their country with a sort of stupid
materialistic efficiency," she said. "What you Americans fail
to understand is that Europeans are an old people, trained to
the godhead. They have a monarchistic mentality. They need
kings and dictators."

"They have had both," I said.

"Fascism would have succeeded in Europe if you Ameri
cans hadn't destroyed it," the doctor said. She poised the tea
pot in mid-air, taking time to think. Then, pouring me a
second cup, she said, "The great American crime has been
the upsetting of the balance of European civilization. You
Americans have come to us with your capitalistic democracy
your passion for reform, and have destroyed the equilibrium
which has kept the simple people of Europe happy for hun
dreds of years."

I said it was my impression from reading Hauptmann
Zola, Dickens, and Tolstoy that the people of Europe had
known discontent, that the "equilibrium" had been destroyed
long before American influence.

"My dear fellow," said the doctor, dancing about the room like an excited child, "that's the mistake Americans always make. You simply can't understand the facts about Europe; you have no concept of European humanity. You can't comprehend the happiness of the Sicilian peasant who has his work, his fornication, his giving of birth, and his religion. Didn't you see them last night in their holy procession? They were living by their emotions and they were happy. Give them more than that and you take away their happiness."

"I can hardly believe," I said, "that the peasant who carries rocks on his back to terrace vineyards for his landlord twelve hours a day is happy, even if he does have ten hours to eat pasta, sleep, fornicate, and give birth."

"You Americans are so naïve," the doctor said. "Always wanting to reform everything to your own corrupted, materialistic concepts. You can't see that the moment you make a materialist out of a simple man he is no longer happy. The most unhappy and troublesome people in the world are the unionized working classes of Germany, England, and America. They are bored with their leisure and they don't know how to spend their money. That is the great danger—teaching men without intellect to live by the intellect. It is the error of America, which has very little intellect and believes it can live by it. Not only live by it but rule the world by it."

"Obviously you do not understand Americans at all, or you would know that the idea of world rule is repugnant to them," I said.

But the doctor was now far too absorbed in her own dialectics to listen. She went on. "The only possible good that could have come out of the last war would have been if America and Germany had found each other and America had helped unite Europe under the strong leadership of Hitler."

I stood up. Since I couldn't enter into a reasonable discussion with the doctor I decided to withdraw. She stepped toward me and continued. "Because of America's blunder her

immediate fate is to become an imperialistic, world-dominat
ing power. America's century will be the century of civil wars
The era of democracy in the world is over. Only in America
it is dying a slower death than elsewhere. In my play Caliban
will bring the world the bloodiest century it has ever known
Of course, America will win many of her wars, but she wil
have sown nothing but hatred and she will reap the abundan
harvest of her sowings. Hitler was never as hated as America
will be. In the end, America will lose, and the world will be
free of her tyranny."

We were at the door of the apartment.

"The country that will eventually rule the world is a coun
try with a sense of direction, a strong political philosophy
and a feeling of certainty about itself. Russia has these things
There is no hope for anything else."

I had to ask the doctor one question before I left. "Are these
the things you teach your students?"

She smiled patronizingly, as if she were talking to a child
"Naturally, when the subject comes up," she said. "Don't you
agree that we educators owe our students the truth?"

"You must be very unhappy to be alive," I said.

"On the contrary," she replied, the lights dancing in her
eyes. "I'm enjoying it. It's going to be the biggest show on
earth. I wouldn't miss it for anything. We can do nothing to
avert it, so for intellectuals there is only one possible attitude
Don't you know what it is?"

I was on my way out.

"It's what Nietzsche calls 'the divine acceptance of our
fate,' " the doctor called after me.

Late that night I went to the Easter Mass in the cathedral
The town was dark, but the white cross of La Madonna dell
Rocca cast its luminous glow far out to sea. The church was
filled. The Monsignor, in still another set of vestments, was
casual and businesslike. At the stroke of midnight light

flooded the sanctuary, the cloths of mourning dropped from the statues and pictures, and the bells of the town rang out. Ilario, Como, and the other young bloods of the town piously received communion, their eyes closed, their hands folded.

Outside I heard tom-toms. I followed their sound down the hill to The Club, where musicians beat out the rhythm on jungle drums, gourds, tambourines, and castanets. The musicians shrieked and the crowd screamed in response. I saw the Countess from Copenhagen, Gilg Mann, and Carolyn, the American student on her junior year abroad. Carolyn was disgruntled and alone at the end of the bar. She was smoking in quick, angry puffs, drinking too fast, and mumbling to herself. Her long hair was drawn back in a ponytail and her décolleté dress revealed a well-proportioned figure.

"The sonofabitch!" I heard her say. My eyes followed hers into the next room, where Gino, her lover of a week, was dancing with a flaxen-haired girl.

"He met her on the beach this afternoon," she said. "He says for Easter he must have a blonde."

I offered my sympathies.

"Someone told him she was an heiress," Carolyn said, emptying her glass.

I bought her another Scotch and asked her what she was studying in Taormina. As an educator, I was interested in knowing how she was spending her junior year abroad.

"I'm not here officially," she said. "Officially I'm in Paris. But I have my travel allowance. Girls," she added significantly, "can travel much cheaper than men. I've been in Switzerland and Holland and Denmark," she said. "The Italian men are the most exciting. They're also the biggest bastards."

What was it she said she was studying?

"We don't really study," Carolyn said. "We work on projects. I am writing a paper on Diane de Poitiers."

A gust of sea wind lashed through the open window. Shutters were drawn and candles were lighted in the wall brackets. A sturdy, blond young man entered the bar. "Are you Swedish?" Carolyn asked him.

He replied he was a Norwegian.

"Do you build ships?" Carolyn asked.

The youth said he didn't, that he was a student on his spring holiday, and he wondered why she thought he built ships.

"Well, of course, everyone in Norway builds ships," Carolyn said. "I never quite know whether I like Norwegian or Italian men best. They're both nice and very different, you know."

He asked her to dance, and she guided him into the other room to show Gino that she too could get a blond for Easter.

I was alone in the bar. A shadow play of figures leaped across the walls. It was a procession: the musicians led their screaming followers in a conga line, in and out of the rooms, under the piano, up the stairs, and into the upper chambers.

I left without knowing where or how it ended. Outside, the electricity was off and the town was dark. I had been under the impression that the dousing of the lights and lighting of the candles was part of the night's festivities. Now I saw that there had been a storm, unnoticed inside because of the drums. Water was running in the gutters. Branches hung low on the trees, and the ground was covered with leaves and broken petals. I made my way through the deserted town, losing myself in the tiny streets. I lit my cigarette lighter, but the wind blew it out. The mountain rumbled softly and the sky to the south glowed as lightning still streaked across the cone of Etna. Ahead of me a huddle of adolescent boys jeered at a drunk leaning against a wall. "I am a poor man," he wailed. I recognized him as a habitué of The Club. One of the boys pushed him. He fell to the pavement, curled up and wept to himself while the boys kicked and shouted obscenities. They gave him a final kick and started noisily down the street. The largest of the group was one of the younger disciples of the Last Supper and the foot washing.

The sea was turning coral. A nightingale sang his farewell to the night. A cloud of steam spiraled lazily over Etna, and on the ledge above the town the white granite cross glowed serenely in the first light of Easter morning.

Near the Mediterraneo I met a fisherman on his way home from his night's work. He was barefoot and had a sack of fish over his shoulder.

"Cristu arrivisciu," he said.

"Christ is risen," I replied.

EASTER IN THE WEST

"The Mediterranean peoples . . . valued emotion for its own sake and sought ecstatic states in which the individual felt himself to be possessed and in some sense united with the deity. They were profoundly impressed by those crises of human existence which arouse the emotions most (conception, birth, and death) and built their religion about these. Their most important deity was still the earth mother, embodying the reproductive principle."

—RALPH LINTON, *The Tree of Culture*
(Alfred A. Knopf, Inc.)

CHAPTER 1

INVASION

RETURNING a later spring for Easter in the west of Sicily, I found the most overrun island of the Mediterranean world in the throes of a new invasion. The noisy army pushing in from the north was not an army of soldiers but an army of politicians.

When I arrived in Palermo by Italian Airlines, Sicily's parliamentary election was still two months off, but the most vociferous campaign in its political history was well under way. Almost nine hundred candidates for ninety assembly seats were combing the island for votes. The big excitement was being whipped up not from the capital of Palermo but from Rome. To Sicily came more than a thousand men, including cabinet ministers and Premier Mario Scelba himself, who let no one forget he was the son of a Sicilian sharecropper. Almost ten billion lire flowed into the island to cover the costs of the battle.

Since 1948 Sicily had been a semiautonomous region of the Italian Republic. Actually, nothing that might happen in this particular election could change a single deputy or senator in the parliament at Rome.

Then why, people outside of Italy were asking, all the fuss?

Since the last Sicilian election in 1951 the Christian Democrats and the Communist-Socialist bloc had been evenly balanced with thirty assembly seats each. Two years later an Italian general election brought to Rome a similarly balanced parliament, which, under Premier Scelba, turned into a sterile, do-nothing government.

The importance of the Sicilian voting to Rome was both prophetic and practical—prophetic because it was to be the first major indication in two years of the strength or weakness of the principal parties; practical because a solid Christian Democrat victory in Scelba's native Sicily would strengthen the premier's power and bolster his government. Anything less would ultimately mean a reorganized government and a new premier.

Posters appeared on every wall. "Eight years of accomplishment," proclaimed the Christian Democrats. The boasts were not idle. Controlling the assembly in coalition with Monarchists and small center parties, the Christian Democrats had inaugurated land reform. Through the Cassa per Il Mezzogiorno (Southern Fund), they had begun extensive industrial and agrarian aid with gifts and loans from America and the World Bank. Sicily had 8,500 new schoolrooms, 3,026 kilometers of new highways, 131,000 rooms in new housing, water systems for 247 towns, new factories and hydroelectric projects, and new luxury hotels for tourists. "Look around you," shouted the Christian Democrat campaigners.

On Communist posters a sinister Uncle Sam in top hat and striped trousers sat on an oil drum. "Stop the American trusts stealing our oil," they said. "Sicilian oil for the Sicilians." The oil issue was the most explosive of the campaign. Unlike the Rome government, which prohibited private and foreign development of Italian oil, Sicily's government was permitting American companies to develop her oil fields. Sicilians hoped that the four hundred tons of medium-quality petro-

leum being pumped daily at Ragusa would lead to untold
wealth for the island. Communist senators who had voted in
favor of American capital were now reversing their position
for political reasons. Communist speakers also asked, "Have
you benefited from the land reform?" and "What has the
government done for the unemployed?" a pertinent question
for at least five hundred thousand unemployed Sicilians.

Skillful as they were with their sophistries, the strategists
on both sides were aware of the fact that Sicily's politics are
inextricably involved with such fundamental problems as:

1. A teeming population of almost five million people,
one tenth of which is totally unemployed.

2. Deforestation and erosion of the mountainous country-
side to such an extent that only sections in the north and east
are productive.

3. The huge feudal estates whose productiveness would be
cut by dividing the land into smaller, less economic units.

4. Poor communications and power supplies.

5. Sulphur mines operated by such primitive methods that
prices must be almost twice as high as those for American
sulphur.

6. The never-ending yearning to emigrate, frustrated by
closed doors almost everywhere, especially in the U.S.A.

7. Widespread illiteracy and lack of special skills.

8. Deep barriers of caste and class and an age-old tradition
of organized banditry as a short cut to social justice.

Though they were keenly aware of all these problems,
speakers for the most part kept to local issues and personalities. It was the only way they knew to appeal to illiterate
voters, who were going to be confronted with a ballot complex enough to baffle a political scientist.

In the background, mighty and unrelenting as Etna, stood
the Church. The Communists reviled the Church and its
clergy and the Christian Democrats recruited Church and

priests in their campaign. Both knew that the Church, far from being blameless for the state of social despair and ignorance, had prevented a Sicilian landslide to Communism.

In squalid piazzas over the island the unemployed, roused from their slumbers in the sun, enjoyed the northern visitors. The Sicilians were attentive listeners. They argued endlessly among themselves but gave few clues as to what they were really thinking. Long used to being the ignored stepchildren of Rome, they made the most of their moment of glory. They weren't forgetting an earlier invasion from Rome which Mario Scelba, then Minister of the Interior, had directed— an invasion of soldiers to flush out like a fox Salvatore Giuliano. The score with Sicilian-born Scelba had never been settled. The drama that was now building to a climax was deeply rooted.

CHAPTER 2

THE LONG WALTZ

IT WAS WEDNESDAY of Holy Week. Palermo was choking under the purple plumes and purple scent of wisteria. A friend pulled one of the tiny blossoms apart to show me the hand of Christ—five tiny stamen fingers buried in each flower— which he said was the springtime miracle of the wisteria.

If the town wasn't to suffocate under the flowers it certainly would under the abundance of the food. Although Sicilians make no great effort to observe Lenten fasting, the end of it is greeted with the biggest orgy of eating in the entire year. Shop windows were loaded with Easter hams and cheeses, cakes in the traditional shape of a dove, and chocolate eggs. The Resurrection egg reaches the height of fantasy in Palermo. Eggs were gilded with gold and silver, and lavishly beribboned. Some had cupid-doll faces and some were hollow and filled with toys. One had a gold clock inside. They ranged from ordinary chicken size to fifteen kilos of chocolate on a pedestal costing twenty thousand lire. I wondered with a shudder who would consume this fantasia of sugar and chocolate which covered the city. Since prices were high, it obviously would be the rich. I had seen their pampered children riding in the open carriages on the *corso* with their fat mothers. Gazing dark-eyed out of their white bunny furs, they appeared soft and pale as maggots. No wonder, eating all those sweets. The thought made me sick at the stomach.

Far more interesting were the paschal lambs. These toylike symbols of Christ made from sugar have been developed into a unique art form. Flocks of ten or more lambs with a shepherd appeared on the tops of pastries, in a flower garden of colored sugar, or among some brightly tinted chickens. There were lambs in all sizes and shapes. Lambs of brown sugar had tiny chocolate hoofs and dainty pink noses. Other long-necked, elegant sheep had bright green feathers between their hoofs. Most of them wore a tiny gold bell and an insipid expression; all had a red spot under the neck to represent the blood of the Crucifixion.

"Do you speak English?"

Standing beside me was a merry-eyed, beaming-faced blond fellow in grease-smeared levis. Assuming he was one of the watch salesmen or confidence operators so common in Italian port cities, I took a cool position.

"I was wondering if you would show me the way to the post office," he said. His accent was so unmistakably cockney that I started to laugh. "Got to buy a stamp for a letter to my missus," he said.

I walked with him toward the post office, listening while he talked. He couldn't have been more than twenty. He was a seaman on an English merchant ship returning from the Adriatic. "Haven't written the missus for four weeks," he said. "Guess she'll be wondering. Haven't seen her for three months. Staying here two days. My first time in Palermo. Maybe you know if there's anything doing here. Women, I'm referring to. Course you can't trust 'em. In Teneri (he pronounced it *Tenereeee*) I met this girl, just as pretty as you could paint. Do you know it, from her I got the works? Gonorrhea, syphilis, and lice. You know when that happens it kinda takes the glory off."

I agreed that such things, especially in combination, might take the glory off.

"She cost me twelve bob. I had to get the doc to shoot me full of penicillin. Took quite a lot to clean me out. We always carry a big supply. Can never tell. You hit a good town you don't need a bit of it, but get into a place like Tenereeee, we need quite a lot. Mighty handy thing, penicillin."

He bought a sixty-lire stamp and I offered to show him where to mail the letter.

"Haven't got it written yet," he said, pocketing the stamp. "Can never tell. Might have time to write it tonight. Didn't have time in Naples. Women crowding right down to the quay in Naples. When women do that, you might say it takes the bloom off the rose. Well, cheerio!"

He left me by still another paschal window. These lambs lay prostrate in death. Bright scarlet sugar blood spurted from their severed necks and lay spattered over the sweetness of the cakes.

In the morning I took the train to Trapani for the Holy Friday *Processione dei Misteri*. A "procession of the mysteries" is part of the Holy Week celebration in almost every Sicilian community; but in Caltanisetta, in the sulphur-mining heart of Sicily, and Trapani, on the western coast, the processions are famous. From what I could learn in Palermo the two are equally spectacular. I chose Trapani because it was easier to get there.

Trapani is a noisy seaport beneath Aphrodite's rampart of Erice. It was dry and dusty. An African wind turned the Dutch windmills peculiar to this part of Sicily, and white sails wafted like butterflies on the bright sea. Disastrously bombed during the war, Trapani is only now rising from its ruins with a frenzy of building. As I wandered through vast areas of rubble, I became more and more depressed. I nursed my despair in a taproom and was well into my second bottle of bad Sicilian beer when someone spoke to me.

"Excuse me. I think you must speak English."

The young man was tall, with the flashing eyes and jet hair of a Spaniard. His white skin and conservative and expensive clothes told me he was well born; his soft voice and tentative but correct English that he was well educated.

"I would be honored if you would let me buy you a drink," he said.

I invited him to sit down.

"I have thought that you might be American," he said. "I would welcome the opportunity of talking with someone in American. If you please, you will correct me whenever I speak a mistake. It is important that I speak very correctly. You see I am soon to visit Pittsburgh. Do you have familiarity with Pittsburgh?"

I had indeed. I replied that for five years I had been a newspaperman in Pittsburgh.

"My name is Gerardo Tuerretta. I must make this trip to Pittsburgh to study the moral position of my future wife."

I had thought him a little pompous but now he seemed absurd. I burst out laughing. His black eyes filled with embarrassment and I realized he was hurt.

"If you would be married," he said, "you must live all the life alone with a woman and that is a very serious thing."

Indeed, I replied, it was.

"I met my fiancée last year in Trapani. She came to Sicily on a holiday with her parents. We became very much in love. She asked me if I would marry her. I said, 'Yes, I like you, so we can be married.' My father whom I love very much told her she must come to Trapani to live. You see, I am the only son of my father, who is old, and he does not want me to part from him. He is a merchant of wine and naturally if I stay with him I have a very good future. Here in Trapani I am rich, whereas in America I would be poor. My fiancée is agreeable. She said she will come to marry here.

"But my father and I have been having uneasy thoughts.

Here in Sicily marriage is a very important thing. It is necessary that a girl be pure. I have heard that in America it is not
important that girls be pure. I see that in your films girls are
very free. It would naturally break my father's heart if I were
to marry with a girl who is not pure. That is why I must make
sure. I must go to Pittsburgh to study the moral position of
my fiancée. It is very important."

How, I asked, did he propose to make this study?

"First I will see how she lives and who are her friends. In
this way I will learn a lot. If I have any doubts, then it becomes a matter somewhat delicate to establish her purity. If
necessary a doctor must be consulted."

As Gerardo spoke my eyes rested uneasily on an unmistak-
able bulge in the sleek line of his jacket. "I have a permit to
carry a gun," he said. "Sometimes I go into the country at
night and there are dogs and bad people."

From somewhere across town we heard the wail of horns.
"The Madonna del Popolo is coming out of her church,"
Gerardo said. "Come. Let us go. I should be happy if you
would permit me to accompany you as your guide. I will be
well repaid if you will speak with me in English."

As we pushed through the crowded streets I marveled at
my good fortune. It was dusk. Everything seemed to be in
flames as the red sun, sinking into the sea, sent its dying rays
over the town. A sharp excitement was in the air. The town
which had seemed so languid and empty an hour before was
filled with moving people.

"The mourning Madonna will move through the streets on
the shoulders of the *fruttivendoli* [fruit vendors]. She will seek
her son who has been arrested," Gerardo said. "It is a cause
for great excitement and sadness because all the people wish
for her to find him. But of course she does not."

In a small market square we passed a Moorish tent richly
lined in red. Inside on a throne of jewels, surrounded with
flowers and flickering candles, was a Madonna. "That is the

Madonna from the Church of the Purgatory," said Gerardo.
"Last night on the shoulders of the *facchini* [porters] she
searched the town for *her* son. Of course she did not find him
either."

It was confusing. I had to remember that while each
Madonna was a representation of the Mother of Jesus, each
had a personality and life of her own, quite independent of
that of her sister Madonnas. I also reminded myself that the
procession of mysteries was not to begin until the next day at
two o'clock. These little processions were merely preliminary
affairs to warm up the populace for the big event.

Night fell quickly and a cold wind blew through the streets.
All the women and many of the men wore black, adding to
the darkness. The music, which was growing louder, was
both macabre and droll; a lugubrious funeral march played
in fast dance tempo.

Suddenly at a corner we came face to face with the Madonna
of the People. She was in a glass shadow box, covered with
beads, brooches, watches, and rings; she rode on a catafalque
covered with arum lilies and carnations and illuminated by
fifty candles one meter high. Two great poles bent and
creaked on the shoulders of eight fruit vendors, identically
dressed in blue denim coveralls and flat caps with pompons,
like French sailors. In the candlelight their faces glistened
with sweat.

The Madonna was accompanied by the wailing band, little
boys in black and little girls in white carrying torches and
black banners, and chanting women cloaked in mourning.
"They are the mothers who help the Madonna in her search
and weep with her," Gerardo said. The end of the parade
was secular: vendors pushing carts loaded with nuts and
sweets, and men with clusters of multicolored balloons.

The procession moved in spurts, for the fruit vendors ran
their heavy burden for a hundred feet or so and then rested.
"It is easier than to carry her steadily," Gerardo said. This,

more than anything, made the spectacle a terrifying one. The carriers, keeping time with the unearthly music, trotted in a sort of jig so that the Madonna rocked and swayed heavily from side to side, like a dancing circus elephant. With every lunge forward the dark-robed women ran sobbing after the Madonna as if she were the lost one and they the searchers. Several fruit vendors with collection boxes gathered money from the crowds on the streets. If the contribution was a liberal one the Madonna turned slowly to bow to the donor. The carriers in the front had to kneel to bring this about.

When the Madonna passed a wineshop the fruit vendors set her carefully on the pavement facing the establishment and went inside to have a beer. The women and children chattered noisily as they waited with the Madonna outside. From the rear came the shrill negotiations of the balloon vendors and the sellers of nuts and candy.

Slowly the Madonna progressed through the town. There was something compulsive about her. Perhaps it was the terrifying effect of the music and the candles. At any rate one could not let go of her. Fishermen coming in from the sea followed her with their lamps and the crowd grew. As she approached the tent of her sister of Purgatory, the tension mounted; the people became hushed and solemn, and the wailing horns rose toward a climax. "When the two ladies meet, that is a dramatic moment," said Gerardo.

It was, and I'm not sure why. The People's Madonna stopped before the Moorish tent with its red and gold awnings and turned to face the Madonna of the Purgatory. There she swayed and rocked, bowing coyly, rolling from side to side, mincing back and forth without changing position. "She is greeting the Purgatory Madonna," said Gerardo.

There was something so suspenseful about her waggling that I broke into a sweat. She seemed a woman undecided what to do. This meeting of the two mothers in the windswept candle gloom was a black parody of the sunlit Tuscan

Visitations of Giotto and Angelico. Eventually the People's Madonna bowed with ultimate graciousness to the Madonna of the Purgatory and continued on her way. "She will continue her search until midnight," said Gerardo. "Then both Madonnas will return sorrowfully to their churches."

We walked toward the harbor, where the moon was rising full into the heavens and turning the sea to silver. Gerardo was back on the problems of his engagement. "If we were to marry, my wife would have to come to live here," he said. "It would be impossible that I leave my mother."

I was beginning to understand the search, the meaning of the two mothers combing the night for lost sons. In Sicily every mother is a Madonna; every son a *Cristo*.

The next day Gerardo came early to indoctrinate me in the procession of the mysteries.

"The clergy have little to do with it," he said. "It is organized by the *ceti*, or trade guilds, which began the *processione* in the sixteenth century. Each guild presents one event from the Passion of Christ and the life of Mary. In the beginning the scenes were enacted by living men as they are still done today in Marsala. A feud developed in Marsala several years ago between the Christ and one of the Roman soldiers taking Him to the Crucifixion. The Christ was angry because the Roman soldier pulled the rope too tightly. After several stops in wineshops, the Christ drew a knife from his robe and threatened to stab the Roman soldier. The *carabinieri* had to calm the Christ before the procession could continue."

Since the seventeenth century the Trapani guilds, like those at Caltanissetta, parade realistic statue groups built of wood and sculptured in *cartapista*, a combination of glue and papier-mâché which gives the figures a hard, stonelike finish. During the year the groups served as Stations of the Cross in Trapani's Church of St. Michael. The church was bombed

during the war and two of the groups were destroyed. One
has been reconstructed by Professor Domenico Li Muli, a
Trapani sculptor who takes care of the groups. The other,
portraying the Crucifixion, was still being built by Professor
Li Muli and had, since the war, been absent from the procession. Eighteen of the twenty are from the original seven-
teenth-century groups. Today the groups are stored in the
old Church of the Collegio, where religious services are no
longer held. The groups and their sponsors are:

Separation of Jesus from His mother	Jewelers
Washing of the Disciples' feet	Fishermen
Jesus in the garden of Geth-semane	Fruit growers
Jesus' Arrest	Blacksmiths
Jesus collapses by the River Cedron	Sailors
Jesus under judgment	Fruit vendors
Denial of Peter	Barbers
Jesus before Herod	Fish vendors
Flagellation	Stonemasons
Crown of thorns	Millers and bakers
"Ecce homo!"	Shoemakers
Sentence by Pilate	Butchers
Climb to Calvary	The people of Trapani
Disrobing	Wine-barrel makers
Crucifixion (not in procession)	Carpenters
Spear thrust	Ropemakers
Deposition	Tailors
Journey to the tomb	Saltworkers
Jesus in the sepulchre	Spaghetti and maca-roni workers
Weeping Virgin	Waiters and chauffeurs

The procession ends with the weeping Madonna searching interminably for her son. Because the search must take her over every street of the city, the long hide-and-seek continues without interruption for more than twenty hours. "Does she find him at the end or doesn't she?" I asked.

"That is the everlasting mystery," said Gerardo. "Every year people argue the same problem. Some say she does; some say she doesn't. No one is sure."

We went to the Church of the Collegio in the heart of the town. At the door a guard was fighting back the crowds to keep them from entering. With a word from Gerardo we were permitted to pass. Inside, flowers were piled everywhere. Orange marigolds, white lilies, roses and carnations, fruit blossoms, iris, tulips, paradise flowers—all lay in stacks like hay. The workers of Trapani were weaving them into blankets, canopies, and every manner of arrangement with which to decorate their statue groups. Gerardo told me it was traditional to award prizes to the guilds for the most beautiful floral decorations as well as for the liveliest dancing of the groups through the street.

The statues were dramatic, the faces filled with anguish or cruelty. Except for the figures of Christ, which were fair in coloring, they were of a dark, African and Moorish cast. The Roman soldiers were men of pomp, glistening with silver and feathers like Paladins in the puppet plays. There was a profusion of silver. Swords were of silver, the column of the flagellation was silver and so was the cross. Each group was supplied with scores of candles, some thick enough to require four wicks. In addition, the groups were wired for electricity, with huge storage batteries hidden in the iron scaffolding underneath. A workman said each group weighed up to eight hundred kilos and took twelve men to carry it.

Burning wax had fouled the air in the church and the heavy odor of flowers was nauseating. We pressed through the crowded streets to the sea front. The day was sunny but windy

and cold. Great waves beat against the quay and on the espla-
nade the tall palms crackled as if they were laden with icicles.
The multicolored clusters of balloons threatened to lift the
vendors into the heavens. We followed the sea to Gerardo's
home, the Villa Nespoli. From the street we entered through
a heavily bolted gate set in a solid stone wall. We walked
through shaded rooms with mosaicked floors of eighteenth-
century fishing scenes, into a cloistered garden of tropical
lushness. On one side colonnades opened on the sea. There
at a table set under a hibiscus tree, Gerardo and I were served
a pleasant lunch of fish and veal and an assortment of vegetables and greens. For dessert we picked the fruits of medlar
trees in the garden. We were alone; Gerardo's parents had
gone to their house in the country for the day. With a touch
of snobbishness, Gerardo said, "The *processione* does not
greatly interest people of culture. Only the poor care deeply
about it."

Two hours later we walked to the Santuario dell' Annunzi-
ata, the church of Trapani's patroness Madonna. The statue
was in the Pisan style, gentle and lovely. Except for heavy
gold crowns on the heads of both mother and child it had a
Hellenic purity and was the most pleasing madonna statue
I had seen in Sicily. Like her sisters in Tyndari and Cagliari,
like Aphrodite up on Erice, the Trapani Madonna is believed
to have been washed in by the sea. Gerardo told me the story.

"Some sailors on a ship saw a box floating on the sea. The
weather was very strong. The sailors caught the box and
opened it. They saw the statue of Our Lady, and they all
noticed the great art of it. As the sea was very stormy, the
sailors begged Our Lady to still the tempest. At once the sea
became quiet. When the ship reached the port of Trapani
the sailors took Our Lady into their city with the intention
to build a large church for her. They put Our Lady on a
wooden cart pulled by six oxen and drove her to the place
they had decided to construct the church. Then the sailors

tried to stop the oxen. But it was impossible—the oxen would not stop. The sailors failed in many efforts to stop the oxen. By this time the sailors knew that the oxen were influenced by Our Lady, because she had a mind to have her church constructed in a particular place of her choice. As soon as the oxen reached this spot where the church now stands, they stopped. The sailors tried to make the oxen move on. But the oxen refused to continue farther. Since it was impossible to make the oxen go on, the people built this church in the place where the oxen stopped."

From his impassioned telling of the story, I knew that Gerardo believed it in every detail.

The procession had begun at two and it was now four. Walking down the Via Fardella we heard its trumpets in the distance, and then we saw it swaying toward us through the dusty afternoon like a caravan in the desert. Leading it were forty figures in bright scarlet robes, their white hoods slit at the eyes. They carried flaming torches. The sight of the procession struck a terror such as only masked unknown figures can. It reminded me of the Ku Klux Klan cross-burnings of my Wisconsin childhood. These hooded men were members of a *confraternita*, a secret society harking back to medieval times. No procession ever moved so slowly or in such curious spurts. The men carrying groups bolted with them for a hundred feet or so and then stopped to rest. Each group of carriers was directed by a captain with a *ciaccola*, a castanetlike wooden clacker with which he controlled their movements. A set of auxiliary carriers in each group rattled coin boxes and begged money from the public. To a generous donor the carriers turned and bowed their statues.

Each group was preceded by a band of twenty-four or more instruments, the largest belonging to the *muratori* (stonemasons), who, in the fever of Trapani building, had become the most prosperous guild in town. Their great bass drum, riding on the back of a small boy, had printed on it in large letters, JAZZ. Bands blared a variety of melodies, including funeral marches from Puccini, Toselli, and Lombardi, and pieces entitled "Weeping Virgin," "The War Dead," "To the Memory of a Valorous Major," "The Gravediggers," and a popular one played by several bands, *Povero Fiore*, or "Poor Flower," in honor of the suffering Virgin. All the bands played in the same slow waltz tempo.

Behind each band marched a black-robed guard of some twenty men. The guards were captained by two standard-bearers, a man and a small boy, both of whom danced in slow motion on the alternate beat, two steps front and one step back.

The combined effect of all this was one of excruciating melancholy. Still there was a counterpoint of gaiety and high spirits among the guild carriers. They were for the most part impious younger men who were still full of animal spirits. They were dressed alike in blue denim coveralls and hats with pompons; many wore the felt and gum shoes worn throughout southern Italy, where leather is expensive. During rests they leaned on their statues and puffed on cigarettes, or reached underneath the statues for a straw-covered bottle of wine which they passed among themselves. Like the dice-throwing soldiers at the foot of the cross, or the impish Serpotta cherubs in the Palermo oratories, they made a merry game of the Crucifixion.

Especially was this true of their dancing. It had a rocking, jungle sensuousness that was like slow-motion jitter-bugging. Gerardo said the movement was a Sicilian hop known as *anmacata*, which was carefully rehearsed for the occasion. The result was a most unseemly jigging of the tragic Crucifixion figures riding on the men's shoulders. As time passed I even became accustomed to the Christ bouncing in his glass coffin. But I never failed to be startled by the *Ecce Homo* Christ, hands bound before Him, naked except for a breechcloth and the crown of thorns. The body, bent in anguish, seemed, each time I saw it, to be bowing to a lady, inviting her to the waltz.

The climax was the appearance of the weeping Madonna, a priestess symbolizing all mother-sorrow. Except for her sacred heart pierced by a dagger and a white handkerchief, she was undecorated. She rode above the crowd like a stark, black-robed Hecuba. But a handkerchief, of silk lace lovingly embroidered with the initial *M* and delicately hung from a little finger, gave her the air of a character in a Victorian melodrama.

She was followed by the sorrowing veiled women of the town, who had medallions of the Virgin pinned to their breasts. Many were old and barefoot, with feet caked by dust. Some wore black stockings worn through at the toes. "These are the penitents," Gerardo said. "To walk barefoot is to be humble. If they have strength to endure the night they will walk to the end." Some of the women carried children, and most of the grandmothers clutched the hand of a grandchild, who trotted alongside. At the end of it all came the colorful, lighthearted auxiliary procession, the balloon vendors fighting the wind for possession of their wares, the *noci* and *caramelle* carts decorated with bunting and pennants, and behind them a contingent of excited and happy children.

Though we did not see the procession again for eight hours, we never stopped hearing it. Most of the early evening it was crawling through the residential streets of the town. A timetable had been made public, and people were ready and waiting wherever it went. At midnight we climbed to the roof of a movie theater managed by one of Gerardo's friends. The new theater was set in a field of bombed rubble and jagged ruins which stood out in bold relief in the bright moonlight. The bands were amplified by the damp night air so that even streets and buildings seemed to be moaning. We caught glimpses of the candlelit procession winding in and out of the narrow little streets and once or twice we saw four or five fragments of it at a time, like the body of a snake coiling in and out the stones. About half an hour past midnight it advanced on to our street.

The torches and thousands of candles had made little impression in the sunlight of the afternoon. Now, in the wild and eerie night, with the city lights turned out, the character of the spectacle was completely changed. The flickering lights sent wild shadows leaping up and down the narrow canyons of the streets. People hung from balconies and windows, in intimate contact with the procession below. The red robes of the *confraternita* glowed like coals; their leader was carrying a cross. It was awesome and frightening.

By now the carriers of the statues had lost their buoyancy. They rested more frequently, almost every fifty feet, and leaned heavily on their burdens when they set them down. Advancing, they laid their arms on each other's shoulders and moved as a unit, rocking the statues gently as if they were putting them to sleep. And they danced. "It is necessary to dance to keep the blood going," said Gerardo. A small boy standard-bearer marching with his father staggered sleepily out of line. His father prodded him back into step with a candle. The black canopies covering the scaffolding underneath the statues were streaked with wax. So was the clothing of the carriers. Said Gerardo, "Wax is difficult to remove from clothing, so the people wear it proudly through the year to show they participated in the procession."

Seen from above, the statue faces appeared human and emotionally overwrought. In the deposition group the wind flapped a beautiful lace shawl around the dead Jesus, and the carriers extinguished some candles to keep it from going up in flames. I could see Jesus in His coffin wearing a watch and chain; the white lilies trembled about the corpse like ghosts. The carriers of the weeping Madonna had put on red robes and white turbans. Waltzing by us into an area of rubble and ruin, the Madonna might have been Persephone entering hell. Mourning women and barefoot grandmothers stumbled silently behind her, while the money gatherers clanked their cans and harvested a shower of coins and notes from roofs and windows.

I had a question which had been bothering me throughout the night. "Whose *festa* is Easter?" I asked. "Mary's or Jesus'?" Gerardo didn't hesitate. "It is a *festa* for both," he said. "But of course it is her son who was crucified and is resurrected."

There it was. *Her son* was crucified, not *Jesus*. The emotions being aroused were not sympathy for his agonies but sympathy for the suffering of bereaved motherhood.

"It was very inconsiderate of Jesus to get himself crucified and bring such anguish on His mother," Gerardo said. "At least many people think so. They will say to you He was a little *pazzo* [crazy]. One who could work miracles could easily have saved Himself. However," Gerardo added with deep piety, "that is not the way I think."

Since it was now three o'clock, Gerardo said good night and I went to my hotel. But the bands wailed on and sleep was impossible. So I put my clothes back on and followed the sounds. The procession was moving along Via Torrearsa toward the Piazza Marina. I ran down a parallel street to meet it head on. People were leaning wearily against buildings; frightened cats leaped in the direction of the harbor. I cut back to the Via Torrearsa and found myself in the fishermen's quarter. At the far ends of a street I saw two large electric signs: PAX and INRI. The occasion had flushed out all the variables of humanity. Hunchbacks and cripples huddled next to mothers with nursing babies. A befurred infant of two jigged to the approaching music. Other children slept on the pavement like corpses. Women in chenille robes and children rolled in blankets looked down from the roofs.

The procession was staggering at a snail's pace now, taking long, silent rests. A boy ran to the rescue of the barbers with several liters of wine. The fishermen entered a tavern to get their own. They drank so long and deeply they held up the procession. Other groups followed their example, and the ropemakers' standard-bearer leaned his cross against a barrel. The wineshops had become the Stations of the Cross.

Some of the bands were stumbling silently along and there was less music. The saltworkers drank from bottles as they moved. One of the fruit growers fell to the pavement; his friends hoisted him up. Women dropped hard-boiled eggs into carriers' gullets like birds feeding nestlings. The silver teeth of the men flashed in the candle glow; their black hair was matted with candle wax. The tiny standard-bearer who had slept four hours earlier was back in waltz step with his father. Little girls wore pink and blue sweaters over their white angels' dresses to keep warm, and the exhausted, barefoot grandmothers leaned on the Madonna to keep from falling. Behind the peanut carts, which were lit up with colored electric bulbs, a brass band was trying to catch up. The musicians had stopped too long in a wineshop and were playing somewhat livelier than usual.

I walked through the town, past movie houses which stayed open all night, noisy cafés, and wineshops. Cafés featured great bowls of hard-boiled eggs, which the people were eating in quantity. Men sang songs. Business was good.

Over the sea dawn was breaking. On the quay fish nets were piled high. Cats, confused by the night-long excitement, still scurried about. Two young men bargained with a prostitute. I could hear the strains of "Poor Flower" echoing over the town and a church clock striking six.

An hour later Gerardo arrived at my hotel refreshed by sleep and a bath. My room had a balcony over the Corso Vittorio Emanuele, the street of the Church of the Collegio, where the procession would end. "The *processione* is finished when the Madonna enters those doors," Gerardo said. "There is always suspense whether or not she will enter by ten-thirty so that the celebration of Easter can begin at noon. Almost every year she is late. Today she is already an hour behind schedule."

The town glittered and the music blew loud against the deep and steady drums. The street below was choked with people, for the population, spread over the city in the night, was now concentrated outside the Collegio Church for the climax of the mysteries. The procession approached from the upper end of the street. The carriers were stumbling only short distances, for the pavements, now coated with candle drippings, were as slippery and perilous as ice. During the long rests the men collapsed on the stones or leaned prostrate on their poles. Their faces were as anguished and tortured as those of the statues they carried. The candles which had brought such brillance to the night, in the sunlight gave only thin spirals of smoke. Ragged children skidded excitedly over the pavements, harvesting wax which hung like stalactites from the statues; it would be salvaged to light the nights of the poor.

So slowly did the procession move that the final thousand feet took four hours. Each guild spent a quarter of an hour carrying its group into the church. Exhausted though they were, the men were reluctant to relinquish their burden. As they approached the church they seemed to tap new wells of energy, like athletes entering the final heat. The bands, all playing different tunes, shook the city like Joshua's trumpets, and a frightened dog, caught in the frenzy, broke through the crowd with a yelp of terror and disappeared. The money-gatherers rattled their cans and brought down a blizzard of currency.

For the carriers it was the last opportunity to compete for the prizes. As each group approached the church steps the men went into an ecstasy of dance. The praying Jesus of Gethsemane, the bloody Jesus of the flagellation, Jesus on the cross, and Jesus dead in His casket—all swayed and bowed, protesting their return to darkness with a final orgy of waltz.

Through the hours of waiting the standard-bearers continued their own curious footwork. Carrying the stonemasons' flag was a golden-haired youth of twenty whose black bow tie and long black gloves had become spotted with wax. Without moving from the spot where he stood, he solemnly kept on dancing, one step front, one step to the side, and a third step back, never smiling, always watching his knee as he crooked it and his slippered toe tip as he pointed. With his eyes fixed lovingly on himself he seemed to be waltzing on a cloud. He reminded me of the narcissistic John the Baptist of the Agrigento museum.

People were anxiously consulting their watches; it was ten-thirty and the Madonna was not even approaching. Finally they saw her coming, the black figure bobbing over a sea of humanity. The blood-colored robes of her guard were clotted with wax and grime. The red-faced, swollen-eyed penitents who plodded behind her waved to friends like victorious athletes. Their number was small, and one who was young nursed an infant. The Madonna's candles flickered low, her lilies were encrusted with wax. A woman tore one off for a souvenir and then throngs of screaming women crushed forward to strip the flowers away. One woman fainted from the excitement. A screeching ambulance plowed through the human ocean like a ship.

For almost an hour the Madonna waited. At a given moment all the bands joined together with "Poor Flower" in lively Viennese tempo, one playing in a higher pitch and a full measure behind, providing an echo of the melody. The avalanche of sound was the signal that the Madonna was at the end of her search. Her carriers were ready on the steps. "This is her moment of indecision," Gerardo said. "She does not know whether to enter or not. She has searched for twenty-one hours and she is tired. If she knew her son were inside she would go, but she is not sure and she knows once she is inside she cannot come back out."

There could be no doubt in anyone's mind that she would enter as she had for the past three hundred years. But rationality had no part in this. I felt myself being caught up in the inexplicable and overwhelming suspense. Gerardo's brow was beaded with sweat, and I felt moisture on my own.

For several agonizing minutes the Madonna jigged and swayed outside the door. As she hesitated the music grew softer and softer until the drums were counting my heartbeats. She began a long to-and-fro movement, starting for the door and withdrawing, reaching closer each time. Below me the people were silent and breathless. It was like watching a human sacrifice. The Madonna swayed toward her fate, to a rhythm that was unabashedly erotic. The music finally faded away, like a wisp of smoke from one of the dying candles.

The world stopped. With a sudden, terrible thrust the Mother of God plunged into darkness. Persephone was swallowed by the underworld.

"*Ecco!*" Cries of relief everywhere. "She's in. It's done. *Così sia!*" As the church doors closed the bands struck up such a thunderous fortissimo of "Poor Flower" that the world could have waltzed to it.

In Gerardo's eyes there were tears.

"Did she find Him?" I asked.

He shrugged. "As you will," he said. "To some she finds Him and her entrance is a triumph; to others it is a defeat, like the closing of the door to a tomb. It is a procession of mystery. You may believe what you will."

The twenty-two hour ordeal was over. The crowd melted away so quickly that it seemed an hallucination.

"In Sicily Jesus rises from the tomb at noon on Saturday," Gerardo said. "The celebration of Easter begins in a half hour." In a tone of voice that was decidedly carping, he added, "The Madonna was an hour late."

CHAPTER 3

RESURRECTION

THE LONG CARAVAN winding up the mountain passes to the roof of Sicily was as brightly colored as holiday eggs. It was Easter morning, and the yellow Buicks, red Chevrolets, and black Humbers were racing through clouds to the Resurrection of Jesus Christ.

Their goal was a mountain village named Piana degli Albanesi. Ente Turismo posters in Palermo had announced in English: "10—Solemn Pontifical, S. Demetrius Cathedral; 12:30—Blessing and distribution of eggs; 16—ralley [*sic*] of costumes and execution of traditional songs." So it was not surprising that the pilgrims, tooting jubilantly to one another, were shouting back and forth in English. They were the British-American colony of Palermo; personnel from the consulates, professors and students, and tourists.

As the name suggests, this mountain town is a colony of 7,500 Albanians whose ancestors emigrated during the Turkish wars of the fifteenth century. For five centuries the people have retained their Albanian dialect and dress. Though their church is affiliated with Rome, they worship, with Vatican tolerance, in the Byzantine rites of the Orthodox faith. The colorful Easter service and the Albanesi women's holiday

273

dress, the most brilliant in Italy, have made Piana degli Albanesi Sicily's most fashionable place for an Easter pilgrimage. Since many of the pilgrims were diplomats, they were quite aware that Piana degli Albanesi is also one of the Communist centers of Sicily.

I made the ascent with George Tomaselli, a young American born of Sicilian parents in Hammond, Indiana, who was studying at the University of Palermo. Though he had a dark, Sicilian face, he was a first-generation American who, thanks to American nutrition, had grown like Indiana corn, taller than either of his parents. He told me he had come to Sicily to get over an inferiority complex.

"I have never in my life been comfortable with Anglo-Saxon Americans," he said. "I was always the wop kid, the foreigner who was not accepted. I was ashamed of being Sicilian because Sicilians were noisy and poor; otherwise they were gangsters. My parents were happy in their Italo-American societies and could not understand why I would not withdraw with them into their way of life. I could not be a Sicilian and I could not be an American. I guess I had the worst inferiority complex in the Great Lakes area.

"So I came to Sicily to find out about this island of my ancestors. I have seen Segeste and Agrigento and the paintings of Antonello. I have read *Orlando Furioso* and I have been to Monreale. Monreale was the big moment. There I felt the greatness of the culture which had produced me. I began to feel differently. I became proud of being Sicilian.

"I am still not quite comfortable in the company of Anglo-Saxons. But it will come. I think the problem of the first-generation American is his lack of roots. I have had to come back to find mine. I have learned to be a Sicilian and now for the first time am beginning to think of myself as an American."

We climbed through towns whose rows of miserable, windowless, one-room huts were overflowing with children and chickens. But rural poverty is never so stark as urban poverty. The morning was sweet with apple blossom and the granite mountains had a dolomitic grandeur. The growth on them was too sparse for sheep, but goats grazed on their thorny foliage.

George was telling me about Piana degli Albanesi. "Just like in an American city, Easter is a women's holiday, time for a fashion show. Only the fashions are those of Albania five hundred years ago. You will see women in the church but not many men. I don't suppose the people have heard of *Lysistrata,* but their politics are on sexual lines, anyway. The men, mostly agricultural workers and shepherds, are Communists; the women are Christian Democrats. Some women will not cook for their husbands and if they cook they will not eat with them because of politics. Still, the men are in the majority and Piana degli Albanesi has had a Communist government since the war."

On the plateau above the passes there were green meadows and a pastoral lake in which the government bred trout. Sheep grazed on its shores. At the head of the lake was the town. It was spankingly clean. Otherwise it was like every other mountain village, one broad main street with cobbled goat paths ascending and descending at right angles. Borders of blue paint around the doorways of the houses gave the town a fanciful appearance. The paint had a practical rather than an aesthetic purpose, for the people believe that blue repels houseflies. The main street was named Corso Giorgio Castriota Scanderbeg, after an Albanian national hero in the Turkish wars. Its widest part, a sort of piazza, was filled with tourists focusing cameras on the modest Cathedral St. Demetrius. "Cameras are an important part of a Piana degli Albanesi Easter," said George. "The town became famous when color film became popular."

For a week the women had shaded their Balkan-white skin, black hair, and eyes under black shawls, mourning the Crucifixion of Jesus with all the women of Sicily. For the Resurrection they were blossoming forth in all their glory. When the sun flashed on them climbing the cathedral steps they were as dazzling as Crivelli paintings of Venetian Madonnas.

The photographers waiting for them were not very successful. Gray clouds covered the sun, and since it was still early in the morning the women were shy and ran squealing into the church. To catch the natives one had to wander up and down the alleys behind the piazza. There they hovered like a strange species of shy bird, but with the genders reversed. The males in grays, browns, and blacks were a somber background to the brilliant female plumage.

Their dresses were made of heavy red, green, and burgundy fabrics richly embroidered in gold. Red or purple jackets were worn over white lace bodices; lace aprons covered the skirts. All wore shawls. The shawls of the older women were black or burgundy; for young women they were a uniform light blue, exactly the shade of the shawl worn by Antonello's Madonna in the Palermo museum. Affluent women wore small gold caps, called *keze*, and carried their shawls, called *mantelline*, on their arms. All women wore an abundance of jewelry, including great gold buckles decorated with images of St. George fighting the dragon, and an extravagance of necklaces, earrings, and bracelets. No two combinations of colors and jewels were quite alike.

The church was packed to the doors, but with the help of a public official who was the father of one of George's school friends, I was squeezed into a choir stall with some bearded, brown-robed old monks. George sat with the official in front of me. A girl from the American Consulate who followed us was sternly turned back because women were barred from the apse. My monks, obviously sanctified in soul, were much less concerned about bodily hygiene. Their odor was heavy and the hair that snarled about their faces, ears, and necks seemed to be filled with nests. It was rather like sitting between two Hungarian sheep dogs. George, fascinated by my companions, kept looking back and giggling. As the monks prayed ardently I began to itch on my right and left. George shook with suppressed laughter. He handed me a note which said that the man who had arranged our seats was the commissioner of sanitation and hygiene.

Our lack of reverence went unnoticed, for everything was as relaxed and noisy as a circus. The church itself had an air of gaiety and light that was appropriate to Easter. It was white and clean and simply decorated in blue and gold. There were no dark, dusty corners with glass coffins and saints' bones, no tasteless chalk saints. The atmosphere was filled with optimism and the joy of spring. The iconostasis that is characteristic of an Orthodox church was in blue and gold and painted with pictures of saints; with its four doors it could have served as a set for a Shakespeare comedy. In the dome, birds darted about and chirped with abandoned ecstasy. I asked Sanitation and Hygiene what kind of birds they were and he replied, "Common birds."

The color motif of the church was sustained by the women, who filled the church with row upon row of blue shawls embroidered in gold. I have spoken of the beauty of the women before, and I must do so again; with their white skin, pink cheeks, dark, wide eyes and black hair, they looked like Antonello Annunciations.

But they were noisy Madonnas. They shook hands, waved to one another, embraced, and chatted in their normal speaking voices. Behind them some tourists had found seats, but most of the *stranieri* were pressed against the walls. On the sides of the platform at the front were rows of stiff *carabinieri*. They stood there without a flicker of an eyelash, expressionless as wax statues, their plumed hats red as turkey cocks. Between them a priest robed like a sultan tried to bring order to a mélange of milling acolytes and photographers. Small boys scrambled like squirrels up some pillars to watch the proceedings, and a photographer climbed the pulpit and popped flash bulbs over it all. I doodled a verse on a paper:

> Zaccharias climbed a tree
> The Lord to see.

The Lord appeared wearing an elaborate jeweled crown, vestments of pure gold embroidered with rubies and emeralds, and carrying a jeweled *pastorale*, or shepherd's crook, six feet high. He had a long gray beard.

It was the Bishop, wearing thick glasses and an expressionless face, surrounded by a bevy of robed attendants bearing candelabra and steaming pots. "God preserve him for many years," two male choirs thundered, Russian style.

Even with the choir roaring "Christ is risen!" the proceedings seemed more like an ill-rehearsed amateur performance of *Boris Godunov* than a religious ceremony. Acolytes looked over the nave searching for friends. No one paid any attention to the choir singing invocations to the Pope and an assortment of cardinals; and the chattering continued. It was a bedlam that would never have been permitted, let us say, at the Folies Bergère, where I have seen an audience watch with silent awe while a chorus of nude women rose to heaven to the strains of "Nearer My God to Thee."

The services lasted about three hours. People came and went as at a continuous movie. With each new invocation, the hirsute men of God at my sides bowed excitedly. The hair of one of them became undone in the back. A twelve-year-old seminarian sang the epistle in a falsetto voice while priests popped in and out of the doors like the gilded figures in a clock tower.

Then came the reading of the gospel, in six languages by six different clerics, one line at a time. An old man quavered it feebly in Latin; a Goliath peeled it in Greek; a young man read it roguishly in French; a stout man boomed it in Rumanian; a mumbler garbled it in German; and a reader with crisp staccato diction hammered it out in Albanian. Sanitation and Hygiene leaned back to apologize because it wasn't also read in English. The English reader, it seemed, was on an ecclesiastical mission to the United States.

All together the readers sounded like a chorus in an ancient play and they seemed to take forever. Each time the six finished a line a bell was rung inside the church. Outside, someone responded with a rumble of drums. The drum sounded official, but Sanitation and Hygiene said it was a crank who had nothing to do with the service. "A man who is angry that his wife is inside," he explained.

The choir responded with a lusty "Glory be to God," and the monk on my left, raising his voice and head in ecstasy, caught a lock in a crack of the ancient stall and let out a small yelp of distress. The Bishop, popping in and out like a weathercock, suddenly was angered by the confusion. He stalked to the foreground, thumped his shepherd's crook on the steps, and scolded the women for gossiping. He reminded them of the solemnity of the Resurrection. "We must be filled with reverence," he stormed, subduing the crowd so that even Zaccharias stopped flashing bulbs and climbed down from the pulpit.

The Bishop then sailed into his Easter sermon, which George warned me would last another hour or so. When the anthems were finished we crept out of our seats and sneaked out the sacristy door like a couple of truant choirboys. Outdoors we found groups of belles who hadn't been to church at all but had remained to preen their plumage in the sun and flirt with the men. They strolled in threes and fours, with arms interlocked, running like rabbits whenever a camera appeared, or they hung bewitchingly over the grillework of balconies, disappearing behind doors when someone looked up. It was the chase they enjoyed, and the men played the game, giving the virgins of Piana degli Albanesi the delicious illusion of wickedness.

There was a running fountain in the heart of the town which was the main source of water for the people. The activity around it was like a Fifth Avenue Easter parade. Newsreel cameramen hung from booms and tourist officials from Palermo, like Hollywood press agents, herded the girls into photogenic groups. The girls, losing their morning shyness, began to preen and pose. Here we lingered, fascinated by two processions, the first of young beauty and the second of old women who came to the fountain with crocks on their shoulders and then returned, slopping the streets as they walked. Sometimes a toothless old crone, humped and swaddled in black, would loiter at the fountain for a glimpse of the color and the excitement.

We bought a bottle of wine and some food and drove down to the meadow by the lake, which was already thick with a score of English-speaking picnickers. As we ate on the water's edge amid grazing sheep, clouds rolled over the saddle of the mountain where the town lay. When we returned to the piazza the weather had turned damp and gray. The girls who had been coy and blushing in the morning now had turned bold and daring and were courting the cameras, anxious to make the most of the attention. Their timing was bad. It had grown too dark for pictures. The gaily colored caravan of visitors was already rolling down to the city. The Resurrection was over.

CHAPTER 4

THE MOTHER

THERE ARE those in Sicily who regard the murder of Giuliano as the crucifixion of their savior by soldiers from Rome. With their Sicilian predilection for mother deities, they will tell you with awe that the mother of Salvatore Giuliano still lives.

I wanted to meet this woman who in vengeance had spoken a language as stark and prophetic as Medea's. It was on Easter Monday morning that I set out to find the mother of the crucified.

In George Tomaselli's car, we turned inland toward the granite hills, leaving Palermo through a ghetto of misery. The day was gray and wet; the clay streets looked as though they were covered with glue. Since it was a *giorno di festa*, families stood idly in doorways, through which radios blared. We climbed back and forth across the hills until Palermo glistened below us in a ray of sun which had broken through the morning gloom. We passed a pillbox which someone had tried to fashion into a dwelling. Occasionally there was a patch of pine seedlings planted by the government. Otherwise it was a dreary landscape with bogs from which the rains could not drain and soil which was too sour to sustain life.

It was eighteen kilometers to Montelepre, but it seemed far

more. We drove on, passing an occasional cluster of houses in the emptiness. This was brigand country where men huddled together for protection. Soon it rained and then we were in the cloud itself, lost in a Stygian gloom of gray rock and mists rolling up the mountain sides. It was also hunting country. George reminisced about how he and some fellow students, getting lost in pursuit of game, had come upon a shepherd's hut and had gone to the door to ask the way. "We found a woman whose husband had not returned from the war and two children who could not have been his living in a small room with an earthen floor and no chimney. We gave the children some chocolate, the first they'd ever tasted, and when we left, the woman asked us if we were from Rome. 'If you go to Rome,' she said, 'tell Mussolini we do not have enough to eat.' "

We pushed on through the midday night, descending finally from the cloud into a fan-shaped valley.

On our left was a high stone wall over which I could see the tops of cypress trees. Across an iron gate between two pink-painted Doric columns were the words *Necropoli Monteleprina*.

The cemetery gate was locked and there was no one around to let us in. There was a slot in the wall for "offerings for souls in purgatory." Peering through the grille we saw a score of imposing mausoleums, one of which contained the body of Salvatore Giuliano. I wondered which. As is usual in Sicily, the city of the dead was more luxurious than the city of the living below.

The wind sighed through the cypress like the exhalations of the dying, emphasizing the terrible silence of the place. The black peaks rising about the cemetery were forbiddingly barren and cold. On a thin terrace someone was nursing a few vines; on a patch of meadow beyond some goats grazed. It was a fierce landscape of rejection. Giuliano had probably hunted in these hills, even though a faded sign near the cemetery said, "Hunting forbidden."

The roofs of the town below were so tightly clustered, they might have been lichen on a rock. Only a church spire and a tower broke the line of the flat, scalelike tiling. The houses were the bright yellow color of limestone. The road curled down into the town. On its outskirts we were greeted with fascist slogans still painted on buildings. "The fatherland is not an illusion," one said; and another, "The fatherland is the greatest, the most human, and the purest reality." Around a corner, we saw an old sign on a house: "Panificio Giuliano & Cusimano." I remembered that the Giuliano family had once owned a bakery, that Turridu had dealt in black-market grain around Montelepre in the dark days of 1943, and that the first of his murders had been over some stolen wheat. Still, Giuliano was probably a common name.

We descended deeper into the town. After wind-swept Trapani and scrubbed Piana degli Albanesi, it looked shockingly mean and poor. Scrawny chickens scratched in garbage piled on the streets and clouds of flies hovered over sewage lying in gutters. Men in the moleskin trousers and boots which had been Giuliano's uniform stood idly in the streets, scowling with boredom. Their hard faces were dark and threatening; among the younger men one saw *his* face, handsome and sullen with rebellion. A few women moved quickly from house to house like black wraiths. I felt eyes following us from behind every door and window. It was a holdover from the months when Giuliano was at large and Montelepre was under martial law. We became aware of a sort of posse behind us, including a middle-aged man and a handful of silent youths who did not let us out of their sight. Everything —the streets, the buildings, the people—seemed sunk in an irredeemable despair. I felt the same hostility and suspicion which I had previously experienced in one of the bandit towns of Sardinia.

We went into the church, called Gesù Cristo Crocifisso named after the Crucified Christ, who is the patron of Giuliano's town. After the brute ugliness outside, the church was startlingly beautiful. It was in Renaissance style and gleamed with gold. I wondered how such a dismal town could have produced such opulence. Obviously an ambitious prelate had spurred on his people to this grandiose effort. Even more startling were the sounds—swooping cacklings that seemed to come from angry peacocks. Actually they were human voices rising in a primitive screech that chilled the flesh. At first we saw only a hunchback sweeping in the back of the church We followed the cries to a small side chapel. There, huddled about a glass-coffined Christ, six old people in black shawls four women and two men—were singing a rosary. One of the women was the leader; she raced through the words so fast that none was distinguishable. The others responded with mumbles and groans. There was something curiously electrifying about this inhuman din; we did not leave until the singers were finished. It happened suddenly and without warning "Ecco!" announced the leader, and the ragged ones quickly parted from one another and crept home.

On the steps of the church a flustered duck squawked angrily at us. Our posse was waiting. The man now addressed us in excellent English. He was an American citizen and his American name was Joe. He told us he was forty-seven years old and had worked in a Chicago meatpacking house for twenty-five years. He had saved his money to return to his home town with his wife and three American-born children. "We Sicilians are like rabbits," he said. "Where we are born, there we like to die." Because he was an American the frustrated young men of the town gathered around him like a band of disciples. It was obvious that he enjoyed his lordly role.

How, I asked, did his American-born children take to life in Montelepre?

"Their grandparents make a big fuss over them and they like it fine," Joe said.

I found it hard to believe.

After some awkward moments the boys became more friendly. One who said he was a barber offered me a free haircut and another asked if I would contact his Brooklyn relatives and find out why they had not sent him the immigration affidavits they had promised. The boys were proud of their town and showed me the fifteenth-century tower which they said was the *palazzo* of a noble family, the last descendant of which now lived in Palermo. They also showed me the handsome new schoolhouse and some new roads, all built with ERP aid. At the bottom of the town we looked out on a green valley dotted with olive trees, grape vines, and plots of vegetables. This agricultural richness seemed to have made little mark on the town.

These idle young men of Montelepre were also proud of their town's noted son. Now that they were no longer suspicious, they all talked about him at once.

"For his own people he did only good things."

"He would have overthrown the rich and returned Sicily to the Sicilians."

"He hated Communists. He knew Communists and priests were bad for Sicily and he was against both. Because of him Montelepre is not Communist."

"He wanted a democratic, people's government in Sicily."

"There was no man strong enough to take over when he died. No one had his capabilities to lead the people."

"He was a god."

The last speaker was the one who had wanted to cut my hair. He was sixteen, a fair-haired, blue-eyed boy who should have been in school but who was an apprentice barber instead.

Joe, the American, said, "The older people of the town do not talk like this. They want to forget Giuliano. They are always afraid for their sons—that they will follow in his footsteps and end as he ended."

"Did Pisciotta kill Giuliano?" I asked the boys.

For a moment they were silent. Finally one of them replied, "No one here believes that he did."

"Who do you believe killed Giuliano?" I asked.

There was a shrug all around and dead silence. I did not know whether the shrug indicated that they did not know or would not talk. I let it pass.

We invited Joe and his satellites for some coffee. The café in the piazza was dark and empty. A bored attendant shuffled in from the back. Coffee? He was out of coffee since yesterday; didn't we know it had been a *festa?* An *apéritif?* The bottles were emptied on Easter. What, I asked, did he have? He frowned and pointed to some sweets which he said were left over from Easter. They appeared to have been left over from more than one Easter.

There were, of course, no restaurants in Montelepre, so Joe directed us to a tiny shop. It was a dark, oppressive cave tended by a surly man dressed in moleskins. There was little to be had. We bought some rusted cans of tuna, some bread and dry cheese, and a few puny oranges. For these we were charged far too much, but we paid without protest, happy to have them. One of the boys ran into the store to report that the caretaker of the cemetery had heard that we were in the town and would meet us at the cemetery gate. We drove back up the hill, past the building on the edge of town which Joe had told us was, indeed, the abandoned bakery of the Giuliano family, who lived right across the street. When we reached the cemetery the caretaker had not yet arrived, so we decided to eat. We had to open the tuna cans with rocks. The bread was sour and as heavy as a brick. We broke off a few hunks and left the rest beside the cemetery wall. "In a hundred years it will be found by an archeologist who will decide it is a grace offering to the dead," said George.

While we were eating this dreary repast the caretaker arrived. He was a small, sprightly bird of a man who carried a clanking ring of keys. A sociable type, he asked at once from what country we had come. It pleased him that we were American. "They come from Sweden, Norway, Switzerland, Belgium, Holland, England, and Germany," he said. "I think you are the first from America."

The slain brigand had become an international as well as a local legend. I had expected the tomb to be an object of pilgrimage for Sicilians, perhaps even for curious Italians, but not for northern Europeans. In retrospect, however, I begin to understand the appeal of this tomb for northerners. Latins build tombs; it is their duty to their notable dead. Romantic northerners turn tombs into shrines. The nonconformist, Giuliano, would be a logical martyr for the frustrated youths of these countries.

"Many who come are students, still boys and girls," said the caretaker. "Some bring wreaths and some pray. Two days ago a young Swiss did both."

He escorted us into the cemetery. It was a small, crowded place with almost twenty family mausoleums and five large chapels for communal interment. The caretaker led us directly to the mausoleum I would have picked—the newest and grandest. It was a small chapel of gray marble that looked like a neat little Venetian *palazzo*. Over the door was a sculptured Madonna holding a sleeping child and the words *Famiglia Giuliano*. On the roof was a Byzantine cross. I had heard that the money for the chapel had been raised by popular subscription; now the caretaker told us it had been paid for by the family. Expensive it certainly was; no doubt some of the fortune Giuliano is reported to have collected in ransoms and given to his *cara mamma* had gone into it.

"It was built two years ago," said the caretaker. "Until then the body rested in a public chapel."

The caretaker pointed to the cemented-up wall of cubicles in a public chapel.

"There is the tomb of Gaspare Pisciotta," he said.

The three and one-half years by which he survived his cousin were troubled ones for Pisciotta. Sentenced in 1951 to life imprisonment in Palermo's Ucciardone Prison, he passed his time writing an autobiography and doing embroidery. It was reported at one time that he so feared being poisoned in prison that he would touch only food and drink brought him by relatives from the outside.

While Pisciotta languished in prison, still new versions of how Giuliano met his death spread through Sicily and Rome. Some versions cast doubt on Pisciotta's confession. Hearing of these rumors, Pisciotta is said to have expressed a desire to reveal some hitherto concealed truths.

One morning Pisciotta, drinking his breakfast coffee in prison, cried out, "I am dying." An hour later he was dead of strychnine poisoning. "Giuliano Does Not Forgive," the headline said, and at the funeral the mother of Giuliano said, "At last the big-mouthed one is silent."

But the stories of Pisciotta's innocence persisted, and after a time even the old mother came to doubt that her nephew had shot her son. For the latest theory about Giuliano's death I am indebted to Gavin Maxwell's book, *Bandit*. According to an account in this absorbing and well-documented narrative, Giuliano was killed in the shadow of the great cathedral of Monreale. The executioner, whoever he was, turned the body over to the soldiers from Rome, who selected Castelvetrano as the setting for the "official" killing and hauled the body there under cover of night. Upon arrival in the courtyard, it was fired with bullets and spattered with blood from a container

Now, in death, the blood brothers were nearly as close as

hey had been in life. I thought of the fierce bond that had ield them together, an emotion far beyond the boundaries of ordinary love and hate. I remembered how Giuliano in a panic had sent to America for streptomycin to cure his beloved riend of tuberculosis; how Giuliano punished Pisciotta for iis lechery with women by tying him to a tree and beating iim. I remembered how Giuliano had written: "What he is I am, and what I am he is. We have made a blood pact, and we have sworn fidelity."

Remembering these things, as I stood there between them under the cypress, I found it hard to believe that Gaspare Pisciotta had killed Salvatore Giuliano.

Who killed him? In his book Maxwell quotes a Monteleprean. "The same man as killed Pisciotta—but the orders in each case came from high up. The arm of the Mafia is much onger than that of the law."

It is possible that one day the identity of the executioner will be known. It is also possible that his name will remain forever a mystery. To the painters of donkey carts and writers of ballads, his identity is not important. The fact that Giuliano and Pisciotta lived and died is. In legend the cousins are already immortalized along with Orlando and Ruggiero of *Orlando Furioso*.

The caretaker unlocked the glass doors and led us into the tomb of the King. To the right, standing on four lion's claws, was a marble sarcophagus. Enameled on it was the famous photograph showing the high, square forehead, the curly black hair, the open shirt showing a V of matted chest. It was the photograph of the King of Montelepre standing aswagger, with thumbs in belt, wearing the moleskin pants and corduroy jacket. The fierce and penetrating eyes gleamed out, challenging you to look into them. Much of the power of the man must have been in those eyes, for it takes strong nerves to face them even now.

Printed in gold letters on the sarcophagus was

SALVATORE GIULIANO

N 16-11-1922

M 5-7-1950

It was a shock to be reminded that he was still four month
short of twenty-eight when he died. Also in gold letters wer
some Sicilian lines from a poem he himself had written.

Oh, my poor blessed dreams of love,
You perished at the height of my enjoyment,
You rose sanguine, but ill-fated,
And vanished like birds in the forest.

On top of the sarcophagus was a plaster head of Christ, a
wreath, and a cross made of laurel, the foliage of kings.

The right and left walls of the mausoleum were divided
into sixteen burial shelves; in due time the hero would be
surrounded in his chapel by his next of kin. Only one, directly
over the sarcophagus, was occupied. It contained the corpse
of the bandit's father, who had died a few months before.

I asked the caretaker if he knew Salvatore Giuliano as a boy
"Everyone knew him," he replied and added solemnly, "Un
ragazzo bravo."

In the front of the chapel was an altar with burning candle
and bouquets of fresh flowers. Some cherubs played over the
altar and above them was a Christ of the sacred heart. The
altar was covered with a spotless white lace cloth. La mamma
herself laundered it, the caretaker told us, and jealously cared
for the chapel. There was a row of chairs. "Whenever the fam
ily wishes there is a mass," the caretaker said. "There is alway
one on the anniversary of his death."

Who, I asked, officiated.

"Sometimes the Monsignor of Montelepre," he replied.

Wreaths and bouquets, natural and artificial, almost filled
the chapel. One fresh wreath of myrtle and lilies was tied with
a white ribbon; upon it in gold letters I read, "Turridu."

The mother's name for her son suggested that the wreath was from an intimate, or a member of the family. It was not from a relative, the caretaker told us, but from the Swiss youth who had left no name. I wondered at the mystic union between a Swiss, of all people, and the spirit of this corpse so nobly encased in marble. The bond was rebellion. In a world demanding more and more conformity at any price, young pilgrims from the north were, in their frustration, seeking out this almost inaccessible, dismal little cemetery, and in a ritualistic gesture of defiance were paying tribute to one who, in his chaotic fashion, had revolted.

It had started to rain softly and the cold winds mourned in the cypress trees. In one of them a solitary bird warbled. I was grateful for this break in the terrible silence. We tipped the custodian, who bowed grandly, and dropped some coins in the collection box for the souls in purgatory.

We rolled back down the hill, stopping at the crumbling remains of Panificio Giuliano & Cusimano. Across the road was the plain little house which was Giuliano's early base of operations. After his death a hidden passage was discovered leading from underneath the house to the open mountainside. On the door was the black band of mourning, with the words *Per mio marito* (for my husband). A heavy, youngish woman all in black was sitting at an upstairs window, presumably knitting. Actually she was watching us. I had been told by the vice-consul in Palermo to ask for a sister named Mariannina who was known to United States diplomats because her husband had been in America and had, under another name, served for a time in the United States Air Force. The woman in the window said Mariannina was visiting in the country and asked who we were.

"I am an American writer."

"We will tell you nothing," she said.

"Is your mother at home?"

"We have nothing to say."

"I have come a long way—thousands of miles—to meet your mother." I hoped the facts would impress her. They seemed to, a bit.

"If you wish to come in you are welcome," she said, shrugging. "But we will not speak."

We climbed a flight of steep stairs and turned left into a small and dark room. It was a combination living and dining room, probably the only room with the exception of the kitchen that wasn't used for sleeping. The woman in the window was one of three dressed in black who sat silent and idle, mourning as if mourning were a physical act that one performed methodically, like baking bread or milking a cow. In addition to the knitter, there was a younger girl who seemed to be about twenty years of age.

The third, a tiny figure, sat motionless in the dark shadows of a corner. I caught my breath. It was *la cara mamma*, the mother of a legend, a Demeter-Mary so loved by her son she had become a legend herself.

The most striking thing about her was her size. She seemed dwarfish—so small that she hooked her heels on the top rung of her chair as a child does. The pose was familiar; it was the way the photographer had caught her the morning after the shooting in Castelvetrano. She was wearing the same drab black cotton of the pictures; a piece of it, knotted into a kerchief, covered her head. Her chin was cupped in a hand, the elbow of which rested on a table.

Awesome she certainly was. She sat there, still, silent, and as inscrutable as a sphinx. I tried to pierce this façade and see the woman who had worn the insignia of brigands and gone to jail with them. The face was old and sunken and on her upper lip was a small mustache. Only the eyes were alive. They were the intense eyes on the tomb, and I could feel them penetrating me like an X ray.

I looked about the room. It was clean, except for the wine-stained cloth on the table and a cloud of flies buzzing about my head. The walls were painted green and there were three small windows. The floor was stone. A door covered by cotton netting led to a kitchen; I could see the rows of pots and pans inside. There was one unshaded light bulb. From a nail by the door hung an assortment of keys and rosaries. On the wall above the mother was a large framed wedding photo with half the glass broken away; it hung at an angle, pulled to the side by its half glass. The pair in the fading photo were young and solemn. The stern little bride in starched white still bore a resemblance to the silent one at the table. Also caught inside the broken glass were communion snapshots of children. Some saints' pictures hung in the room. I was surprised to see that there was not a single photograph of Giuliano in the room.

The silence had to be broken. I addressed the mother. "I am interested in the story of your son."

She made no response. The girl escaped the pain of the moment by going into the kitchen. Finally the knitter at the window said, "We are mourning for our father and we are filled with sorrow. We do not wish to be disturbed."

"I am sorry. I did not know. I have come a long way and would be grateful for your patience."

"They come from Brussels, from London, from Munich," the knitter said. "For all the same. Nothing."

"I carry greetings from the United States Consulate for Mariannina."

"You can wait for her if you wish. But it will be no different. She will not speak," the knitter said.

By the table la cara mamma stirred. I could see she was preparing to speak.

"Do you come from Hollywood?"

It was a simple, direct question and it took a moment for me to collect myself for a simple, direct answer. The dark eyes narrowed.

"Do you wish to make a film about my son?" she asked.

"*Signora*, I am not from Hollywood. I am not going to make a film."

"*Come lei desidera*," she said. "As you wish."

Perhaps she was right to want a film. The heroics of Giuliano could cover the widest screen on earth with cinematic glory. In Hollywood and in Rome the project had been discussed, but so far caution and prudence had prevailed. Perhaps it was only that the time was still too soon. Perhaps, if she lives long enough, the mother of the King of Montelepre may yet see her son a celluloid hero in the eyes of the world.

I realized that no further communication between me and the old woman was possible. I got up to say good-by. The young woman returned from the kitchen. All three nodded but said nothing. As I clattered down the stone stairs I heard the old woman laughing.

Outside, it was raining hard and the blanketing clouds seemed to choke the town. We could see only a small distance. The world seemed to have shrunk to the proportions of the little woman huddling in the house, a small, dark thing. As we crawled through the storm, I saw a crack in the ceiling and a shaft of light fell diagonally on the golden shell of Palermo. Thank God, there was still a sun.

CHAPTER 5

THE RESULTS

ELECTION DAY—a Sunday in June—dawned fair. There was a spirit of *festa* over the island. To get to the polls in Montelepre, voters rode out from the mountain passes on donkeys and mules. In Piana degli Albanesi bearded Orthodox priests and nuns of the Greek rite bustled between church and polls. In Trapani, groups of voters rode to the polls in the black limousines usually reserved for Communist officials. In each town the people milled around the polling places long after they had voted, but few voices were raised and everything was orderly.

It took three days for the villages and towns to file their returns. When all the votes were in, the Christian Democrats had seven new assembly seats in Palermo, bringing their total to thirty-seven. The Communist-Socialist bloc, making no gains, had held its thirty seats.

The results in the three towns I had visited were:

	Christian Democrats	Communist-Socialist bloc
Trapani	10,559	11,796
Piana degli Albanesi	1,150	2,640
Montelepre	1,242	389

In Trapani there were 4,834 Monarchist votes and 7,071 Neo-Fascist votes. In Piana degli Albanesi there was one vote for the Contadini, or peasant party. As the young men in the piazza of Montelepre had said, there were not many Communists in Giuliano's town.

In Rome and Milan the press celebrated the election as "a defeat of extremists"; in America as "a resounding victory for the Christian Democrats."

But thoughtful, less exuberant observers suggested there was less to the victory than met the eye. Gains by the Christian Democrats were largely at the expense of minor rightist parties which had been part of the governing coalition in Palermo. The Christian Democrats had increased their popular votes, but so had the Nenni Socialists of the Communist bloc. Reporting for England's London *Telegraph*, Anthony Mann wrote:

> The blind neglect and exploitation of centuries cannot be made good in a decade, and vast resources of cash, labor, and tact will be needed before Sicily can be restored to her ancient prosperity. It is still an open question whether political deterioration or economic recovery will win the race.

The voting, though it had limited repercussions in Sicily, had, as everyone feared, far-reaching results in Rome. Indirectly, but very decisively, Sicily, island of the vendetta, finally settled her score with a native son. Premier Mario Scelba lost a parliamentary vote of confidence and a Sardinian, Antonio Segni, was appointed to succeed him. As Sicilian Scelba discovered, though the King of Montelepre was dead, a legend was very much alive.

ABOUT THE AUTHOR

HERBERT KUBLY'S *Swiss ancestry goes back to the fifteenth century and the Canton of Glarus. He was born and reared on a farm in New Glarus, Wisconsin, making him a fifth-generation American of pure Swiss descent.*

Mr. Kubly attended the New Glarus public schools and the University of Wisconsin. Part of his college expenses were paid for out of his earnings from writing magazine articles and pulp fiction. Graduating from the university in 1937, Kubly went to Pittsburgh, where he worked as a reporter and, later, art critic on the Pittsburgh Sun Telegraph. *Five years later he came to New York and to jobs as reporter on the New York* Herald Tribune *and music editor of* Time *magazine. His first play,* Men to the Sea, *was produced in New York in 1944 under the direction of Eddie Dowling; his second,* Inherit the Wind, *at the Playhouse Theatre, London, in 1948.*

In 1950 Kubly accepted a post as Associate Professor of Speech at the University of Illinois. The following year he was granted a Fulbright fellowship, which took him to Italy and Sicily by way of Germany, Austria, and Switzerland and resulted in his first book, American in Italy, *winner of the National Book Award for the outstanding work of nonfiction in 1955. His short stories and articles have appeared in* Harper's Bazaar, Town and Country, Vogue, Mademoiselle, The Atlantic Monthly, *and* Esquire. *As this book goes to press, he is completing two plays—*The Cocoon *and* Beautiful Dreamer.